United Nations University Series on Regionalism

Volume 18

The United Nations University Series on Regionalism, launched by UNU-CRIS and Springer, offers a platform for innovative work on (supra-national) regionalism from a global and inter-disciplinary perspective. It includes the World Reports on Regional Integration, published in collaboration with other UN agencies, but it is also open for theoretical, methodological and empirical contributions from academics and policy-makers worldwide.

Book proposals will be reviewed by an International Editorial Board.

The series editors are particularly interested in book proposals dealing with:

- comparative regionalism;- comparative work on regional organizations;- inter-regionalism;- the role of regions in a multi-level governance context;- the interactions between the UN and the regions;- the regional dimensions of the reform processes of multilateral institutions;- the dynamics of cross-border micro-regions and their interactions with supra-national regions;- methodological issues in regionalism studies.

Accepted book proposals can receive editorial support from UNU-CRIS for the preparation of manuscripts.

Please send book proposals to: pdelombaerde@cris.unu.edu and lvanlangenhove@cris.unu.edu.

Tullo Vigevani • Haroldo Ramanzini Junior

The Challenges for Building Regional Integration in the Global South

The case of Brazilian Foreign Policy towards Mercosur

Springer

Tullo Vigevani
Sao Paulo State University
Sao Paulo, Brazil

Haroldo Ramanzini Junior
Federal University of Uberlândia
Uberlandia, Brazil

ISSN 2214-9848 ISSN 2214-9856 (electronic)
United Nations University Series on Regionalism
ISBN 978-3-030-93347-0 ISBN 978-3-030-93348-7 (eBook)
https://doi.org/10.1007/978-3-030-93348-7

This Springer imprint is published by the registered company Springer Nature Switzerland AG
The registered company address is: Gewerbestrasse 11, 6330 Cham, Switzerland

Contents

Chapter 1
Introduction

The purpose of this book is to evaluate and provide an analytical overview of the Brazilian foreign policy in relation to Mercosur and the South American regional integration. We will analyze the bloc's development, with focus on the state and Brazilian domestic actors. We will identify the results obtained, the causes for the difficulties, and the reasons for the impasses which have arisen during the 30 years of Mercosur's existence, which will be celebrated in 2021. From March 1991 until today, it has been possible to observe a qualitative transformation in the pattern of relationships between the member states considering that a customs union came into existence from December 1994, with the signature of the Ouro Preto Protocol. The agendas and domestic interfaces of regional issues have been significantly broadened, as has the interest in the intra-bloc trade, albeit with strong oscillations.

This book is aimed at analyzing these very issues. At the same time, difficulties regarding the consolidation of regional institutions, cooperation, and integration amongst states can be verified. It is important to understand this development for the scholars of regional integration and Latin American politics. We likewise seek a dialogue with the established theories concerning the motivations of states and the consequences of regional integration. Some of the key concepts applied in this book,—such as developmentalist-distributivist, autonomy, interdependence, and paymaster—contribute to our central argument, that Brazil, even in a situation in which there was an effective interest in regional integration, did not develop the necessary agency-capacities to decisively drive this process. This was due to the opposing interests of large parts of elites[1] and certain structural weaknesses, particularly the mode of insertion within the political and economic international system.

[1]In this book, we consider Dahl's concept of elites, formulated as: "A ruling elite, then, is a controlling group less than a majority in size that is not a pure artifact of democratic rules. It is a minority of individuals whose preferences regularly prevail in cases of differences in preference on key political issues" (Dahl, 1958, p. 464). In addition, we consider that the concept of elites includes union leaders and others of social sectors leaders.

T. Vigevani, H. Ramanzini Junior, *The Challenges for Building Regional Integration in the Global South*, United Nations University Series on Regionalism 18,
https://doi.org/10.1007/978-3-030-93348-7_1

With this in mind, we hereby seek to strengthen future analytical capacities. Mariano (2015) discusses the differences between the integration wave of the 1950–1960s, centered on the European experience, and the processes of integration within Latin America, which often did not revolve around defining a common stance in relation to foreign powers, but mainly emphasized attempts at cooperation between regional states. Within existing literature, we encounter a debate about the utility of theories developed within the field of studies of European regional integration in order to explain the motivations and difficulties related to integration processes in other parts of the world, particularly the Global South. According to Acharya (2016, p. 7) "the EEC was basically conceived as a project to tame nationalism and constrain state sovereignty; non-Western regionalisms were inspired by exactly the opposite motivations, to advance nationalism and preserve sovereignty after centuries of colonial rule".

Within this book, we seek to explain how the regional integration process within Mercosur relates to Acharya's (2016) perspective. The emphasis on notions such as nationalism and sovereignty was not directly contrary to the integration process, but neither did it converge clearly with it. We can identify this contradiction within the Brazilian state. In contrast to the EU, where the regional integration process was aimed at overcoming nationalism, for developing countries, regional integration was viewed as a means to strengthen nationalism and autonomy. Within Mercosur, autonomy would serve to shape regional institutions, but this very same autonomy would also impede its institutional development (Krapohl, 2020; Burges, 2009; Malamud, 2005). Krapohl (2020) specifically highlights the difficulties encountered within regional integration processes marked by strong asymmetries between countries. A central conclusion of this author, therefore, is that "The empirical analyses of ASEAN, MERCOSUR, and SADC support the hypothesis that regional cooperation in the Global South only takes place as long as it does not contradict the extra-regional economic privileges of regional powers" (Krapohl, 2020, p. 26). In this book, we emphasize that in the case of Brazilian policy in relation to Mercosur, an explanation which encompasses other factors becomes important. This does not least regard the way in which the region relates to the patterns within Brazilian foreign policy. Another important aspect concerns the role of extra-regional actors along with the global geopolitical evolution and its relation to the Brazilian elite's interests. We argue that Mercosur is not a case of the regional integration process contradicting or favouring extra-regional privileges of the largest member state. On the contrary, we rather highlight the difficulties which the state and political elites' have had in terms of envisaging the regional environment as a sphere which is apt to promote its interests, be these either economic or political.

Briceño-Ruiz and De Lombaerde (2018, p. 263) highlight that "using the specific knowledge and theorization within the context and case at hand is not incompatible with the use of more general theoretical frameworks which permit a comparative work between regions and the flow of inter-regional knowledge". In this book, we aim to do this. That is, within the analysis of Brazilian policy in relation to the regional integration process, we highlight experiences of both success and failure. We apply integration theories with a universalist scope, particularly those that arise from the analysis of the experience of European integration, contraposing it with the experiences from the Southern Cone, especially those of Brazil. We can reveal that our conclusions will reflect the reality with which we are confronted: a relative failure in the formation of this bloc, albeit some achievements obtained are recognized. We engage with the underlying reasons for this, which include the process of formation of Brazilian elites as well as structural questions. This means analyzing the insertion of Brazil and Mercosur within the international system and the persistent conditionings which have not been overcome.

Thus, the book adopts an ecletic analytical framework aiming to discuss the strength and weaknesses of several approaches to understand Brazilian foreign policy towards Mercosur. Domestic, regional and global aspects are treated to understand the trajectory of Brazilian foreign policy and the challenges of Mercosur. We enquire to what extent Brazilian foreign policy towards Mercosur is conditioned by each level of analysis and identify the factors present in different periods in each level and how they condition the norms, rules and interests that orient foreign policy. Our analysis focused on Brazilian foreign policy, provides evidence for how perceptions and the insertion of a state in a world region evolves depending on how patterns of interaction between the domestic, regional and global levels develop across time. This perspective provides an understanding of the differences in how autonomy is implemented within foreign policy as well as its impact in the making of regional orders. At the same time, we underline that structural variables, such as states fragility, the patterns of engagement with the global economy and the limited capacity to increase regional economic interdependence limits the emergence, design and functions of regional institutions in the Global South.

Alden et al. (2010, p. 3) higlight that the South is a "phrase used to describe those regions of the globe that have in common a political, social, and economic history rooted in the inequalities of a colonial or imperialist power". The term also encompasses an "ideological expression for the range of concerns facing developing regions, which themselves are growing in economic and political diversity and experience" (Alden et al., 2010, p. 3). The notion of Global South "is not simply the land below the equator. It is an ideological concept highlighting the economic, political, and epistemic dependency and unequal relations in the global world order" (Mignolo, 2011, p. 166). Concerning the rise of the Global South term in the 2000s, Alden et al. (2010, p. 221) argue that it involves a "deliberate de-centring of the geographic certainties which framed the use of South as a proxy for the former colonial and developing countries, seeks to simultaneously capture the rise of economic powers of the South and concurrently the emergency of substantial middles classes within these societies producing both new affluence and the spectacle of enduring poverty. At the same time, the use of the term reflects the changing dynamics in the North, with its burgeoning immigrant communities—whose orientation remains fixed in many ways in the South as well as the relative decline of European and American working classes—whose quiet slide into poverty puts them in increasingly close economic proximity to the circumstances found in the developing world".

Our attempt to incorporate the notion of Global South and examine its contexts and challenges through an analysis of Brazilian foreign policy towards Mercosur is in tune with Acharya's (2014) global International Relations (IR) perspective. For him "Global IR calls for theoretical and epistemological pluralism and eclecticism, across the mainstream-critical theory divide" (Acharya, 2015, p. 2). The perspective advanced by Acharya (2015, p. 2) ascertains that "the future of IR should involve multiple but overlapping conversations. It should not be an exclusive discourse within the Global South community of scholars, but a dialogue among different theoretical and epistemological approaches. It should not run parallel to other debates about the future of IR, but intersect with them". Thus, the focus of this study on Brazilian foreign policy allows one to broaden the understanding of why states seek regionalism and the specific challenges for building regional integration in the Global South. The book's findings may be useful to understand other countries and regionalism difficulties in other Global South regions, such as Southern Africa or South Asia.

The intent to provide an overview of Mercosur has been a strong motivating factor behind this work. Within this perspective, we consider the composition of Mercosur as that of the four original member states (Argentina, Brazil, Paraguay, and Uruguay), as Venezuela, which adhered in 2012, was suspended in December 2016. According to Botto (2015, p. 25), who also analyzes the bloc, "the knowledge of the scope of the past permits us to better understand the possibilities of the future and hereby avoid creating false expectations and a sense of dismay". For this purpose, we make use of Hirschman's (1971) formulation. This author has been a strong critic of the automatic reproduction of models, underscoring the importance of analyzing each specific national experience. In other words, the question of the agency of the regional actors, the emphasis on the dimension of autonomy, and the centrality of aspects such as context and specific regional trajectories, emphasized within the perspective of comparative regionalism (Acharya, 2012; Fioramonti & Mattheis, 2016; Ramanzini Junior & Luciano, 2020), can serve to create a dialogue and incorporate theoretical aspects developed within the field of studies of the EU, though, without being exclusively limited to those.

Considering the specific characteristics which motivated Mercosur, we situate the case within the theories of regional integration which mainly were developed with point of departure in the European case. We consider the spatial situatedness, the historical trajectories, and the characteristics of each member state, in particular Brazil. The motivation for integration, in this case, was never to substitute the state with a supranational entity. In the same way, we argue that the manner in which regional integration functioned in Mercosur was not defined by alliances between economic actors interested in a supranational bureaucracy, as neo-functionalism would predict. It is true that there was a certain degree of signaling in this regard, but initially only with a proposal for integration of the car manufacturing sector,—a goal which eventually lost priority. As Hooghe and Marks (2019) underline, within the neo-functionalist perspective, the regional integration process advances if groups inside the state believe that supranational institutions are more suitable to promote their interests than their national equivalents. Therefore, without neglecting the value of integration studies based on comparative methods, as some important research projects have done (Hurrelmann & Schneider, 2015), we want to stress that this method does not structure our analysis, which is more in tune with historical institutionalism (Pierson, 1998).

As we shall see in this book, neo-funcionalist expectations did not arise in the case of Mercosur, partly due to the lack of businesses and technology. The member states,—and not only Brazil, but also Argentina, Paraguay, and Uruguay—did not prefer a path of deepening of the integration process. With this, the perspectives focused on agency within the regional integration process lost prevalence. Alternatively, the member states' governments chose ways which can be classified as a "*salto in avanti*". There was little insistence and a low capacity for productive complementation and the construction of intra-regional value chains. Inversely, the goal became redefined in the direction of social and political objectives, or even in the broadening of the bloc. This was meant to generate the least possible amount of resistance towards it. It was thereby believed that the negative effects of the integration process would be diffuse and the positive effects, focalized. Consequently, there would be less resistance from negatively affected groups. Analyzing the regional integration process in North America, Pastor and Wise (1994) show how such cases in fact can spur its advancement. Within the chapters in this book, we discuss the structural difficulties through a Brazilian foreign policy perspective, and how low adherence from society and the elites eventually provided obstacles for the deepening of the regional integration process.

The focus of attention of the different forces either directly or indirectly involved with the regional integration process is the state. In this regard, as Moravcsik (1998) highlights, aspects such as economic interests and relative power play a central role. Within the liberal-intergovernmental perspective, regional cooperation in the process of construction of the European Union occurred in three steps: "the domestic formation of national preferences, intergovernmental bargaining, and the creation of European institutions to secure agreements" (Hooghe e Marks, 2019, p. 1116). In this case, there are also tensions with regards to the suitability of the liberal-intergovernmental perspective in order to understand Mercosur. In particular concerning the third aspect, related to the capacity of regional institutions to guarantee negotiated agreements, this became only partially evident with respect to Mercosur. Apart from this, contrary to what liberal-intergovernmentalism would suggest, Mercosur, which dates back to the cooperation between Brazil and Argentina from the end of the 1970s, did not arise from the previous economic interdependence and neither from the strong demands from interest groups within member states—despite the fact that, as Gardini (2010) demonstrates, epistemic groups have retained certain importance. Acharya (2012) and Fioramonti and Mattheis (2016) emphasize the need to broaden the knowledge about the motivations and reasons for the difficulties and the impact of regionalism on other experiences, to shed light on and contribute to the comprehension of this phenomenon, be this either concerned with its development or decline. Contributing to furthering insights about motivations as well as difficulties is part of this book's central aim.

Can developing countries proceed in the direction of successful regional integration? As we shall emphasize, the fact that the countries within Mercosur have been inserted within the global economy in a similar way as raw material exporters and having low rates of national savings hence, being dependent on external financing and technology, makes them highly vulnerable to oscillations of international commodity prices and dependent on extra-regional dynamics. In the case of Brazil and Mercosur, their low agency-capacity appears to have cemented the perpetuation of this vulnerability. In the same way, the low economic interdependence provides obstacles for the integration process. Observing trade data, we can see that from 1991 to 2018, the Brazilian intra-bloc trade fell in relative terms from 9% to 8%, as we shall discuss in Chap. 6. These data are fundamentally different from those which can be verified in other blocs, where complementarity and regional value chains lead to a noticeable rise in interdependence.

In this book, we confirm Krapohl's (2020, p. 2) argument that "economies in the Global South are economically less developed, less diversified and less interdependent with regional neighbors. They are more dependent on trade with and investment from well-developed regions like Europe, North America, and increasingly, Northeast Asia". From this, the author concludes that the "extra-regional interests of the regional member states motivate and constrain regional economic integration". Yet, differently from Krapohl (2020, p. 4), in our research, we do not observe that in Mercosur "the main goal of regional integration in developing regions is to improve the regions' relations with extra-regional investors and trade partners". In Mercosur,—which also is true for Brazil as we shall see in the period of thirty years from 1986 to 2016,—the bloc and South America were by themselves effectively part of the interests of the regional states. This does not contradict the fact that the aspirations towards a broadening of trade partners, investments, and technological assets originated from a predominantly national point of departure, focused on national and not regional gains. This discussion is an important theme within this book, particularly in Chap. 4, *The Grounding of Regional Integration for Brazil: Universalism, Sovereignty and Elite Perceptions*. This ambition has gained an asynchronous expression within the four countries.

With point of departure in case studies from ASEAN, Mercosur, and SADC, Krapohl (2020) sustains the hypothesis that regional cooperation in the Global South only becomes possible in so far as it does not run counter to the extra-regional privileges of regional powers. In Mercosur, this would be a relevant point to evaluate with regards to Brazil. One of the arguments within this book points to another explanation, that which highlights the weakness of Brazilian as well as Argentinean governments from the crises of 1999 and 2001, and how this has compromised the integration process. This weakness should be understood as a parallel consequence of the structural insertion within the international system and the bloc's internal power structure.

The concept of post-hegemonic regionalism (Riggirozzi & Tussie, 2012) refers to the period from 2003 to 2015, which was marked by developmentalist-distributivist governments in the Mercosur countries, as those which have partaken in the integration project. From the *ex-post facto* vantage point, as we shall discuss in the following chapters, we demonstrate that this engagement was not sufficient to impede the growth of the interests contrary to the integration process. From 2015, these interests contributed to the weakening of governments in certain members states. In the case of Brazil, the strong instability which led to the impeachment of President Dilma Rousseff in 2016 further deepened the crisis within the bloc. This was further stimulated by a new context in which the weakening of the centralizing capacity of Mercosur resulted in a hemispheric wave which led to the downgrading of the goals concerned with autonomy. Not only did relations with extra-regional investors and trade partners gain a higher degree of importance, but geopolitical interests were also becoming more directly felt.

We identify the complex inter-relationship between domestic and international factors which influence the Brazilian foreign policy and help to understand Mercosur's trajectory. We agree with Farrell et al. (2005, p. 3) when they highlight that "economic and political motivations certainly play their part in the actions of actors; however, the importance of identity and self-perception should also be recognized". These are relevant aspects to be developed. Thus, the perception of the country's role in the world and of how regionalism converges,—or not,—with this conception is as relevant as the economic and political aspects. The book hereby contains two interrelated analytical dimensions, which are (1) the ideational and identity-related dimension, (2) the dimension concerned with behavior and the agency of political and economic interests. In the same way, we aspire to be attentive of the dimension of the global influences and the opposing influences of the United States and China, as processes of regional integration develop with the global environment as their point of reference.

Within the first dimension, which we treat in Chap. 2 (A Long Perspective on Latin American Regional Integration seen from Brazil) and Chap. 3 (Brazilian Thinking and Regional Integration), the book engages with the *longue durée* historical trajectory with regards to the Brazilian foreign policy positions in relation to regionalism, from 1902 to 1991, or rather, from the beginning of the Republican period and the term of the Baron of the Rio Branco as Minister of Foreign Affairs and until the signature of the Asunción Treaty, which marks the surge of Mercosur. Still, within this dimension,—and particularly pronounced from the second half of the twentieth Century,—we will study how schools of thought, represented by significant figures within the fields of politics, economics, and diplomacy perceived the issue of regionalism and integration with neighboring states in the case of Brazil. We shall scrutinize the reasons why the issue of regionalism became protracted and encountered difficulties in terms of becoming rooted within the Brazilian social and political thinking.

The second dimension is present within Chap. 4 (The Grounding of Regional Integration for Brazil: Universalism, Sovereignty and Elite Perceptions), Chap. 5 (The Social Mercosul within a Brazilian Foreign Policy Perspective), Chap. 6 (The Brazilian Economic Interests in Regional Integration: Mercosur and Latin America), and Chap. 7 (Between Alliances and Disputes: Brazilian Attitudes Towards OAS, CELAC, Unasur, and Mercosur). These chapters will analyze the policies of varying Brazilian governments in relation to Mercosur and the regional integration process.

They will also study the concrete forms of the country's agency. In other words, they will treat the analysis of Brazilian foreign policy in relation to the bloc and its functional dynamics and transformations in the period from 1991 to 2020.

Having analyzed the political and institutional aspects, we examine the economic and social indicators of member states as well as trade data, in addition to the Mercosur and Brazil's relations with other regional and hemispheric institutions, and global dynamics. Amongst these are Unasur, Celac, and the OAS. The role of the United States constitutes an undeniable backdrop for the structural comprehension of these policies and their changes.

Within this second dimension,—the analysis of Brazilian policy,—we can observe how the historical foundations identified within the first dimension become concretely evident from 1991. With this, a specific question arises: do the successive changes in the Brazilian elites' perceptions with regards to Mercosur and South America, and even also the hemispheric relations with the United States, concern the "historical delay" treated in the Chaps. 2 and 3? An answer to this question might only be found within the field of normative proposals or scenarios. This has not been our goal. The Chaps. 4, 5, 6, and 7 provide the basis for our conclusions regarding the role of Brazilian elites. Their consequences have significantly influenced official policies in relation to regional integration and cooperation.

In the 1980s, the idea of universalism, which became important due to its interconnectedness with autonomy, gradually evolved in the direction of a tightening of relations with Argentina. There was a reevaluation of ideas in this regard, leading to a convergence around the goals of regional integration and cooperation. The national interest would be defended through a process of extensive integration. In this book, we discuss the moment of construction and implementation of this type of state strategy. Our empirical analysis shows that at the end of the 1990s and the beginning of the 2000s, a tendency of increasing divergence between prevailing perceptions of national interest and regional integration became evident. We leave it to be up to the reader to reflect upon the relation between these difficulties and the secular isolation in relation to the region, including the weight of pro-Americanism on Brazilian elites.

According to Hettne and Soderbaum (2000, p. 461) "regionness" is the process whereby a geographical area is "transformed from a passive object to an active subject capable of articulating the transnational interests of the emerging region. Regionness thus implies that a region can be more or less. The level of regionness can both increase and decrease". During certain moments, Mercosur developed a sense of "regionness", meaning that the bloc acted in conjunction during certain negotiations, such as for example in relation to FTAA in the period from 1994 to 2005. In other situations, the bloc did not have joint policies, which illustrated the differences in trade policies, as well as the distinct political positions (the Gulf War, the increase in the number of permanent members of the Security Council, etc.). As we shall see, these differences gradually became increasingly salient.

The concept of autonomy,—which is a common thread throughout the book,—led to certain ambiguities in the relation to Mercosur, as the capacity for autonomous national agency was increasingly accentuated at the same time as intergovernmental regional institutions were strengthened. We argue, that the evolution of Mercosur to a wide extent reflects the centrality of the notion of autonomy for Brazil. The peculiarities of the bloc's institutional design and the difficulties of advancing regarding the construction of a community of interests is a result of this. A relevant concept from within the literature on regional integration in order to explain the possibilities of success of the integration project is that of a paymaster. Mattli (1999, p. 14) highlights that "a key supply condition for successful integration, namely the presence of an undisputed leader among the group of countries seeking closer ties. Such a state serves as a focal point in the coordination of rules, regulations and policies; it may also help to ease distributional tensions by acting as a regional paymaster". In the case of Mercosur, as we will discuss in the Chaps. 4 and 6, Brazil did not assume this role; at least not in the sense which Mattli's (1999) perspective would lead to assume.

We also treat the Brazilian difficulties,—if not outright incapability—of assuming this role. Technological, military, financial, and industrial weakness constrains it, even though its GDP constitutes approximately 75% of that of the bloc. According to Hermida et al. (2015, p. 623), "In the case of the countries which together make up the Southern Common Market,—Mercosur, Argentina, Brazil, Paraguay, Uruguay, and more recently, Venezuela-, a productive specialization which is highly based on exports of primary commodities and manufactures with a high degree of raw material inputs predominates. These products, due to their technical characteristics (a low intensity of labour and value-added inputs) generally are not very well integrated into global value chains". In this book, we intensely discuss an argument highlighting the Brazilian shortcomings which impede the country from more consistently assuming the role of a paymaster. This expectation of leadership attributed to a country with enormous economic and social disparities, and with an HDI lower than those of other members states such as Uruguay and Argentina, eventually encumbered the integration process, even during the post-hegemonic period.

In addition, even if we consider Brazil as a regional power, as a state whose foreign policy has a significant effect in the region due to its territorial dimension and population, the political and economic dynamics within Brazil limits the possibilities for managing the asymmetries in the region and building regionalism. Nolte (2010, p. 893) highlights that a regional power is defined, among other aspects, as a state "which displays the material (military, economic, demographic), organisational (political) and ideological resources for regional power projection; which truly has great influence in regional affairs (activities and results). In addition, it is expected that a regional power is a state which is economically, politically and culturally interconnected with the region". Through the analysis in this book, we will show that Brazil can only partically be identified as economically, politically and culturally interconnected with the region. Indeed, since 2016, Brazil has become evermore economically, politically and culturally distant from the region.

We answer the following questions:

- What are the limits between a worldview according to which regional integration has its place, and one in which the integration process is viewed as instrumental, albeit still important? From the analytical viewpoint, this made us discuss how the issue of regional integration was internalized, and how the interests of the state and society were engaged in this respect.
- How can we understand the development from an idea of regional integration strongly based upon commercial concerns, even considering the continued relevance of political issues and worldviews, towards one which was marked by the weakening of the commercial pillar and by economic integration emphasizing political, social, and cultural integration?
- What is the relation between notions of regional integration based upon the deepening of the process and those aimed at its expansion. In other words, what is the relation between focusing on Mercosur and at the same time strengthening other regional bodies, such as Unasur, Celac, and others which still contain a technical or sectorial character?

After high initial expectations, nurtured by the growing process of cooperation with Argentina, which had its beginning in 1979 with the Tripartite Treaty for the utilization of waters from the *Paraná* River, but mainly due to the agreements of 1985 and 1986, and the Programme for Economic Integration and Cooperation (PICE), Mercosur's institutional and economic advance encountered greater difficulties from 1999. The initial pro-integration conception, prevalent in the period from 1986 to 1994, which considered the risks of regional isolation in relation to the world,—which at the time was rapidly globalizing and expressed through the materialization of regional blocs (Moreira, 1989),—remained present. Yet, it did not achieve sufficient density for spillovers to become evident (Malamud, 2020), which would be necessary for a deepening of the process. One of the reasons,—which so far has not been sufficiently analyzed—was the attraction of central countries in general, and the United States in particular. From the 2000s, China gradually became a very relevant economic partner for all of the Mercosur countries. This permitted the diffusion of tensions which hereafter again would become evident within the four countries, and more generally in Latin America.

The US diplomat, Thomas Shannon (apud Magnotta, 2019, pp. 167–179), explores this evolution of the United States' perception of the region. In an interview with the researcher, Fernanda Magnotta (2019), he outlines the changes within the United States' government regarding the insertion of China within South America: "during the Bush's administration the major perception was that we should cooperate with China and try to integrate China into the global order.... We certainly didn't see China as a geopolitical threat in Latin America. In fact, in the 2008–2009 international economic recessions they were helpful. Their commodities purchases actually helped stabilize Latin American governments and ended up being very important for our benefit. Not just for the benefit of Latin American countries, especially South American countries, but also for the United States .... I don't think we stopped interacting, but there was less openness to a Chinese presence". As it becomes evident in the interview with Shannon, what truly spurred the US concerns regarding the Chinese presence, not least from the point of Hu Jintao's travels to South America in 2004 and 2010, and in particular concerning Brazil, was the possibility that China could serve as an element to counterbalance the United States. According to the diplomat, this was especially evident regarding the Workers' Party governments. He shows how this array of positions accentuated the contradictions within the Brazilian diplomacy. Shannon thus stresses "And so it was the beginning of a change in how we understood China's presence in the region". Hence, throughout the latter part of the first decade of the 2000s, there was a change in the way that the United States viewed the Chinese presence. This perception became increasingly evident throughout the 2010s, hereby contributing to the reorientation of US policies, which also would influence Brazilian policy. This geopolitical movement occurring beyond the region would therefore wield a more direct impact on the South American regionalism, contributing to its weakening.

In this book, we analyze the ambivalent Brazilian behavior, of its governments, its political forces, and high officials, in relation to the region. In a dialogue with other interpretations, we consider the Brazilian capacities, without overemphasizing them, as well as the principles which inform the country's international insertion, just like the internal and international conditioning factors. We supplement some of these analyses with certain necessary elements, and long-term perspectives of both political and material character, which explain the oscillations, resistances, and oppositions to the deepening of Brazilian regional integration. We hereby seek to explain the factors which influence the level of regionness within the Brazilian international insertion and highlight their consequences regarding Mercosur. It is therefore interesting to seek to understand Borzel's formulation (2018, p. 482): "If discourses become more nationalist and practices more non-compliant, we need theories that tell us how and when these tendencies of disintegration will undermine economic transactions, regional institution-building, and the dependable expectations of peaceful change among Europeans. If we tackle these challenges, there is no need to worry about the future of EU studies". In the case of Mercosur, it is not exactly that which is the focus. Hence, the future of EU studies helps us to understand its effectiveness and continuity, due to its success and motivations, as we consider the continuity of research about the reality and the context of the European bloc. In Mercosur, as we shall see in this book, more significant perplexities become evident, or rather, a preoccupation in relation to the future of the bloc, which gains expression through institutional, ideational, and economic and political foundations with a lower degree of resilience. Therefore, there are reasons to be preocupied.

In this work, we do not pretend to formulate a theory of regional integration or disintegration. We adopt another point of reference in order to reflect on how a theory and school of thought can be constructed. Discussing what could be viewed as a school of international relations, Wang and Buzan (2014) frame the question in other terms. For them, the English School gained relevance due to its adherence to certain standards of universal interest. Wang and Buzan's (2014) reasoning serves a very specific goal: to evaluate that which would be a Chinese school of international relations. With point of departure in research on Brazilian foreign policy, we study how regionalism and regional integration within the Southern Cone have been defined, considering its historical trajectory and motivations.

Studying the Brazilian policy in relation to Mercosur, our goal is to contribute to a systemic understanding of the events, therethrough defining its rationale. Indirectly, this relates to a process of incorporation of geo-cultural epistemologies, be this either in times of decay or in ascent for Brazilian foreign policy. The *longue durée* perspective, informed by historical institutionalism, contributes to the systematization of Brazilian foreign policy in relation to Mercosur. That is, our analytical process thereby supports the discussion of both integration and disintegration theory. Perotta's (2018, p. 33) idea that "the field of regional integration responds or reacts *ex-post* to *la politica en América Latina*" which is incorporated to analyze the Brazilian case. This does not concern an instrumentalization of research, or, as Cox (1987) would say, a "problem solving" theory, constructed at a later moment in order to explain theoretically unresolved facts. Rather, the goal is to contribute to the construction of theories which seek to understand the reasons and difficulties of regional integration, considering this phenomenon's global dimension.

We hope that this book can provide an important contribution for those who are interested in theories of international relations and regional integration, as well as Brazilian foreign policy and international organizations. We hereby make a theoretically and empirically detailed contribution focused on furthering the understanding of the factors which condition states' engagement in relation to processes of regional integration. Likewise, we also provide subsidies for understanding the role of large emerging countries, discussing the potentials and limits of their regional and global roles.

Authors' Notes
The next three chapters are modified versions of published articles that have been revised with this book's central aims and analytical framework in mind, which is defined in the introduction above. Chapter 2 is a modified version of an article published in the journal *Contexto Internacional* vol. 36 n. 2, 2014. We thank Clodoaldo Bueno, co-author of this article and an important academic figure within this theme for the opportunity to revise and publish it in this book. Chapter 3 is a modified and updated version of an article of our own authorship, published in the journal *Contexto Internacional*, vol. 32, no. 2, 2010. Chapter 4 is an adapted and updated revised version of an article published in *Revista Brasileira de Política Internacional*, vol. 51, no. 1, pp. 5–27, 2008. We thank Gustavo de Mauro Favaron and Rodrigo Alves Correia, co-authors of the article in question, for their authorization of its revision and publication in this book. We also highlight the valuable collaboration of André Mellini for the research and systematization of the international trade data used. Likewise, we are also thankful to Niels Soendergaard for his work in translating the chapters within this book and for his help in the organization of the material.

We are thankful to the National Institute of Science and Technology for Studies of the United States (INCT-INEU) that led to this book, and to the National Council for Scientific and Technological Development (CNPq) and to the Research Support Foundation of the State of São Paulo (FAPESP).

References

Acharya, A. (2016). Regionalism beyond EU-centrism. In T. Börzel & T. Risse (Eds.), *The Oxford handbook of comparative regionalism* (p. 7). Oxford University Press.

Acharya, A. (2015). *An IR for the global south or a global IR? E-international relations*. Available at: https://www.e-ir.info/2015/10/21/an-ir-for-the-global-south-or-a-global-ir/

Acharya, A. (2012). Comparative regionalism: A field whose time has come? *The International Spectator, 47*(1), 3–15.

Acharya, A. (2014). Global International Relations (IR) and regional worlds a new agenda for international studies. *International Studies Quarterly, 58*, 647–659.

Alden, C., Morphet, S., & Vieira Marco, A. (2010). *The South in world politics*. Palgrave Macmillan.

Borzel, T. (2018). Researching the EU (studies) into demise? *Journal of European Public Policy, 25*(3), 475–485.

Botto, M. (2015). *La integración regional en América Latina: quo vadis? El Mercosur desde una perspectiva sectorial y comparada*. Editorial Universitaria de Buenos Aires (EUDEBA).

Briceño-Ruiz, J., & De Lombaerde, P. (2018). Regionalismo latino-americano: produção de saber e criação e importação da teoria. *Civitas - Revista de Ciências Sociais, 18*(2), 262–284.

Burges, S. (2009). *Brazilian foreign policy after the cold war*. University Press of Florida.

Cox, R. (1987). *Production, power and world order: Social forces in the making of history*. Columbia University Press.

Dahl, R. (1958). A critique of the ruling elite model. *The American Political Science Review, 52*(2), 201–215.

Farrell, M., Hettne, B., Langenhove, V., & Van, L. (2005). *Global politics of regionalism: Theory and practice*. Pluto.

Fioramonti, L., & Mattheis, F. (2016). Is Africa really following Europe? An integrated framework for comparative regionalism. *Journal of Common Market Studies, 54*(3), 674–690.

Gardini, G. L. (2010). *The origins of Mercosur. Democracy and regionalization in South America*. Palgrave.

Hermida, C., Avellar, A. P. M., Xavier, C. L., & dos Reis Azevedo, B. M. (2015). Desempenho e fragmentação da indústria de alta tecnologia do Mercosul. *Revista de Economia Política, 35*(3), 622–644.

Hettne, B., & Soderbaum, F. (2000). Theorising the rise of regionness. *New Political Economy, 5*(3), 457–472.

Hirschman, A. O. (1971). *A bias for hope: Essays on development and Latin America*. Yale University Press.

Hooghe, L., & Marks, G. (2019). Grand theories of European integration in the twenty-first century. *Journal of European Public Policy, 27*(8), 1113–1133.

Hurrelmann, A., & Schneider, S. (2015). *The legitimacy of regional integration in Europe and the Americas*. Palgrave Macmillan.

Krapohl, S. (2020). Games regional actors play: Dependency, regionalism, and integration theory for the Global South. *Journal of International Relations and Development, 23*, 840–870.

Magnotta, F. (2019). *A política dos Estados Unidos para a China na América Latina no início do século XXI: acomodação versus confrontação*. Tese de Doutorado PPGRI - San Tiago Dantas - UNESP, UNICAMP, PUC-SP.

Malamud, A. (2005). Presidential diplomacy and the institutional underpinnings of Mercosur: An empirical examination. *Latin American Research Review, 40*(1), 138–164.

Malamud, A. (2020). *Mercosur and the European Union: Comparative regionalism and interregionalism*. Oxford Research Encyclopedias.
Mariano, K. L. P. (2015). *Regionalismo na América do Sul: uma novo esquema de análise e a experiência do Mercosul*. Editora da UNESP.
Mattli, W. (1999). *The logic of regional integration*. Cambridge University Press.
Mignolo, W. (2011). The global south and world (dis) order. *Journal of Anthropological Research, vol., 67*(201), 165–188.
Moravcsik, A. (1998). *The choice for Europe*. Cornell.
Moreira, M. M. (1989). *O Brasil no contexto internacional do final do século XX*. Lua Nova, no. 18, ago. pp. 5–23.
Nolte, D. (2010). How to compare regional powers: Analytical concepts and research topics. *Review of International Studies, no., 36*, 881–901.
Pastor, M., & Wise, C. (1994). The origins and sustainability of Mexico's free trade policy. *International Organization, 48*(3), 459–489.
Perotta, D. (2018). El campo de estudios de laintegración regional y su aporte a las Relaciones Internacionales: una mirada desde América Latina. *Relaciones Internacionales, 38*, 9–39.
Pierson, P. (1998). The path to European integration: A historical-institutionalist analysis. In W. Sandholtz & A. S. Sweet (Eds.), *European integration and supranational governance* (pp. 12–26). Oxford University Press.
Ramanzini Junior, H., & Luciano, B. T. (2020). Regionalism in the Global South: Mercosur and Ecowas in trade and democracy protection. *Third World Quarterly, 41*(9), 1498–1517.
Riggirozzi, P., & Tussie, D. (2012). *The rise of post-hegemonic regionalism: The case of latin America*. Springer.
Wang, J., & Buzan, B. (2014). The english and chinese schools of international relations: Comparisons and lessons. *The Chinese Journal of International Politics, 7*(1), 1–46.

Chapter 2
A Long Perspective on Latin American Regional Integration Seen from Brazil

2.1 Introduction

This chapter aims to discuss Latin-American integration, with special attention to the Brazilian positions, in order to understand the elements of continuity between the foreign policy of the first years of the Republic of Brazil, particularly the period of the Baron of Rio Branco (1902–1912), and the present days. We seek to analyze the roots of the Brazilian regional integration policy that culminated in the Mercosur proposal in the 1980s. Accordingly, in this chapter, we examine the Brazilian policy in relation to its neighbors throughout the twentieth century. We focus on policy and strategy coordination experiments that aimed to maximize the interests of the countries of the region. Such is the case with the ill-fated ABC agreement, which was discussed at the time of the Baron of Rio Branco. Other attempts were made throughout the twentieth century. One such attempt was the November 1941 Free Exchange Agreement signed by Enrique Ruiz-Guiñazú and Oswaldo Aranha, respectively, foreign ministers of Argentina and Brazil, which however never came into effect. The question was taken up again with the important free trade agreement proposal submitted by Juan Domingo Perón of Argentina in the 1950s, and with the attempt by the Humberto de Alencar Castello Branco government in 1967 to negotiate a Trade Union with Argentina's president, General Ongania, an idea immediately dropped with the inauguration of General Artur da Costa e Silva. These are significant attempts insofar as they establish the existence of twentieth-century regional rapprochement agreements, mostly between Brazil and Argentina, which until the 1980s had, nevertheless, always been superficial agreements. During the period under analysis in this chapter, from the Proclamation of the Republic in 1889 until 2011, the end of the Lula government and the beginning of the Dilma Administration, Brazil's relations with its neighboring countries were driven by rivalry, approximation and differentiation, and finally, by distancing.

T. Vigevani, H. Ramanzini Junior, *The Challenges for Building Regional Integration in the Global South*, United Nations University Series on Regionalism 18,
https://doi.org/10.1007/978-3-030-93348-7_2

Before the Mercosur, discussions in Latin and South America concerning integration were of a romantic, or merely trade-related, character, as were the cases of the Latin-American Free Trade Association (LAFTA) created in 1960, and the Latin-American Integration Association (ALADI) from the 1980s. From the point of view of the Brazilian foreign policy, it is only as of the mid-1980s that the regional sphere begins to be viewed as a structuring axis of the country's international behavior. Previous attempts to foster regional cooperation were not necessarily guided by the logic of integration. Until the 1980s, pursuing autonomous national development in the Latin-American context was a clear aim. In other cases, pursuing a privileged relation with the US was the main driver, not only because of the context-bound, strategic heritage but also because of the benefits the largest economy of the continent can offer.

An interpretation reiterated by some authors is that 1985 marks the passage from the romantic to the pragmatic phase of the integration, as attested by the evolution of the Argentina–Brazil relations in the Raúl Alfonsín and José Sarney governments (Barbosa, 1996). From then and onwards, these relations overcame decades of mutual fears, thus enabling an economic integration hinging on the partial complementarity of the two countries' economies rather than on traditional multilateral schemes. Brazil preserved the 'universalist' nature of its foreign policy, while on the domestic front the country made it a priority to strengthen and widen relations with its neighboring states, particularly with Argentina. Integration efforts, both in the bilateral phase and in the ensuing Mercosur phase, would change interactions of the countries of the Southern Cone, with the resolution of the Itaipu–Corpus dispute, followed by the Brazilian solidarity with Argentina during the Malvinas/Falklands War in 1982, as milestones.

Bearing the foregoing aims in mind, the text is organized as follows. In the first section, we discuss the trajectory of the Brazilian regional integration policy from the Baron of Rio Branco era to the 1958 Pan American Operation. In the second section, we analyze the ECLAC and LAFTA experiences, aiming to identify their meaning regarding the Brazilian integration and cooperation policy. The third section is dedicated to analyzing ALADI. Lastly, the fourth section aims to analyze the Mercosur considering its difference in relation to the previous experiences. We also seek to identify the elements of continuity in the Brazilian policy in relation to the countries in South America, from the beginning of the twentieth century until the end of the first decade of the twenty-first century.

2.2 From Rio Branco's ABC to Operation Pan American (1902–1958)

The Baron of Rio Branco was the Minister of Foreign Relations during the period from 1902 to 1912. He served under four different presidents: Rodrigues Alves (1902–1906), Afonso Pena (1906–1909), Nilo Peçanha (1909–1910) and Hermes da

Fonseca (1910–1914). Throughout his tenure at the head of the Ministry of External Relations (MER), the Baron of Rio Branco spoke with elevated rhetoric in favor of good relations with all the nations of the hemisphere, despite being aware of the limits of South-American solidarity. Accordingly, even when he had already become a prominent figure in the region, he was careful enough not to ever let his country appear as if it sought a leading role. The sensitivity which Hispanic-American nations exhibited in matters involving Brazilian interests made him realize that Brazil had little chance of influencing them alone. Rio Branco, and leading elites, considered their country different from all the others in Latin America, which at that time was marked by endless political turmoil. Chile would be the sole exception. According to Rio Branco, the most efficient way to shield Brazil against such attacks would be to guarantee the region's political stability to ensure the end of its age of revolutions. Rio Branco's broad foreign policy guideline concerning South America was underpinned by a search for equilibrium to avert imperialist dreams or hegemonic projects originated in its own space, which convinced him to abide by an *entente cordiale* policy with Argentina and Chile (Lins, 1945, p. 613). In the official letter to the minister plenipotentiary of Brazil in Buenos Aires, dated 22 November 1904, he clearly formulated his thoughts and suggested the creation of a binding instrument governing peace- and order-driven attitudes in the region by the three South American countries.

In Argentina, President Julio Roca (1880–1886 and 1898–1904) also advocated joint action by the three main republics of South America, forming the then so-called "ABC triangle". In 1904, Roca and Foreign Minister José A. Terry conditioned the recognition of the new State of Panama to a joint recognition, thus resulting in the first concrete ABC measure (Fraga, 1994, p. 44). In advocating shared influence, Rio Branco acted, above all, with pragmatism. The three nations' friendship, in addition to their equilibrium, would prevent interventions by one of them in less powerful republics, and also allow Brazil to feel more at ease within the sub-regional context. In an official letter, he stated that "(...) the close friendship between Brazil and Chile has served to contain their [the Argentineans'] vague desires for open intervention in the Chilean-Peruvian dispute, in the one we had with Bolivia, and in the one we still have with Peru" (AHI, 1906). The three nations' rapprochement gained a character of an entente of the South, which brought fear, especially to the Peruvians, as informed by Joaquim Nabuco, Brazil's ambassador in Washington.

The 20th of October 1907, in Santiago, Puga Borne, (Chile's Foreign Relations Minister) and Lorenzo Anadón, (Argentina's representative in that capital), wrote a draft treaty to regulate relations between the ABC countries. The draft they outlined, though including rules on immigration and accession by other countries, had the character of a military alliance as it even provided for a "discreet equivalence" in the three naval forces. The subject subsided mostly because of the tense bilateral relations between Brazil and Argentina at the time, quite different therefore from those defining the period of President Roca. Rio Branco saw no possibility of cordiality between Brazil, Chile and Argentina as long as his rival in the Misiones dispute, Estanisláo Zeballos, who had "vague desires of hegemony and intervention in others' matters", was the minister of foreign relations. The Brazilian foreign minister wished to examine the entente affair only further ahead, "with time and calm" and in such a way as to not harm "intimacy with the American government" and to foster closer friendship with Chile too (apud Conduru, 1998, pp. 106–10; 77–8).

The 13th of February 1909, in Brazil, Rio Branco received a minute for a preliminary draft treaty from Puga Borne, then Chile's former minister of foreign relations, who was on his way to Europe to assume his country's representation in Paris. Rio Branco prepared another draft and had it delivered on the 21st day of that same month to the aforementioned diplomat, but opted instead to have Chile submit the proposal to Argentina. According to Conduru (1998), Rio Branco's draft preserved the formula of the Puga Borne draft in Article 1, in stating that the three countries were in "most perfect harmony" and wished to "keep it and strengthen it, always seeking to proceed in agreement with each other in all matters relating to common interests and aspirations and in those designed to ensure peace and stimulate the progress of South America". Ricupero (1995) holds that the "core of the agreement was in its Article 1". By Article 2, the parties agreed to "submit to arbitration disagreements of any nature that should arise between them and which had failed to be settled by diplomatic means", provided they did not involve "the vital interests, independence, sovereignty or honor of the contracting states". Article 6 provided for rules to be complied with in the hypothesis of serious divergence between them that failed to meet arbitration requirements. Rio Branco's concern with the region's order and stability is reflected in Article 9, which provided for the obligation that the contracting governments prevented, in their respective territories, émigrés from gathering and arming themselves. The two following articles further detailed the procedure by prohibiting trade with insurgents from bordering countries and providing for exiles to be disarmed (Conduru, 1998, pp. 75, 84, 110–2; Lins, 1945, p. 770–1, 1965, p. 522–3; Ricupero, 1995, p. 95).

It is worth reiterating that the ABC draft, as conceived by Rio Branco, made no mention to economic issues, nor to trade between the nations involved and naval equivalence in the Southern Cone, which he vehemently ruled out, and reaffirmed that the Argentina-Brazil-Chile rapprochement was not intended to counterbalance US influence. This allows us to conclude that in the vision of the Brazilian foreign minister, the ABC subsumed the idea of what can be called an oligarchic condominium of nations, for the benefit of peace in South America. In July 1906, on the occasion of the 3rd International Conference of American States, held in Rio de Janeiro, in a notorious interview to the correspondent of Buenos Aires newspaper *La Nación*, he stated that, among other things, if there was to be an agreement between Argentina, Chile, and Brazil, these nations, given the fact that they were the "strongest and most progressive [...] would exert influence on the others, preventing all too frequent wars in some countries". The Baron held that it was impossible to sign an accord with the 21 republics, "We think that an agreement in the interest of all, to be feasible, should only be attempted between the United States of America, Mexico, Brazil, Chile, and Argentina." Brazil, in particular, could only exert some influence over Uruguay, Paraguay, and Bolivia if acting in line with Argentina and Chile. Brazil was distant from the other countries, due to lack of communications,

(La Nación, Buenos Aires, 26 July and 9 August 1906; AHI, dispatch to Washington, 10 March 1906, in Lins, 1945, pp. 757–61).

The idea was that Brazil, Argentina and Chile should mutually support each other and, as that possible entente would not take up an anti-US character, it would increase the prestige of the three nations and contribute to preventing imperialist aggression by Europe. At Rio Branco's time, the ABC Treaty failed to go beyond the preliminary negotiations phase. Nonetheless, the three nations would still attempt concerted action at the 4th International Conference of American States, held in Buenos Aires in 1910. Brazil took the initiative of secretly establishing a previous understanding with the other two countries on a settlement formula in support of the Monroe Doctrine, drafted by Joaquim Nabuco shortly before his death. As details of the negotiation were leaked, prompting reactions from the representatives of the other American nations, Brazil and Argentina, backed by the United States, were led to withdraw the resolution from consideration at that conference (Burns, 1966, p. 154–5). The New York Herald issue of September 4, 1910, published a story by its correspondent in Buenos Aires in which the proposal to enlarge the Monroe Doctrine to be submitted by the Brazilian delegation failed because of the Chilean delegates. Still, the idea of the ABC would reappear further ahead, during Lauro Müller's term of office, though in another context of the hemispheric relations.

The pacifist treaties were a reaction to the escalation of the crisis of the age of empires in the first decade of the twentieth century. Treaties were signed and leagues formed both with offensive and defensive purposes, as well as compacts designed to avoid disruptions of peace by providing for appeasement and dispute resolution mechanisms. Rio Branco's successor at the Ministry of External Relations, Lauro Müller's visit to Argentina in 1915 took place in the wake of the mediation by the ABC in the United States–Mexico bilateral relations' crisis and was a milestone in terms of cordiality between the two most important Atlantic nations of the Southern Cone. On the 25th of May, in Buenos Aires, the Brazilian foreign minister, together with his peers José Luis Murature and Alejandro Lyra, respectively, of Argentina and Chile, signed a Pacifist Treaty, and also designated the ABC Treaty, for the friendly settlement of potential issues arising between the signatory countries not covered by arbitrations provided for in previous treaties. Just as was provided for in the American treaty, disputes not settled by arbitration or direct diplomatic means would be submitted to a permanent committee, made up of one delegate from each country. There should be no hostility until this committee had made a ruling or within 1 year of its constitution. The difference compared to other US pacifist treaties is that the ABC was tripartite. The subject matter of the treaty was modest while its purpose was to freeze conflicts for one and a half year since the deadline for issuing a ruling could be extended for another 6 months (Burns, 1977, p. 394; Ferrari, 1981; Ministry of External Relations Report, 1914–15, pp. 144–9).

The 1915 ABC Treaty, according to the Brazilian ministerial report, presented no special feature when compared with the pacifist treaty Brazil had signed with the United States. The 1915 treaty was smaller in scope than the 1907–1909 ABC proposals and complemented previously signed bilateral arbitration treaties. Thus, the 1915 Treaty was unique in that it neither had regional scope nor provided for a military alliance, naval equivalence, or (as had been proposed by Rio Branco) anti-insurrectional cooperation (Conduru, 1998, p. 12). Müller's initial idea was to sign a treaty of perpetual friendship with Argentina. His Argentine peer, José Luis Murature, however, received the proposal as if it were similar to those that had already been signed by the United States.

The conception that the Argentine government had of the Brazilian ABC Treaty initiative was regarded by the French representative to Buenos Aires as mere international courtesy. This appears as an obvious conclusion, since the Argentinean government, though moving toward the ABC Treaty, would not give up its arms policy, as noted by *La Mañana*, a Buenos Aires newspaper. The Brazilian Chamber of Deputies passed the May 25th treaty, and so did the Senate on November 3rd, 1915. The president of the republic sanctioned it on the 12th of the same month. The treaty was also approved by the Chilean Senate, while Argentina's Senate passed it by unanimous vote after the speech delivered by rapporteur Joaquim Gonzáles. Yet, it failed to pass in the Chamber of Deputies, where its opponents found no reason not to extend it to all the other republics, besides having seen signs of hegemonic and interventionist intentions. Luís Maria Drago and Zeballos stood out as the most vocal among the opposition.

In Argentina, the ABC treaty was interpreted as limiting the country's foreign policy options, as it would be obliged to go along with Brazil and Chile, a view that can be traced as far back as 1912. Luis P. Tamini, thereby envisioned an approximation with the ABC. As the *Radicales* reached power, the treaty was shelved in Buenos Aires. In March 1917, *La Gaceta*, a Buenos Aires newspaper, reported on the "cooling of the active fraternity brought about by the former administration of *Doctor* Plaza" (Ferrari, 1981, p. 70; *La Gaceta*, 1917).

In Heitor Lyra's interpretation (1992) the Brazilian diplomacy's poor timing and lack of skill in presenting the ABC treaty had led to its failure. Hence, the treaty's poor reception on the Continent, mostly in the "Bolivarian" countries, who felt sidelined. Müller's initiative was also criticized at home. Federal Deputy Dunshee de Abranches—an international relations scholar and former collaborator of the Baron of Rio Branco—criticized Minister Müller's initiative during the session on the 6th of October, 1915, in the Chamber of Deputies with, among others, the argument that the treaty was unnecessary. Pandiá Calógeras, in 1918, classified the treaty as a "disaster" because "in international politics, a useless action is a dangerous action, for it solves no problem at all and, for its declarations, may be invoked in other unforeseen circumstances". Three other bilateral arbitration agreements between Argentina, Brazil, and Chile were already in force. Thus, he asked why a possible discussion between two contracting parties ought to be replaced with one involving three parties, potentially leading to "a grouping of two against one". Moreover, as it was a "treaty of perpetual friendship" setting out "principles of continental fraternity", Calógeras insisted there was no way it could avoid accession by other South-American powers, and asked, "Being Chile one of the signatories, what [would be] the attitude of the ABC if Peru and Bolivia joined [it], and by Brazilian initiative (since we have had the case) relive the palpitating Tacna and Arica question, the Alsace-Lorraine of our Continent? Dormant, today, the

Itamaraty's clumsy stewardship would have come to awaken it" (Conduru 1998, pp. 71–73). Calógeras's conclusion was emphatic, "Result: from friendly to every republic in the Pacific, Brazil has become the threat to peace in America" (Calógeras, 1987, p. 502).

Yet Müller, if he was sincere in the words he said aboard the *Gelria* on his return from the [River] Plate, such as reproduced by the newspaper *La Razón*, saw the ABC Treaty as unrealistic, for he expected it, despite the indifference of some politicians, "to have a repercussion of transcendental importance in international politics". Thereafter the South American countries would have more weight in international politics because "before, they were considered as an inactive part of the overseas policy, they will now have a firm vote which it will be necessary to consider and appreciate" (La Razón 1910).

We must stress that the 1915 Treaty contained nothing in terms of resistance against any political and economic penetration of the United States or even of Europe. The informal ABC alliance had not been received with hostility by the United States, as the country was reshaping its tutelage over its Southern neighbors. The First World War led to a total crisis of the international order in which the ABC was embedded. As a consequence, the ABC disappeared without ever being able to reemerge during the interwar period. The ABC policy finally collapsed in early 1923 because Argentina's foreign affairs office refused the Brazilian proposal for a preliminary meeting with the three countries in Valparaíso to address the naval armaments issue, before the launch of the 5th Pan-American Conference in Santiago (Donghi, 1972, p. 292–3; Ferrari, 1981, p. 70; Smith, 1991, p. 80).

The Great War interrupted the sequence of American international conferences which led to the weakening of hemispheric solidarity in the 1920s, made evident in the 6th International Conference of American States (Havana, 1928) where the schism between the US and Latin America became evident. In the context immediately preceding the Second World War, once again the United States turned to Latin America by pursuing a rapprochement policy led by President Franklin D. Roosevelt, who named it as a "good neighbor". In October 1930, the Getúlio Vargas era began in Brazil, during which Pan-Americanism was enhanced and applied in the Leticia question (conflict between Peru and Colombia) as well as in the mediation, together with Argentina, of the Chaco War. In the world order of the post-Second World War, the UN Charter provided for the creation of regional organisms. Thus, in 1947 the Inter-American Treaty of Reciprocal Assistance (TIAR) was signed in Petrópolis, which provided for peacekeeping and hemispheric security mechanisms. The Organization of American States (OAS), created in 1948 by the 9th International Conference of American States, in Bogotá, is the successor to the Pan-American Union, created in 1890 and responsible for the ensuing conferences. With the TIAR and the OAS, hemispheric regionalism was integrated into the post-second world war order.

After the end of World War II (May 1945), in which Brazil fought on the Allied side, more precisely in October, Getúlio Vargas was ousted. With democracy restored, Marshall Eurico Gaspar Dutra was elected by a direct vote on December 2, 1945, and took office in January of the following year. The new president's foreign policy, in the wake of the wartime military alliance, continued to be focused on close US-Brazil relations (despite serious economic divergence). Domestically, the president administered the national economy and finances in line with liberal principles. Therefore, Dutra took, at home and abroad, a course that differed from that of Argentina, which under Juan Domingo Perón's leadership moved toward nationalism and away from the United States, factors that kept Brazil on guard and against any sort of international rapprochement project of the ABC type. This situation changed with Vargas's return to power in 1951, as the dubiousness which characterized his governing style returned with him, leading to greater distance with the US. To head the Ministry of External Relations, Vargas appointed João Neves da Fontoura, an advocate of political proximity with the US and an opponent of closer relations with Buenos Aires, to whose embassy he sent an old companion, João Batista Lusardo. Like himself, Lusardo was also born in the Rio Grande do Sul state, a supporter of the ABC entente and a friend of Juan Domingo Perón, who longed for the union of the three most important nations of the Southern hemisphere.

Domestically, those against the rapprochement denounced the treaty as a pretext for Perón's expansionist pretentions in the continent's southernmost part. This stemmed from the fact that, in face of the antagonistic power blocs led by the US and the Soviet Union, Perón proposed a "third position"—a South America led by the ABC nations. The liberal opposition and part of the press warned of the danger represented by the establishment of a labor republic. After a period of hesitation and infighting, Vargas secretly contacted Perón in 1953, using an intermediary to ask him about his willingness to reestablish the ABC. Upon returning an affirmative answer, the Argentinean president kept waiting for some manifestation by Vargas, who, nonetheless, failed to proceed with the subject, likely because of the crisis at home. The delay prompted Perón, in a secret conference at Argentina's National School of War, to accuse Vargas of weakness, and to state that the Itamaraty created obstacles to the two countries' union. The text leaked and in Rio de Janeiro fell into the hands of oppositionist Carlos Lacerda, who published it in *Tribuna da Imprensa*, turning the affair into a national scandal. Vargas was accused of betraying the country, particularly by the supporters of the vehement journalist Carlos Lacerda. At this point, the Vargas government was already losing support. Months later, on August 24, 1954, he would commit suicide amid a political crisis with internal and external components. Shortly afterwards on September 21, 1955, Perón was overthrown from power (Bandeira, 1987, pp. 25, 30–32). But the prospects of an ABC-type agreement were dead before that (Cavlak, 2008, pp. 56, 65, 169, 171, 176, 182, 195 and 201).

Brazil's relations with Latin America once again gained prominence during the Juscelino Kubitschek de Oliveira administration (1955–1960), with the launching of Operation Pan American (OPA) in 1958, a hemisphere-wide international cooperation plan designed to ban poverty and underdevelopment from Latin America, which were seen as a path of entry for antidemocratic ideologies. OPA's debut took advantage of an escalation of anti-US sentiment, which hampered US relations with the nations of the Southern Hemisphere, as they had not received the benefits of the economic cooperation the US extended to other areas of the world. The Brazilian president asked the US President Dwight Eisenhower for an economic translation of the political Pan Americanism since that would be the most efficient way for the hemisphere to oppose "the materialistic and anti-democratic threat of the Soviet bloc". Kubitschek thought not only of Brazil but the whole of Latin America in defending the strengthening of democracy, as it would be incompatible with poverty. To him, the OPA was not "a mere program, *but a whole policy*" adjusted "to the new forms of the world crisis, at a critical moment for the West". The proposal called for studies on investments in backward areas of the continent increased credit by international bodies, a strengthening of the economy, discipline in the primary products' market, the establishment of regional markets, enlarged and diversified technical assistance, and the need for public capital for basic sectors and infrastructure. Despite Secretary of State John Foster Dulles' unwillingness to deliberate on the matter, an idea he found inopportune, given the issue's international repercussions, the US government could not avoid discussing it. The OPA, though well accepted by the Organization of American States (OAS), which set up a special committee with representatives of its 21 member countries (Committee of the 21) tasked with the execution of the operation, had very little to show in terms of practical results. The creation of the Inter-American Development Bank (IADB) is singled out as its only concrete result, coincidently a long-standing aspiration of the region (Bandeira, 1973, pp. 378, 381–2; 137–44; VI, 116–23; Leite, 1959, pp. 26–43; Sette, 1996, p. 251).

To Latin Americans, regional integration until the early 1950s had a political character. Trade relations, incipient in some subregions, were governed by bilateral agreements. Trade integration and economic cooperation only began to be viewed as enabling economic growth in the region in that decade (during which the Juscelino Kubitschek administration held office in Brazil), also driven by examples from abroad, namely, the Treaty of Rome (1957).

2.3 Brazil, ECLAC and LAFTA

Rubens Barbosa (1996, p. 135) considers that the period of discussions conducted by ECLAC, the late 1950s and early 1960s, should be defined as romantic considering the concrete proposals for, and the possibility of, integration. Discussions at the ECLAC started in 1953 and were driven by the real problems that existed in Latin America and which, thus thought the Commission, could at least be attenuated by a process of economic integration between the countries of the region, construed then mostly as industrial integration. Most importantly, ECLAC viewed regional integration as a means to strengthening national capacities.

To ECLAC industrialization was seen, in the 1950s and 1960s, as a long-term solution for the problem of external vulnerability, which was assumed to be an intrinsic characteristic of peripheral industrialization processes. Regional integration was also stressed as a possible response to the problem. ECLAC was directly involved in the creation of LAFTA as it understood that the new regional agreement could contribute to a process of export diversification spearheaded by the countries of the region themselves through the "theoretically" easier way of intraregional trade. The Latin-American common market would have the virtue of broadening transactions across demanding industrial sectors, thus contributing to deepening a process of import substitution (Bielschowsky, 2000). However, ECLAC's goals regarding integration and other steps of a greater magnitude proved difficult to meet because national policies failed to assume integration as critical to development. According to Cervo (2008, p. 155), ECLAC's thought, underpinned by concepts such as industry, employment, protection, domestic market and self-sufficiency, materialized in policies whose ultimate, though unintended, consequence would constrain the very same integration processes. With regards to Brazil, the ECLAC theses strengthened the perspective of those who defended the ideas of development and national projection.

Since 1953, ECLAC had recognized the need to enhance intraregional trade, which should be premised on the reduction or elimination of the customs tariffs that apparently constrained it. At the November 1954 meeting of ministers of economy, on the occasion of the 4th Extraordinary Session of the OAS Inter-American Economic and Social Council, ECLAC documents were presented which discussed the role of regional trade as a driver of development (United Nations, 1954). Against this backdrop, in 1956 ECLAC created a Trade Committee whose purpose was to study the impediments to regional trade. This committee created a Working Group on the Latin-American Regional Market, which first convened in February 1958 in Santiago and released the document *Bases para la Formación del Mercado Regional Latinoamericano*. Raul Prebisch's conceptions were clear. As ECLAC's senior director, he was the head of the Secretariat for the Regional Market group, which included Brazil's José Garrido Torres, chairman of the National Economic Council, and Argentina's Eustaquio Méndez Delfino, president of the Buenos Ayres Stock Exchange. This milestone text recognized the social demand for development. The paths would be the technification of agriculture and the progressive industrialization of the regional states. "Industrialization requires a broad market without which it will not be possible to reach, within our countries, the elevated productivity of the great industrial centers. Latin America could have a broad market, yet, it is fragmented in twenty separate compartments" (United Nations, 1961a, p. 41). Undoubtedly, as we shall have the opportunity to see when studying the reasons for the LAFTA crisis and the feebleness of ALADI, the idea of a Latin-American market comprising all the countries of the region seems to have been one of the reasons that prompted some to classify ECLAC's proposals as romantic. That is, a diversity of interests and even the impossibility of a comprehensive Latin-American vision were not taken into account. While ECLAC's document of February 1958 recognizes differences in affirming that "the less advanced countries shall be the subject of special treatment" (United Nations, 1961b, p. 43), the advantages of the bigger countries—Argentina, Brazil and Mexico—do not appear clearly. On the other hand, the potential advantages of these bigger countries will be decisive in determining their adhesion to LAFTA. ECLAC suggests not only a free trade area but the prospect of a common tariff regime *vis-à-vis* the rest of the world, as GATT's regulatory framework provided for, and allowed customs unions. The impact of the Treaty of Rome, of March 1957, which created the European Economic Community, was evident in these debates.

Concerning LAFTA, there is wide analytical consensus that its first years of functioning, until 1967, can be positively assessed. At this point it is fit to highlight the reasons, if not for the failure, then most certainly for the withering away of LAFTA; one of an economic character, the other of a political nature. If an integration process fails to impact strategic governmental stewardship actions this is a strong sign of the precariousness of the whole process. In the case of LAFTA and other regional integration processes in Latin America, except for the Andean Pact, no attempt was made by the governments to bring these same processes under the framework of a new institutional structure that would entrench the theme and transform it into a relevant national fact. Particularly in the case of Brazil, the geographic environment, with a few exceptions as in the case of the 1961 Uruguaiana agreement, barely had any bearing on the country's international undertakings and objectives in the 1960s, the 1970s, and part of the 1980s (Cervo & Bueno, 2011).

LAFTA's first years were certainly positive, yet they hardly had any impact on the regional economies, since the main ones, especially Brazil and Mexico, sought growth from within and constant improvement of relations with the central countries. In analyzing the economic reasons for the waning of LAFTA, it is important to consider the serious differences arising across countries for various reasons. As the negotiation prompted tariff reductions of non-competitive products which could be bought at lower prices in countries outside the Association, tensions rose. At the same time, more and more situations of unequal distribution of costs and benefits (a key issue in every regional integration process) arose. While some, mainly Argentina, Brazil and Mexico, had positive results, particularly in manufactured goods trade, others were at a disadvantage. Conflicts over tariff treatment of important products, like oil and wheat, increased tensions. Surely this was an important reason behind the decision of a group of countries to sign the Cartagena Agreement, in May 1969, when Bolivia, Chile, Colombia, Ecuador and Peru created the Andean Pact. Perceived losses by some of the smaller and middle countries eventually affected the bloc's credibility.

In the period preceding the Montevideo Treaty of February 18, 1960, political convergence across Latin-American countries was at a low, a situation that, despite some important attempts, would not change over the following years. Though Operation Pan American had been proposed by the Kubitschek government with Latin America in mind, US cooperation was absolutely essential. Accordingly, the United States had an active role in the creation, on October 1, 1960, of the Inter-American Development Bank (IADB), which, however, featured no programs directly linked to the integration of Latin America, then at the center of the debate. A reflection of the existing situation in the region was the Uruguaiana Meeting, on April 20, 1961, between the Presidents Arturo Frondizi and Jânio Quadros. On that occasion, talks focused on the two countries' relations—political, military and economic—as well as on relations with other countries in the region and with the United States. The terms of the Convention on Friendship and Permanent Consultation and the Declaration of Uruguaiana presented joint action on behalf of Argentina and Brazil in the resolution of international problems. Though talks focused on greater integration, no specific reference was made to the possible meaning of LAFTA regarding the integration process (de Melo Franco, 1968). However, it does not suffice to explain these attributes solely through the apparent contradictions and incoherencies to the two countries' foreign policies or their conceptions of regional integration. The domestic situations and Brazil and Argentina did not allow for a high level of coherence in their foreign engagement. As we know, the following years were intense in critical events that led to resignation and *coups d'état*.

It is worth signaling that, for its founders, Brazil in particular, LAFTA had a seemingly limited character in that some characteristics are enshrined that will not disappear from the debates over the two last decades of the twentieth century. As perceived at the time, the Montevideo Treaty was the outcome of a conference of a technical nature. In the Brazilian interpretation, a Free Trade Zone did not require "modifications in domestic economic policy or trade policy *vis-à-vis* the other members". Nor did it require a supranational authority for its functioning but, rather, intergovernmental bodies to run it (Resenha, 1960, p. 110). The Treaty created the Permanent Executive Committee and a Secretariat—the latter the only joint administrative body that was to remain in the second Montevideo Treaty of 1980. To a certain extent it served as a model for the Mercosur's secretariat, also headquartered in Montevideo, in 1991, and featuring technical characteristics and devoid of political power.

Regional integration processes at the level of free trade areas do not need to be premised on development policies. But any regional integration process must be perceived by states and society as in their self-interest. In the case of LAFTA, from its inception, but more emphatically in the mid- to the late 1960s, and despite growing exchange, the integration effort stagnated. Likewise, the ECLAC goals of the 1950s and 1960s proved impossible to accomplish, even if they might have provided some scope in this regard, as more daring steps were ruled out by national policy guidelines. Another likely decisive cause for the withering away of the integration perspective in Latin America is the role of the nation-state, as well as and foremost, the nationalist perspective from which the integration had been considered, particularly for the cases of Argentina and Brazil. This perspective remained until a new phase began in November 1985 with the signing of the Iguazu Declaration. It is important to mention that, with the Iguazu Act, for the first time Brazil's foreign policy centered on a South American country as a strategic partner. This was a more symmetrical partnership, significantly different from the partnerships established between Brazil and Germany and Japan in the 1970s, or even with the United States at different junctures.

We may affirm that the 1960s was a very intense decade in terms of initiatives aimed at overcoming underdevelopment: the Conference of Alta Gracia, the Second United Nations Conference on Trade and Development, with the creation of

UNCTAD, and the Group of 77. None of these initiatives, however, was driven by integration. The new Brazilian government that emerged from the military coup of March 1964 signaled that the integration should be understood primarily as an instrument for the promotion of Brazil's trade in the region: "we shall do everything toward the strengthening of LAFTA, to increase the presence of Brazil in the Latin-American market" (Leitão da Cunha, 1965, p. 136). It is also worth pointing out that, even in the period beginning in 1967, when authoritarian-nationalist and, partly, third-worldly conceptions were reintroduced in Brazil's foreign policy, regional integration was never a major concern. And not even when the Costa e Silva government (1967–1969) reintroduced features of the independent foreign policy of the Quadros and Goulart era did regional integration receive greater attention.

Hence the great relevance of the changes effected as of 1985 signaling a deep reorientation: a structural change in regional policy and the creation of an integration policy. This statement must be well situated. The Brazilian foreign policy, both in its autonomist and 'universalist' versions, or even from its global trader perspective, has always favored independence. The resolute adhesion to the integration with Argentina and to the Mercosur, in 1985 and 1990, must be understood as a tool for national strengthening, aligned therefore with a realist perspective of foreign policy, which accepts integration when seen to be in the country's self-interest and for its relative strengthening.

2.4 ALADI

In analyzing the LAFTA stalemate that led to the creation of ALADI, 1969 stands out as a milestone. The Caracas Protocol extended the end of the transition period defined for the creation of the free trade area, besides lowering the annual tariff reduction quantitative targets and laid out the blueprint for negotiations to start adapting the 1960 Montevideo Treaty to a new integration phase. These negotiations, which only started in 1974, continued throughout 1975 yet produced no immediate results. They were nonetheless instrumental in consolidating a broad consensus around the need to render more flexible the operational mechanisms that had been set out in 1960, by eliminating quantitative targets and timeframes for accomplishing previously established goals aimed at the creation of a common Latin-American market. The ALADI model began to be designed in this phase: the promotion of partial agreements between two countries or groups of countries, limiting the regional agreement to a trade preference zone. Preferential treatment for economically less developed countries was the subject of inconclusive debate. In November 1978, the 18th LAFTA Conference decided to formally open negotiations for a new Treaty. The meetings held in 1979 and in the first semester of 1980 ended at the 19th LAFTA Extraordinary Conference in Acapulco, in June 1980. The 1980 Montevideo Treaty was signed on August 12, 1980 (Moavro, 1992, pp. 180–6). To understand the differences between the two treaties, it is important to bear in mind that ALADI reflects a strong belief in the impossibility of a regional integration policy—a stance fully shared by the Brazilian government.

The 1980 Treaty gives up the goal of establishing a free trade zone. This is arguably the most important aspect from the political point of view; hence the dispensation of all quantitative and provisional commitments. In practice, it creates a tool for keeping a record of agreements between two or more countries and harmonizing them with GATT rules. Substantively, the agreement reflects the different political, social, and economic perspectives of the member countries. The Andean countries insisted on higher levels of integration, such as a common external tariff, an industrial development program, and equal treatment to foreign capital—objectives rejected by Brazil, which maintained a high tariff protection policy which was further strengthened as the foreign exchange crisis intensified. By contrast, the liberal policies of Argentina, Chile, and Uruguay had eroded the preference margins set out in the LAFTA framework. From 1980 and onwards, the oil crises and, especially, the foreign debt crises, starting with that of Mexico in 1982, accentuated the trend for every country to seek to increase its own exports. In this context, ALADI started to assign more value to the individual interests of the member countries to the detriment of the communitarian vision (Barbosa, 1996, p. 146).

While prospects of Latin-American or at least South-American, integration faded, other circumstances hint at new developments. New and more adequate references help explain the reductionist character of ALADI, which was adapted to the context of its creation. In 1977, the first Argentina-Brazil nuclear cooperation agreement was signed. More importantly, in October 1979, the Jorge Videla and João Baptista Figueiredo governments—once resistance from military sectors with noncooperative readings of national sovereignty had been subdued—signed the agreement that allows the tri-national utilization of the waters of the Paraná River, thus making it possible to build the Itaipu and Corpus hydroelectric power plants. Highly significant for this agreement was the influence of sectors interested in positive outcomes which were not at the core of the national states' decision-making process—in the Brazilian case, companies Itaipu Binacional and Eletrobrás, and in the Argentinean case, economic interests concerned with the energy sector (Caubet, 1991). Soon after the signing of the Second Montevideo Treaty, Brazil's Minister of Foreign Affairs, Minister Saraiva Guerreiro, expressed concern over the continent's relationship. For him, "to translate into actions and undertakings the vocabulary of Latin-American solidarity" signaled a pragmatic course of action—no longer that of general agreements. The military government thus discussed new pathways, but no direction arose to prevail. Although relations with Argentina stand out to some extent, they are vague and difficult to clearly distinguish from those with other countries (Saraiva Guerreiro, 1980, pp. 38, 40).

In its first years, ALADI partly consolidated what had been attained between 1960 and 1980, the so-called historical heritage. The low-profile Regional Preference Tariff Agreement signed in 1984 continued to produce little trade effect. Throughout the 1980s, intraregional trade declined, after peaking at US$24 billion in 1981. For the purpose of the discussion on Latin-American integration and Brazilian policies, it is worth signaling that trade preferences failed to increase regional trade, whereas the possibility created by ALADI for the negotiation of bilateral agreements provided an additional instrument that was to be extensively used in the following years, particularly in Argentina–Brazil relations, and by both in their relations with Uruguay. In 1986, a new attempt to strengthen ALADI was made with a call for a Regional Round of Negotiations, which ended in March 1987, when the organization's Council of Ministers approved the Program for Trade Recovery and Expansion. According to Roberto Martínez le Clainche (1984), the low priority assigned to integration is also expressed through the apparent lack of technical preparation for the negotiations, though poorly qualified staff, lack of clear instructions, compounded by poor coordination in the public and private sectors involved in the integration (le Clainche, 1984, p. 173). ALADI was a self-declared technical and record-keeping institution. Although political and social benefits are considered integral to integration processes and were considered as such by LAFTA and the Andean Pact, they were not among the goals of the Montevideo Treaty of 1980. Some years later, and in the context of a different relation and project, political and social goals were revitalized.

The development of Argentina–Brazil relations from 1985 and onwards corresponds, as we have seen, to the phase that Barbosa (1996) calls pragmatic. Leaving behind decades of mutual fears, some of which we have discussed in preceding pages, by initiative of Buenos Aires, the presidents of the two countries decided to start a process of economic integration outside multilateral schemes but hinged on the partial complementarity of their economies. In the Brazilian perception, Minister of External Relations Olavo Setúbal, and supported by President Sarney, who summoned the finance, agriculture, and mining and energy ministers, suggested that "Latin-American integration could only be achieved with the previous integration of the Southern Cone, which, in turn, would depend on the integration of Brazil and Argentina" (Barbosa, 1996, p. 149). By opting to accept bilateral initiatives and Economic Complementation Agreements, ALADI naturally came to endorse the process that was beginning. From then on, the Brazilian policy for Argentina has been grounded in a cooperation logic both in the political sense (consolidation of democracy and increased bargaining power in the international system), and in the economic, in which high inflation and foreign indebtedness represented the common face of the challenge both countries faced. Writing this book after the strong intensification of institutional tensions in Brazil from 2016, with strong consequences regarding the relations with Argentina and with Mercosur, it becomes necessary to consider the decrease in the relevance attributed to these same relations. From 2019, it is even likely that a change in direction has occurred.

2.5 Mercosur

A string of agreements led to important changes in the relations between Brazil and Argentina, with impacts on the whole of Latin-American relations. The most important of these agreements are (1) the Iguazu Declaration of November 1985, signed by Presidents Sarney and Alfonsín, which amongst other points emphasized the importance of consolidating the democratic process in the two countries and a union of efforts aimed at defending shared positions in international forums, (2) the Program for Integration and Economic Cooperation—PICE, July 1986—establishing 24 sectoral protocols targeting the integration of specific productive sectors, and (3) the Integration, Cooperation, and Development Treaty of November 1988, whereby Brazil and Argentina set a 10-year deadline for the creation of a common economic space.

To Celso Lafer (1997), what we might call the transformation of the regional system, would be the result of (1) the 1979 trilateral agreement for the use of the waters of the Paraná River; (2) the Brazilian position regarding the Malvinas/Falklands War; and (3) the democratization process, with an emphasis on development, civilian control over the military, and transparent and trustworthy nuclear relations. The broad corollary represented by the Asunción Treaty gave rise to the Mercosur. The radical innovation in the preceding regional relations pattern is derived from political cooperation whose starting point is a new perception of international positioning, a novel understanding of what political cooperation is, and, with the active participation of epistemic groups that included the military, the dismantling of the hypothesis of confrontation between the two countries.

The Argentinean and Brazilian governments in the years of 1985 and 1986 considered integration as a radical change in the attitudes of each state toward its partner. The idea of the pragmatic and realist phase reflects such perception. "The Brazilian government defined, at the presidential level, a clear policy in relation to the regional integration process. Integration and economic cooperation with Argentina are assigned the highest priority; Latin-American integration would only be made possible with the previous integration of the Southern Cone and this, in turn, would depend on the integration of Brazil and Argentina." (Barbosa, 1996, p. 149). To Luiz Felipe Seixas Corrêa (1996, p. 374), drawing on an idea of Rubens Ricupero, one of the formulators of the Brazilian policy in that period, "perhaps the main and longest-lasting foreign policy line of the Sarney government has been the reformulation of the Brazil–Argentina relationship, through the overcoming of rivalries and misgivings outliving the past and the concomitant setting-up of the preferential space for democratic understanding and economic integration that came to be the Mercosur".

After the Mercosur had been established, the fact that Argentina, Brazil, Uruguay, and Paraguay submitted joint positions before other countries and organizations is reasonably unprecedented. These coordinated actions yielded results, as is attested by the position of the bloc in response to the Enterprise for the Americas Initiative, first proposed by President George Bush in June 1990. On the occasion, the Four plus One Agreement, or Rose Garden Agreement (Amorim and Pimentel, 1996), laid down the principle that the regional bloc would negotiate as such with the United States. In 1994, with the Ouro Preto Protocol, the Customs Union of the Mercosur countries was established, a legally binding agreement whereby member countries are obliged to adopt joint positions in international trade negotiations. The position of the Mercosur countries was a key element in bringing the negotiations for a Free

Trade Area of the Americas (FTAA), to an end—the continuity of the Bush initiative—at the Mar del Plata meeting of 2004.

The Brazilian regional integration policy, as we have seen, while anchored in the Mercosur, also yielded other initiatives. The proposal for the creation of the South America Free Trade Area (SAFTA) in 1993, in the Itamar Franco government, and the Union of South-American Nations (UNASUR) in 2008, during the Luís Inácio Lula da Silva administration, show the Brazilian interest in strengthening the prospect of subcontinental integration. These initiatives stemmed from policymakers' concerns across the region, which led to the creation of the geopolitical concept of South America and, at the same time, from concerns with the stability of the whole of the subcontinent.

Intra-bloc trade flows increased significantly in the Mercosur's first years of functioning. However, after 20 years, deadlocks arose in face of which the Brazilian state will still have to take a position, while there is no consensus in society and among the elites on how to consolidate the process. The Mercosur is not only a trade integration bloc; it is also economic in the broadest sense. Just how state instruments, financial, fiscal, institutional, should be allocated to deepen the process is still unclear. The bloc's recent agenda has been marked by the question about the distribution of the benefits of the integration, by discussions on how to strengthen its institutions, and by a greater internalization of the logic of the integration in the member countries. The establishment of the Mercosur Structural Convergence Fund (FOCEM from the Spanish acronym), the Olivos Protocol, the discussions about the Mercosur Parliament (Parlasul), and the Consultative Forum of Mercosur Municipalities, Federated States, Provinces, and Departments (FCCR), procedures designed to facilitate regional production chains, all these themes are encompassed by the goal of strengthening the integration process. They are indicative of important prospects whose outcomes have not been assured. Successive Brazilian governments, including the Dilma Rousseff administration (2011–2014, 2015–2016), were clearly favorable to the continuity of the integration; yet, political will is not sufficient to guarantee the advances intended. The economic crisis, including the European Union crisis, surely impacted this process. Since 2019, when Bolsonaro took office, political will towards regional integration has been radically reduced and Brazilian foreign policy has ceased to act as a mediating and constructive factor in the region, while gradually moving towards fragmentation and polarization.

2.6 Final Remarks

Our discussion demonstrates that almost until the end of the twentieth century, the theme of regional integration had not been at the center of the debate in the state and in Brazilian society. Neither at the political level nor at the economic, not even at the cultural. Although the literature on the theme of Latin America appears sporadically, the country's continental dimensions have not fostered its embedding in the great national debates. There are explanations. Nearly all of the other countries share a common Spanish colonial origin, a fact that counts even though, in some cases, negatively. Latin America, especially the River Plate Basin, was considered the natural environment for the expansion of the Brazilian influence, though that was still not about integration. This expansion faced competition from a powerful state, Argentina. At the time of the ABC treaties, as we have discussed, consideration was given to political cooperation. Only in the 1980s did regional integration start to be seen as an instrument for national strengthening. In earlier decades of the 1940s, 1950s, 1960s, integration-driven initiatives appeared sporadically. None of them was successful. We have discussed the difficulties that faced LAFTA, initially proposed as a free trade area, which, eventually, was downgraded to a trade regulation instrument, just as ALADI had been. The idea of integration as an instrument for the enhancement of the a country's international position is not exclusive to Brazil. All processes of integration hinge on the assumption that they will be beneficial for the country itself, the whole of society, and its elites.

Brazil, like nearly all other countries in Latin America, was conditioned in the twentieth century by its relations with the United States. Themes like rapprochement with that country, how to benefit from such a relation, how to reach autonomy, and strengthen a nationalist project, all were and are part of a permanent debate. The outcome was the non-urgency of a regional integration project, continuously postponed to a point "later on" which is increasingly distant. The LAFTA, ECLAC, and ALADI proposals have not contributed decisively to introduce the theme of integration in Brazil. The economic and political changes of the 1970s and 1980s spurred the passage from an idealist formulation of integration to the formulation of a concrete project. The notion of development eventually found common ground with the notion of integration. In the end of the first decade of the 2000s, the creation of UNASUR suggested that the concern for integration had spread to the whole of South America. However, since 2016, the dismantling of UNASUR and the progressive loss of a cooperative space in South America, evidence that regional integration had not been totally absorbed by the Brazilian state and its elites. Notwithstanding the currently critical political and economic situation facing Brazil and the region, this chapter aimed to analyze the historical trajectory that helps to understand the difficulties for inserting regional integration as a main priority in Brazilian foreign policy.

References

Amorim, C., & Pimentel, R. (1996). Iniciativa para as Américas: o acordo do Jardim das Rosas. In J. A. G. Albuquerque (Ed.), *Sessenta anos de política externa brasileira (1930-1990)* (Vol. Vol. II). Cultura/NUPRI—USP/FAPESP.

Arquivo Histórico do Itamaraty (AHI). (1906). Diplomatic mail from Asunción, Buenos Aires, Montevideo, Washington, Santiago; Private archive of the Baron of Rio Branco; Documents of the 1st and 3rd International Conferences of American States.

Bandeira, M. (1973). *Presença dos Estados Unidos no Brasil (dois séculos de história).* Civilização Brasileira.

Bandeira, M. (1987). *O eixo Argentina-Brasil: o processo de integração da América Latina*. Editora Universidade de Brasília.
Barbosa, R. (1996). Brasil e a integração regional: a ALALC e a ALADI (1960–1990). In J. A. G. Albuquerque (Ed.), *Sessenta anos de política externa brasileira (1930–1990), Volume II, Diplomacia para o Desenvolvimento*. Cultura Editores Associados/Núcleo de Pesquisa em Relações Internacionais da USP/FAPESP.
Bielschowsky, R. (Ed.). (2000). *Cinquenta anos de pensamento na ECLAC*. Record.
Burns, E. B. (1966). *The unwritten alliance; Rio Branco and the Brazilian-American relations*. Columbia University Press.
Burns, E. B. (1977). As relações do Brasil durante a Primeira República. In FAUSTO, B. (Org.) (Ed.), *História geral da civilização brasileira Rio de Janeiro: Difel*, t. 3 (Vol. 2, pp. 375–400).
Calógeras, P. (1987). *Idéiaspolíticas de PandiáCalógeras* (Introduction, chronology, bibliographic note and selected texts by Francisco Iglesias). Senado Federal; Fundação Casa de Rui Barbosa.
Caubet, C. G. (1991). *As grandes manobras de Itaipu. Energia, diplomacia e direito na Bacia do Prata*. Editora Acadêmica.
Cavlak, I. (2008). *A política externa brasileira e a Argentina peronista (1946-1955)*. Annablume.
Cervo, A. L. (2008). *Inserção internacional: formação dos conceitos brasileiros*. Saraiva.
Cervo, A. L., & Bueno, C. (2011). *História da política exterior do Brasil* (4th ed.). Editora Universidade de Brasília.
Conduru, G. F. (1998). *A política externa de Rio Branco os tratados do ABC*. Master's dissertation. Universidade de Brasília.
de Melo Franco, A. (1968). *Planalto—Memórias*. Livraria José Olympio Editora.
Donghi, T. H. (1972). *História contemporánea de América Latina* (3rd ed.). Alianza Editorial.
Ferrari, G. (1981). *Esquema de la política exterior argentina*. Editorial Universitária de Buenos Aires.
Fraga, R. (1994). *Roca y el Brasil*. Editorial Centro de Estudios Unión para la Nueva Mayoria.
Gaceta, L. (1917). *Newspapers-Buenos Aires: La Gaceta de Buenos Aires*. La Mañana.
Heitor, L. (1992). *A diplomacia brasileira na Primeira República (1889–1930) e outros ensaios Nota bibliografia de Hélio Antônio Scarabôtolo*. Instituto Histórico e Geográfico Brasileiro.
Lafer, C. (1997, July/December). Relações Brasil-Argentina: alcance e significado de uma parceria estratégica. *Contexto Internacional, 19*(2), 249–265.
le Clainche, R. M. (1984). *La ALALC/ALADI*. El Colegio de México.
Leitão da Cunha, V. (1965). Palestra do ministro das Relações Exteriores na Associação Comercial do Rio de Janeiro, em 11 de novembro de 1964. *Revista Brasileira de Política Internacional, Year One, VIII*(29), 12–30.
Leite, C. (1959). Banco Interamericano de Desenvolvimento. *Revista Brasileira de Política Internacional, 6*, 26–43.
Lins, A. (1965). *Rio-Branco* (2nd ed.). Nacional.
Lins, A. (1945). *Rio-Branco*. José Olympio.
Ministry of External Relations. *Report* 1914–15.
Moavro, H. R. (1992). *La decisión: aportes para la integración latinoamericana*. IFEDEC.
Razón, L. (1910, September 4). *Newspaper-La Razón*.
Resenha. (1960). *Zona de Livre Comércio na América Latina* (Vol. 10). Revista Brasileira de Política Internacional, ano III.
Ricupero, R. (1995). Um personagem da República. In R. Ricupero & J. H. P. de Araujo (Eds.), *José Maria da Silva Paranhos, Baron of Rio Branco*. Fundação Alexandre de Gusmão.
Saraiva Guerreiro, R. (1980). Conferência pronunciada pelo ministro das Relações Exteriores na Escola Superior de Guerra, em 5 de setembro de 1980. *Revista Brasileira de Política Internacional, Year, XXIII*, 89–92.
Seixas Corrêa, L. F. (1996). A política externa de José Sarney. In J. A. G. Albuquerque (Ed.), *Sessenta anos de política externa brasileira (1930–1990) Volume I, Crescimento, modernização e política externa*. Cultura Editores Associados/Núcleo em Pesquisa em Relações Internacionais da USP/FAPESP.

Sette, L. L. (1996). A diplomacia econômica brasileira no pós-guerra (1945-1964). In J. A. G. Albuquerque (Ed.), *Sessenta anos de política externa brasileira (1930-1990)* (Vol. 2, pp. 239–266). Cultura Editores Associado/Núcleo de Pesquisa em Relações Internacionais da USP.

Smith, J. (1991). *Unequal giants; diplomatic relations between the United States and Brazil, 1889-1930*. University of Pittsburg Press.

United Nations. (1954). *A cooperação internacional na política de desenvolvimento latino-americana*. United Nations.

United Nations. (1961a). Recomendaciones acerca de la estructura y normas del Mercado Común Latinoamericano (informe de la Segunda reunión del Grupo de Trabajo, México, 16–-27 February 1959). In *La cooperación economica multilateral en America Latina. Volumen I, Textos y Documentos*. Naciones Unidas.

United Nations. (1961b). Bases para la formación del Mercado Regional Latinoamericano (informe de la primera reunión del Grupo de Trabajo, Santiago de Chile, 3 a 11 de febrero de 1958). In *La cooperación economica multilateral en America Latina, Volumen I, Textos y Documentos*. Naciones Unidas.

Chapter 3
Brazilian Thinking and Regional Integration

3.1 Introduction

This chapter's aim is to analyze the ways some schools of thought, represented by significant individuals, have considered the issue of regional integration in Brazil. We focus on the second half of the twentieth century, seeking to understand the conceptions of the country's regional and international projections, that underlie the possible scope for integration. To this end, we discuss a range of issues, such as the role of the state, the vision for the country, nationalism, economic development and underdevelopment, international recognition and the perceptions of neighbors (Gardini & Almeida, 2016). The idea of Brazilian uniqueness in relation to neighboring countries is an element which is present in the works of intellectuals and policymakers. This idea can be found in many countries, including others within this region. We also seek to understand how this idea evolved over time, culminating in the 1980s with the acceptance of the existence of a community of interests with the countries of the Southern Cone as well as the rest of South America.

Brazilian ideas about regional integration are influenced by the country's continental dimensions and by the aspiration towards playing a distinguished role within the international realm. This perception has been influenced by the country's history, its process of state formation, and territorial consolidation. Some of these ideas, together with centuries-old rivalries in the Rio de la Plata Basin persisting in the twentieth century, weakened the prospects for integration (Ricupero, 2017). Over time, however, due to domestic and external factors, there was a significant change in the perception of regional integration. The changes that occurred and the emergence of new conceptions have not entirely overcome the structure of previous ideas, which in turn contributed to difficulties of integration. Ideas are only transformed into actions if they become recurrent. This process normally lasts a long time and is linked to certain interests. The predominant idea, as we saw in Chap. 2, changed from the 1980s, but encountered difficulties in terms of becoming deeply rooted. We

T. Vigevani, H. Ramanzini Junior, *The Challenges for Building Regional Integration in the Global South*, United Nations University Series on Regionalism 18,
https://doi.org/10.1007/978-3-030-93348-7_3

can, therefore, affirm, *ex-post-facto,* that its shallow embeddedness can help to explain phenomena which occurred from 2015 and onwards.

We seek to discuss the tradition of Brazilian thought regarding regional integration, identifying those moments when it existed, and the forms it took, as well as those moments when it simply did not become evident. In Brazil, there are lineages of Americanist/anti-Americanist, developmentalist and nationalist thought, but there is no long-running tradition of Latin Americanist thought. This does not mean that different thinkers or currents of thought were against integration, but rather that their reflections underlying the project for an idea of Brazil, for the most part, did not include integration with neighboring countries as an important variable. Darcy Ribeiro (1996) and others in the 1950s and 1960s discussed the importance of integration in the light of what they considered essential for unity among the countries of the region against American imperialism. In those decades, members of the Brazilian geopolitical current of thought, like Golbery do Couto e Silva (1967), who wielded significant influence over the National War College (*Escola Superior de Guerra—ESG*), also centered their concerns on national interests. During the same period, the concept of development as formulated by members of the Higher Institute of Brazilian Studies (*Instituto Superior de Estudos Brasileiros—ISEB*) did not identify integration with neighboring countries as a fundamental concern. In their views, the main preoccupation was national integration.

The idea of Brazil as a major power (*Brasil potência*) was central to the National Security Doctrine (*Doutrina de Segurança Nacional—DSN*) during the military regime (1964–85). The national-developmentalist school of thought and the import-substitution model of industrialization, as well as readings of the theses espoused by the Economic Commission for Latin America and the Caribbean (*Comisión Económica para Américana Latina y el Caribe—CEPAL*), strengthened the perspective of national development and international projection.

Though not the only determinants, and not dissociated from other interests, ideas do influence the cultural context in which the international positions of countries are formulated. Ideas are gathered on the basis of an understanding of historical problems to which they relate and on the basis of their institutional connectedness (Goldstein & Keohane, 1993). Hence, it is necessary to take into consideration the specific contexts in which they are formulated and discussed. In Brazil's case, the idea of the country's economic and political development is a powerful matrix in the intellectual field.

Until the 1980s, the issue of regional integration was not on the national agenda in Brazil. After the Second World War, the problem of development/underdevelopment, industrialization, and discussions of the participation of foreign capital in the economy focused on a strictly national perspective. Yet, these debates were still internationally connected, though mainly focused on developed countries. In the sphere of international projection, the debate revolved around the need for a more independent foreign policy less aligned with the United States (US). In the 1970s, particularly during the Emílio Garrastazu Médici (1969–74) and Ernesto Geisel (1974–79) governments, the *Brasil Potência* idea gained ground, which led to difficulties in relationships with other countries in the region, chiefly Argentina. In the 1980s, in the midst of the re-democratization process, the debt crisis, and of spiraling inflation, the theme and possibility of regional integration emerged more concretely in the perception of some Brazilian intellectuals. Authors such as Celso Lafer (1973) understood the importance of an agreement between Brazil and Argentina as early as the 1970s.

This chapter is organized in the following way: in the second section, we analyze the way in which ISEB perceived Brazil and the implications of its relations with its regional environment. In the third section, we discuss the independent foreign policy with a basis in the ideas of San Tiago Dantas and Araújo Castro. In the same section, we consider the responsible pragmatism, with a point of departure in Azeredo da Silveira's thinking, in light of the partial existence of certain analytical overlaps. In the fourth section, we analyze the ESG doctrine, mainly the ideas of Golbery do Couto e Silva, which wielded considerable importance during the Brazilian military regime and contributed to the formulation of regional relations. In the fifth section, we engage with the way in which CEPAL's ideas were absorbed in Brazil, with special emphasis on Celso Furtado's conception, relating these to the visions of Latin America. We also discuss the ideas of two Brazilian intellectuals connected to the Dependency Theory, Fernando Henrique Cardoso and Ruy Mauro Marini. In the sixth section, we take a look at the recent ideas about regional integration, mainly Celso Lafer and Samuel Pinheiro Guimarães, whom we identify as very representative within contemporary thinking. In the final considerations, we delineate the main aspects which constitute the Brazilian thinking about regional integration. We argue that while the regional question was not the center of attention in the nineteenth century and in most of the twentieth century, there was a significant change in the 1980s and 1990s, and now in the twenty-first century in the direction of incorporating the idea of regional integration as a substantial intellectual and political issue. We claim that this important evolution also was associated with a certain degree of difficulty in terms of becoming more deeply embedded within certain social sectors and epistemic groups.

3.2 ISEB Conceptions About Brazil and National Development

The ISEB was created in 1955 under the leadership of a group of Brazilian intellectuals coordinated by Hélio Jaguaribe. It counted with the participation of Álvaro Vieira Pinto, Cândido Mendes, Alberto Guerreiro Ramos, Nelson Werneck Sodré, Roland Corbisier, among others. During its 9 years of existence (1955–64), it became a center for the theoretical formulation of a national-developmentalist project, and it left a legacy of ideas that would strongly influence the Brazilian intellectual debate. Pécaut (1990) believed the ISEB's developmentalist ideology gradually became the guideline towards which public opinion was inclined. As will be treated in the following sections, the idea of Latin America was absent from the institute's thinking, except as part of a more general bloc that could counterpose imperialism. At the level of ideas, the ISEB became a counterpoint to the ESG in the 1950s and 1960s. While the ESG, under the influence of officers such as Couto e Silva, Cordeiro de Farias, and Castelo Branco saw the world through an East–West perspective, ISEB developed a nationalist and developmentalist matrix of thinking. The main subject and decisive factor was the nation.

The ISEB's objective was to formulate studies and spur debates that supported the making of a national development policy or strategy. In a similar manner, it sought to contribute to the emergence of Brazilian thought with propositions for great national issues, with an emphasis on the cultural and socio-political dimensions of development. According to Luiz Carlos Bresser Pereira (2004), with the election of President Juscelino Kubitschek (1956–60), the ISEB was transformed into the main center for nationalist and developmentalist thinking. Its ideology was conceived by this group to lead the country to overcome cultural alienation and economic backwardness through state action, taking the form of a broad multiclass alliance, economic intervention, and planning. Toledo (2005) argues that although the ISEB was not an ideological apparatus at the service of Kubitschek's developmentalism, its intellectuals were clearly in tune with the government's industrialization project, particularly in the early years of the administration. The key concern was to reflect upon development and, as far as possible, influence the government to adopt its recommendations. It is worth to notice that from 1953, and with a renewed impulse from 1958, as we saw in Chap. 2, discussions took place among Latin American countries under the auspices of CEPAL that led to the signing of the Treaty of Montevideo in 1960, constituting the Latin American Free Trade Association (*Associação Latino Americana de Livre Comércio*—ALALC). This negotiation, however, did not have significant repercussions on the members of the ISEB, and was relegated to the technical aspects of trade. In Brazil, the major currents of thought remained distant from the integration theme.

Despite having different theoretical and ideological hues, members of the ISEB converged in so far as they considered that historically, Brazil's elites had not oriented its interests according to the needs of society as a whole. They agreed on the diagnosis that the country could only overcome underdevelopment by intensified industrialization conceived of as a national phenomenon not connected to a potential regional market. Even initiatives relating to integration formulated by Juan Perón's Argentina did not resonate in the intellectual debate of the period. Industrialization was seen as the dynamic element of development. The policy needed to be nationalistic and its implementation would bring changes in the political system, weakening the country's old ruling elites and consequently reducing the weight of actors linked to large-scale mercantile landed interests, thus defying the hegemony by the agrarian ruling class. The view that business entrepreneurs might constitute the nucleus of development was later criticized by Fernando Henrique Cardoso (1972, p. 14), who sought to demonstrate the fragility of the "ideology that affirmed the feasibility of the alliance between the national bourgeoisie, part of the urban masses, and the state to produce structural transformations capable of spurring economic development on a national basis". Within the perspective of strengthening national capitalism, the idea of closer relations with its geographic vicinity did not emerge, as it appeared that there was no motivation for it. In fact, throughout the underdeveloped world, even when political agreements between countries were sought and non-alignment and neutralism were part of such agreements, the perspective of integration and the idea of a common identity never emerged. In the 1950s and 1960s, the idea of integration and community only developed in Europe, motivated by specific economic, geopolitical, historical and social circumstances.

In the ISEB's view, the defence of the democratic-bourgeois revolution, termed national-populist ideology by some (Cardoso, 1972; Weffort 1978) implied a need for unity among the national bourgeoisie, the peasantry, the proletariat, and other social segments interested in national industrialization to combat the major landowners linked to the export trade. According to Alberto Guerreiro Ramos (1960, p. 70), "all factors that contribute to the formation of psychosocial, political, ideological, institutional and economic pressures that tend to weaken Brazilian capitalism should be considered adverse to national objectives" (Ramos, 1960, p. 70). For him and other members of the ISEB, the groups linked to the agro-export economy, as well as international imperialism were the elements most threatening to the national-developmentalist project. This worldview, albeit part of the ideational context of the period, related to the national debate and to national solutions for problems. Understanding this perspective is fundamental to see why there was a certain lack of knowledge about the region. The regional states with which Brazil shared interests were in the underdeveloped category but did still not identify with the nationalist and anti-imperialist perspective, which had a stronger presence in other continents.

Adopting part of the language of the Third International, Sodré (1967) focused on the hindrances to development, considered as the relations of production, and emphasized the negative role of imperialism. In his view, the presence of "feudal relations" in rural areas, the pernicious influence of foreign capital, and imperialist domination were the main elements hindering capitalist development in Brazil. This can thus be viewed as a perspective focused on national advances. The Brazilian revolution was related to the end of the power and hegemony of landowning classes and imperialism, which reinforced colonialism and hindered the formation of a national economy (ibid). The solution was situated within a national perspective. This, however, did not emerge as a counterpoint to South America or in connection with the countries of the region, as there was an absence of connectivity. Major landowners' monopoly on land and imperialism obstructed economic growth and had to be combated at the national level. Sodré thus emphasized the need for planned industrialization on a national basis to make national capitalist development feasible and prepare the passage to socialism (Bielschowsky, 2004).

For the ISEB, the concept of development involved a process of capital accumulation, incorporation of technical progress, and raising the standard of living of the population, beginning with a capitalist and national revolution. According to Pereira (2004, p. 58), it would be a process of sustained growth in the population's income under the strategic leadership of the state, with Brazilian entrepreneurs playing a leading role. Development would, therefore, be national, owing to the fact that it would take place domestically under the aegis of institutions defined and guaranteed by the state. On the international level, the key concern was the effort to overcome external dependence and its consequences. As argued by Corbisier (1968, p. 33), "if the development project seeks to promote national emancipation, its fulfilment will previously imply the negation of dependence, that is, it will enter into a contradiction with the domination of our economy by any foreign hegemonic center". With the benefit of hindsight, it can thus be sustained that this form of analysis led to Brazilian problems as being exclusively identified within a center-periphery contradiction, with possible identification with neighbors being subsumed below this.

According to Ignácio Rangel (1962), Guerreiro Ramos (1960), and Hélio Jaguaribe (1958, 1972) overcoming underdevelopment by means of industrialization was related to overcoming mercantile capitalism. With the passage from mercantile to industrial capitalism, capitalist accumulation combined with the systematic incorporation of technical progress would make it possible for incomes to rise in a sustained fashion and for the population's standard of living to improve. The national revolution was to be the association of various sectors of society in favor of a national project. In this sense, nationalism would be the ideology of the national revolution. According to Sodré (1960, p. 33), "nationalism grows out of the need to compose a new picture, conjugating class interests, reducing them to a common denominator, in the struggle in defence of what is national within us. It is the imperative for overcoming the contradiction between the national bourgeoisie and the working class that adopts nationalism as the opportune expression of a policy".

As we have seen, issues of industrialization, the possibility of an alliance between classes in favor of development, a national project, foreign investment, nationalism, and cultural mimicry were some of the main items of intellectual debate in the period. In the international arena, another central theme for the ISEB was a critique of imperialism, demonstrating the differences between the developmental processes of the center and the periphery. These issues were discussed by CEPAL. Unlike the center, in the course of its development process, the periphery would have to overcome the interests of international capitalism and alienated local elites linked to imperialism. As Corbisier argued (1968, p. 53), "one notices that there is nothing in common, other than the term itself, between the nationalism of underdeveloped countries fighting against oppressor nations and to win political sovereignty and economic independence, and the nationalism of industrialized countries, eager to maintain their rule over colonial areas and in winning or enlarging markets for their manufactured goods". This conception left the issue of the South American region as an underlying question. There was a potential convergence of interests, but it did not materialize. Herein lay the difficulty in reflecting upon the question of Latin America—the region ended up "not being seen" and thus failed to be integrated into the cultural, economic, and political concerns of current thought. The theme of regional integration understood as the discussion of possibilities for denser relations between the countries of the region was not present in Brazilian thinking at the time. The way in which intellectuals thought about Brazil and national development could not be contextualized in a regional integration process, which by definition, assumed loss of autonomy in some functions of the nation-state in order to recompose them at a regional level (Mariano, 2007; Mattli, 1999). When Latin America appeared in the ISEB's reflections, the principal focus was not on regional integration, but on understanding the historical causes of underdevelopment. As we shall see, this perception had some parentage with other lines of Brazilian thought such as the Dependency Theory, but with some marked differences. The lack of reflection about the region was not incidental. It derived from the ISEB members' conceptual fundamentals based on the idea that the state was the resolving locus, and consequently, attention was drawn in its direction.

3.3 The Independent Foreign Policy and Responsible Pragmatism

In the early 1960s, the affirmation of a new socio-political profile of Brazilian society, the strength of nationalist ideas, the radicalization of some political and social groups, transformations in the external environment, and the quest for an autonomous international role are aspects that help to understand the context in which the Independent Foreign Policy (*Política Externa Independente*—PEI, 1961–64) emerged. In general, the literature attributes its formulation to Francisco Clementino San Tiago Dantas. Beginning with the Jânio Quadros government (1961), Brazil experienced 3 years of significant change in priorities and in the implementation and guiding conceptual framework of its external relations, which were to some extent interrupted by the 1964 military coup d'état. These priorities were in part resumed from the mid-1970s, albeit with marked differences. The following section discusses some conceptual aspects of the PEI and Responsible Pragmatism (*Pragmatismo Responsável*—PR, 1974–78) resorting to the ideas of San Tiago Dantas, Araújo Castro, and Azeredo da Silveira.

The basic principles of the PEI were an autonomous formulation of economic development plans; an enlargement of the external market; general and continuous disarmament; non-intervention in the internal affairs of other countries; peace maintained through peaceful coexistence; respect for international law; self-determination of peoples; and support for the full emancipation of non-autonomous territories (Dantas, 1962). Some of these principles were already present in Brazil's foreign policy, but others were new, such as support for the full emancipation of non-autonomous territories. This changed Brazil's position *vis-à-vis* Portugal's Salazar regime. This position also enjoyed support from conservative groups. This is the case with the newspaper *Estado de São Paulo*: the Mesquita Family emphasized its traditionalist and liberal origins, positioning itself in opposition to the Salazar dictatorship and colonialism.

The PEI sought to transform the country's international role and projected a position less aligned with the US. According to Fonseca Júnior (1998, p. 363), "the period was one of the universalist openings of foreign policy and the gathering of a broad range of bilateral relations [...] Links with African countries were established or renewed, the presence in the Middle East was enhanced, and most importantly, ties with Latin America gained new density". Along the same lines, Dantas (1962, p. 11) stated, "The rapid enlargement of the external market for our products has become an imperative within the country's development [...] Winning markets must be the key element of our foreign economic policy. Our policy has turned to Latin America, in the first instance and in the second, to socialist countries, without disregarding the possibilities for increasing trade with the US and Western Europe". Gilberto Freyre (1962, p. 294) believed, "this policy of instituting an effective system of closer relations between the new African and Asian nations and Brazil must be implemented with tact and wisdom. This because it implies both greater independence for Brazil in the face of older alliances, and its natural leadership of a whole new group of tropical nations with problems similar to those already being solved among Brazilians". Concerned about relations with African countries, Gilberto Freyre dissociated himself from the PEI, signaling that Brazil's leadership of tropical nations should be compatible with old alliances which he associated particularly with Portugal.

Within the framework of the PEI, Brazil participated intensely in international initiatives on the issue of overcoming underdevelopment during the early 1960s, and until 1964. The concern with national development projects was strong enough to be incorporated into the logic of a broader process of integration. The quest for development was seen as possible only as a consequence of the national effort, which had to apply an internal focus. The question of integration with other states, even in the surrounding areas, did not appear as a relevant issue in this period. As Amado (1996, p. 284) notes, "for many observers, the PEI instituted in the Quadros government resulted from an awareness that Brazil could no longer remain confined to the principles of Pan-Americanism".

Brazil's deepening industrialization within the framework of the PEI and under the influence of the ISEB assumed that the country would have a more autonomous position *vis-à-vis* the US. The PEI's conceptual formulation was permeated by a broad range of ideas grounded in the national developmentalism of the time. Fonseca Júnior (1998, p. 302) reinforced this interpretation when he stated that the PEI, "is born out of a political project, out of an intellectual conception" that included a critique of the international status quo and of the way the issue of development was discussed. Castro, an important foreign policymaker during this period, was critical of how the question of development was dealt with internationally, "There are attempts to convert the serious problem of underdevelopment into a mere problem of stabilization, forgetting the fact that if one were to stabilize many countries at the present economic level, one would proceed to stabilization at an extremely low level" (Amado 1982, p. 201).

José Honório Rodrigues (1966, p. 187) argued, "The independent policy was soon accepted by public opinion and by the more progressive sectors. Brazil wished to pursue an open-door policy, without being committed to ideological or military blocs". With the PEI emerged the universalist paradigm (Faverão, 2006; Mello, 2000) or the globalist paradigm (Pinheiro, 2004) of Brazilian foreign policy. The worsening political, economic, and international crisis in the João Goulart years

(1961–64) hindered the effective implementation of PEI proposals. With the PR of Foreign Minister Silveira during the Geisel government (1974–79), these were partly taken up again from the mid-1970s, under different political conditions and resting on different social bases (Fonseca Júnior, 1996).

According to Dantas (1962, p. 5) the PEI aimed at "the exclusive consideration of Brazil's interest, seen as a country that aspired to be developed and economically emancipated and to historically reconcile the democratic regime and social reforms capable of eliminating the oppression of the working class by the property-owning class". Nationalist ideas of the 1950s and 1960s and the PEI as formulated by Dantas and Castro represented not only a position in the face of the outside world that sought to drive Brazil's industrial development and increase exports but also contained the proposal to project the country as a relevant actor on the world stage. In Castro's (Amado, 1982, p. 212) perspective , "Nationalism is not an attitude of isolation, prevention or hostility [...] It is an effort to position Brazil in the world through the use of every means and with the participation of all the countries that wish to collaborate with us in equating and solving world problems". In this formulation, there was an evident interest in cooperation with the countries of Latin America, but these were seen as part of a wider set of countries and the specificity of regional relations was not evident. Apart from the nationalist component, the PEI project incorporating part of the ISEB's reflection related the domestic aspect of the integration of vast social sectors to the project of national development, the foreign policy included. As stated by Dantas (1964, p. 525), "to develop always means to emancipate oneself. To emancipate oneself externally through the extinction of links of dependence on political or economic decision-making centers located abroad. And to emancipate oneself internally, which can only be achieved through transformations in the social structure".

The independent aspect of the PEI was displayed at the Punta del Este Conference of the Organization of American States (OAS) in January 1962, when Dantas defended a position of neutrality *vis-à-vis* Cuba, opposing the idea of a possible invasion of the island with OAS support, clearly distancing himself from the US position. Brazil opposed sanctions against Cuba and together with Argentina, Bolivia, Chile, Ecuador and Mexico abstained from voting on a resolution suspending the Cuban government from the OAS. For that moment in time, the Cuban question symbolized an important aspect of hemispheric relations. In particular, it signaled how relations with the US, continental solidarity, the problem of communism, and the principle of non-intervention were perceived (Vizentini, 1994). The convergence with Latin American countries was in counter-position to the US and not due to any explicit agreement between the states of the region, which would imply common thinking. However, there were moves towards rapprochement with neighboring countries during the period of the PEI, particularly with Argentina, as demonstrated by the meeting of Quadros and the Argentine President Arturo Frondizi in the border town of Uruguaiana in 1961.

Some formulators of the PEI and PR directed their attention to the debate about the structure of the international system, as they were concerned with the premises to achieve peace. In Araújo Castro's perspective, peace would grow out of a combination of economic, security, and social development, rather than a situation of equilibrium between powers. Castro (1970) took the view that a potential evolution to a stage of supra-nationalism and interdependence presupposed a prior level of sovereignty and complete economic and political independence. This idea was strong in both the PEI and PR and must be understood in reference to Brazil's relations with developed countries, as well as underdeveloped states, including its Latin American neighbors. That is why relations with Brazil's neighbors, above all Argentina, were difficult during the period of the PR and why conceptions linked to the national security school of thought coexisted with the PR. Such difficulties were only overcome towards the end of Geisel's administration in 1978, in the João Baptista Figueiredo government (1979–84), and more so during the José Sarney years (1985–89).

For an accurate picture of the beliefs of the PEI's formulators *vis-à-vis* the region, it is important to remember that the universalist idea present in their midst included closer ties with Argentina as one of the guidelines, especially for San Tiago Dantas. According to Dantas (1962, p. 19), "the improvement of our relations with the Argentine Republic will be worthy of particular attention, in relation to which sentiments of collaboration, support and affection animate us, sentiments capable of leading us to constant integration of the economic and cultural order in the interest of all the other nations of this hemisphere". After the military coup that toppled Frondizi in 1962, Argentinian policy toward Brazil hardened as the ideas of conservative nationalist groups that warned against the risks of Brazilian "hegemony" gained strength (Fausto & Devoto, 2004). In his 1963 "Three Ds" speech (decolonisation, development, and disarmament) at the UN, Castro (Amado, 1982) stated, "Brazil does not belong to blocs, but is part of a system, the inter-American system, which we conceive of as an instrument for peace and understanding among all members of the community of nations". Discussing Brazil–Argentina relations during the period of the PEI, Amado Luiz Cervo and Clodoaldo Bueno (2002, p. 312) state, "the rhetoric of solidarity, of cooperation for development, the enlargement of markets through customs associations and the desire to unite efforts so that both countries might acquire greater participation in international affairs appear in the speeches and joint communiqués". Hence, the regional question and relations with neighboring countries did not go unnoticed, even though the central theme for the formulators of the PEI was universalism and Brazil's projection in the world. The non-centrality of the regional theme was often attributed to instability in neighboring countries, although the Brazilian instability was often overlooked.

Within the framework of the PEI, particularly in the perspective of San Tiago Dantas and Castro, relations with Argentina and other countries in the region were important but did not constitute the policy's conceptual nucleus. There was a strong component of Third Worldism and a critique of the policies of dominant powers, the so-called "freezing of world power". The main aim was to position the country against demands for alignment and attain a certain level of autonomy in the face of the poles of power in the Cold War—the US and the Soviet Union. There was an aspiration to affirm Brazilian national interests as essentially different from the interests of the great powers, explore areas of convergence with countries that shared an underdeveloped condition, and intervene with its own position in debates on major international questions. Lafer (1973) held the view that the PEI set out to articulate a single united front of underdeveloped countries in the international system. The search for a higher level of independence in the country's international relations, symbolized by the relationship with the US during this period, may also be contextualized in relation to the case of relations with Argentina and other countries of the region. For Jayme Azevedo Rodrigues (1965, p. 36) the juxtaposition of the relations of independence that Brazil maintained both with the US and with Latin America was significant. "The understanding with the US, like the harmony with Latin America—with the addition of the free trade area today—is a legitimate affiliation we should maintain for our security and development" (Rodrigues 1965, p. 36). Thus, regional integration, though it was indeed contemplated, did not constitute the PEI's key concern.

The influence of the PEI was not circumscribed to ideas on international politics but rather reflected a certain worldview. It was delineated in a magazine called *Política Externa Independente* (Independent Foreign Policy), whose three issues were published in 1965 and 1966, during the military government by a group made up mostly of intellectuals from Rio de Janeiro. The journal had strong connections with the PEI and with perspectives that were universalist and national developmentalist. It was concerned with the Third World and the interest in Latin America derived from this, as well as the publication's anti-colonialism and anti-Americanism. It defended closer ties with underdeveloped countries, particularly in Africa, as well as the argument that independence and self-determination should be the guiding principles of the international order.

It is noticeable that the Latin American question gained space within the magazine. The general idea of its first issue was that "a solid and cohesive Latin American front should not be content with the unified defence of common demands but rather seek to establish modes of coexistence with the exclusive participation of Latin American countries capable of contributing to the progressive integration of their economies [...] The true and great alliance of the underdeveloped countries of Latin America is that which congregates them with the other underdeveloped countries of Africa and Asia" ("Foreword", *Política Externa Independente*, 1965, p. 6). The theme was highlighted but in the strong Third Worldist context of the time. Specific questions of integration were stressed in the journal and the document by Felipe Herrera, Carlos Sanz de Santamaría, José Antonio Mayorbe and Raúl Prebisch about the creation of the Latin American Common Market was also published in it.

Criticism of the US—anti-Americanism even—was also a strong presence, manifest in the denouncement of the OAS's submissiveness to the superpower and the radical condemnation of the invasion of the Dominican Republic (1965). This critique was immediately associated with the tough position of the Brazilian military government presided over by Castelo Branco, whose foreign affairs minister was Vasco Leitão da Cunha.

Latin America appeared in the context of the debate on development. It is interesting to notice that most of the analyses identified common aspects of the countries of the region in the context of the Cold War, especially from a national development perspective. As Luciano Martins (1965, p. 202) stated, "the political viability of Latin America will have to rely more and more on the action of its internal social forces. For this reason, my understanding is that the problems of development must be equated more and more based on the here and now, as a function of the specific interests of each Latin American nation, breaking with the system of international alliances that each nation, that each of the social classes of these nations, had until now been led to sustain and to submit to". Contained in this statement was a critique of imperialism, of international alignment with central countries, and an indication of the potential of national but not regional development.

Latin American themes present in *Política Externa Independente* were principally related to the need for autonomous positions in the foreign relations of the region's countries, chiefly against the US. Thus, the question of integration did emerge but was not central. It was subordinate to the broader question of development and the necessity of a rupture with the hegemony of central countries, especially the US.

The term PR, or Responsible Pragmatism or Responsible and Ecumenical Pragmatism, was also used by Geisel to characterize the foreign policy of his government in 1974. At the time, it was structured within the realm of the Ministry of External Relations (*Ministério das Relações Exteriores*). Letícia Pinheiro (2000, p. 464) argues that the broad outline of the PR was drawn up during meetings between president-elect Geisel and Silveira, the prospective foreign minister. Central to this work are the ideas of Silveira regarding Brazilian foreign policy, which are largely in consonance with Geisel's, and very central to the conceptual formulation and implementation of the PR.

According to Souto Maior (1996, p. 340), the PR imposed both a need and a consequence on Brazilian foreign policy. The need was for a political rapprochement with other developing countries, a process which had begun in the early 1960s with the PEI, but lost ground after 1964. The consequence was the "acceptance of a certain degree of friction with the great economic powers, the main beneficiaries of the international order which was sought modified". One of the PR's objectives was to increase Brazil's room for manoeuvering in the international system, given the strict limits imposed by the Cold War.

The PR brought many important foreign policy changes: in relations with the US, the Río de la Plata Basin (especially Argentina), Andean countries, as well as with Africa, China, Europe and the Middle East. There was greater approximation with the Federal Republic of Germany, with the aim of assimilating nuclear technology for peaceful ends, with electricity production in mind (Almeida, 2015). The objective was development and increasing power in the field of international relations. According to Silveira (1976, p. 62), "We do not want a new status for Brazil because we are motivated by ambitions of prestige and by power for power's sake. What is of interest to our country—and the present foreign policy seeks to interpret this desire faithfully—is to increase our role in the major decisions that affect the lives of nations, so as to permit the mobilization of the necessary resources for the economic and social development of our people under the best possible conditions".

The PR contained strong realistic fundamentals in terms of its understanding of the international dynamic. It represented a deepening of the perception that negated the convenience of an ideological alignment with the US and emphasized the idea of national autonomy. In comparatively analyzing the PEI of Quadros and Goulart, as well as Geisel's PR, Fonseca Júnior (1996, pp. 329–330) stated that with regard to doctrinal formulation, both put the quest for autonomy on the agenda "in contrast with what the hegemonic (powers) advocate(d)". Alternatively, as argued by Faverão (2006), Brazilian diplomacy at both moments distanced itself from the battles of an ideological character relating to the East–West conflict and put forward reformist proposals for world order.

There are, however, important differences between the projects of the PEI and PR, mainly on the perception of the relationship with Argentina. During 1975–78, relations between Brasília and Buenos Aires became significantly strained, largely owing to the ideas of Geisel and Silveira, as well as the weight of the Brazilian geopolitical school of thought, while geopolitical ideas simultaneously also grew in importance in Argentina. Silveira was opposed to the traditional Brazilian policy of accommodating the neighbor. According to Matias Spektor (2004, p. 208), "for Silveira, the Argentinian decline opened the way for a new regional arrangement in which Brazil would abandon its timid position. In Silveira's analysis, there was incongruence between the South American power structure (Argentina no longer had the material or social means to put pressure on Brazil as it had done before) and the behavior of the units (Brazil of the late 1960s continued to act as if Argentina had the capacity to put pressure on it)". Due to this perception, the period witnessed Brazilian policies that made no effort to defuse the contentious atmosphere surrounding the issue of international rivers. It also becomes interesting to note how Argentina also was excluded from Brazil's multilateral initiatives. In Silveira's (1976, p. 57) words, "A country with increasingly global interests, in a universe with ever more solidarity and interdependence, cannot circumscribe its policy to a certain region". For Lafer (2004) the PR was characterized by the exacerbation of the dispute over Itaipu, with all the inevitable consequences that a difficult relationship with Argentina brought to the preservation of a climate conducive to cooperation for development in South America. This situation was gradually surpassed towards the end of the Geisel administration due to a number of reasons, particularly because of the intervention of epistemic communities, including those connected to national electrical agencies, in a wider context of petroleum shock and scarcity (Gardini, 2011).

In the formulation of the PR, Brazil needed to play the role of a protagonist in Latin America, which would be the basis of its international actions. The country's insertion would not be restricted to the region and it would seek to project itself globally. This idea was not new in the way of thinking about Brazil's destiny. The policy of drawing closer to Latin and South America, although considered important in its own right, did not lose sight of the global level. According to Silveira (1974, p. 21) "it will not be possible for Brazil to remove itself from developments in other areas, given the growing dimension of its economy and of its national power, and the fact that it is projecting itself in a world where the coexistence between nations is becoming closer". In a critical review of some of the guiding concepts and ideas of the PEI and PR, and considering above all Brazil's regional positions, Ferreira (1975, p. 63) argues that "the denunciation of the freezing of world power and the reiterated statements that power politics should give way to a fair international legal order (which began in the Médici government and later was continued), as well as the refusal to recognize the existence of zones of influence—all of this sounds like an attempt at self-affirmation on the part of a country that resents the minor position in which it finds itself, though from its position it exerts the very same policy it condemns in others within its specific ambit of action". That is, there was a discontinuity in positions. In relation to the "strong" there was a search for the redistribution of power. For the PR, the country's power in the region would be sufficient to justify it having greater influence. In this case, the PR differed from the PEI (Pinheiro, 2004).

For the PR, the role attributed to the region and to the relationship with neighboring countries could not imply positions that might attenuate the universalist/ecumenical character of foreign policy. Silveira worried about risks for Brazilian regional policy when he stated, "As Brazil dives into the Southern Cone, it loses out in universalization terms, which must be the key to our foreign policy. Furthermore, we would need to remind ourselves, that despite our complexes in relation to the 'white' South, our neighbors are everywhere and speak languages different from Spanish. Excessive concern on our part with the 'whites' of the South costs us dear in Latin America and in the rest of the world. Hence, it is improper for Brazil to have an alliance with Argentina" (Azeredo da Silveira, 1979 apud Magnoli et al., 2000, p. 43). Not necessarily in contradiction to such considerations, Silveira also considered, "Any nation, whatever its level of industrialization and natural resources wealth, needs to interrelate with others, above all those that are near it, so as to better achieve its fair imperatives of progress and well-being." He also highlights that "The Geisel government introduced 'ecumenism' also in our regional relations, if I may express myself through an apparent paradox. In fact, the thirty months of the current government have witnessed an enormous intensification of our contacts with the countries of South America situated outside the Platine region, while not harming—of course—the maintenance of the high level achieved in relations with the countries of the mentioned area" (Silveira, 1976, p. 59).

In the thinking of San Tiago Dantas and Castro, Brazilian universalism was not counterposed to the quest for approximation and cooperation with its regional peers. The approximation failed, owing to specific concrete reasons, mainly instability. The region was considered a part of underdeveloped countries, with which there was a common destiny. The PR and the PEI coincided inasmuch as they placed universalism and the fight against the freezing of power at the center of their concerns, with a view to the projection of Brazilian power. However, they differed concerning relations with Brazil's neighbors. Silveira considered these relations, at least in part, as contradictory to the aspiration towards universalism.

3.4 The ESG and Geopolitical Thought

This section analyses elements of the ESG doctrine, showing how this institution reflected upon the country, its development, and international insertion. From this point of departure, we discuss its understanding of Latin America and integration. A special emphasis is laid on the ideas of Couto e Silva, one of the most influential formulators of geopolitical thought. The analysis concentrates on the period from the college's founding in 1949 to the end of the military regime in 1984.

From its creation, the ESG was linked to the armed forces' staff, representing a privileged forum for joint doctrinal formulation by the Army, Navy, and Air Force. The objective of the college was to develop and consolidate the knowledge required to plan national security. In this environment, various considerations about geopolitics and military strategy found fertile ground to develop, generating ideas that were to influence Brazil's relations with its neighbors until the mid-1980s. Part of the ESG's conceptions and the DSN were influenced by the conservative thinking of Alberto Torres and Oliveira Vianna, developed in the first half of the twentieth century. They considered a strong state necessary to make up for the selfishness of the elites and the lack of preparation of the masses for political activity. Part of the institute's thinking had as its reference the experience of the Brazilian Expeditionary Force (*Força Expedicionária Brasileira*—FEB) in the Second World War. According to Moura's understanding (1996), FEB was considered by part of the Brazilian military as the nucleus of a political project for strengthening the armed forces and providing the country with a position of prominence in Latin America, and global importance as an ally of the US (Alves, 2007; McCann, 1973).

The ESG doctrine may be understood as a national development project. The *Brasil potência* view was popular among the officers of the college. Power was to bc based on a trans-nationalised capitalist development process under the stewardship of a civilian–military elite. The idea of the "construction of power" (Cavagnari Filho, 1987) brought with it the expectation that the country's rise to higher levels in the international hierarchy would have as a corollary the enhancement of the military capabilities in defence of national interests abroad. As we have seen, the idea of transforming Brazil into a relevant actor in the international system was not exclusive to the ESG or the armed forces, but it was in the military milieu and through the DSN that it was transformed into a project of the Brazilian military dictatorship. For the ESG, sovereignty was the "power of self-determination, without any interference. It was the original power source that ruled over and legally disciplined the population found in the territory of the state" (Dreyfuss 1987, p. 167).

For the ESG, sovereignty was to be ensured by strengthening national power and a greater international projection. Most of the studies produced by the ESG held that Brazil would achieve such projection owing to its geographical position and continental expanse. This idea did not belong exclusively to the ESG but gained a specific dimension through it. The concern with making Brazil a viable power was present from the college's creation. As argued by Shiguenoli Miyamoto (1995, p. 123), "there are no reasons to doubt that from the beginning, the ESG sought to formulate a model of development to make the country gain a place of relevance in the international concert of nations".

The idea of *Brasil potência* was strong among Brazilian geopolitical thinkers (geopolíticos), particularly in the late 1960s and 1970s. The notion of Brazil as a world power as presented in the book *Brasil, Geopotitica e Destino* (1975) by Carlos de Meira Mattos went beyond the ideas of Mário Travassos (1935), who thought in terms of Brazil as a continental power. This discussion originated in the first half of the twentieth century when authors such as Elyseo de Carvalho and Leopoldo Nery da Fonseca discussed it (Miyamoto, 1995).

The main concepts of the DSN were security, strategy, national objectives, ideological borders, ideological and subversive wars. The doctrine was influenced by the international context of the Cold War period, which Couto e Silva (1967, p. 130) characterized as "the picture of the present dominant antagonism between the democratic and Christian West and the communized and materialist East". From its formulation the ESG's doctrine had an anti-communist grounding and a realist view of the international system. In this sense, as argued by Alfred Stepan (1975, p. 132) if communism was an enemy, "the US, being the main anti-communist country, was a natural ally". Even so, doctrinally speaking, Brazil's capacity to make independent decisions was emphasized as the need for more robust national power, allowing the state to gain sufficient strength to trail its own path in a world dominated by the cold logic of interests, with a view to the creation of a new independent center of power in South America (Garcia, 1997).

According to Pécaut (1990), the DSN was not merely a conception of anti-subversive action, often repeated after 1964. Importantly, it also included an industrialization programme for Brazil, which as Couto e Silva stated, was a "plan to reinforce the national potential". With the 1964 military coup, the set of ideas brought together in the DSN contributed to the political guidelines of the new regime. According to Rodrigues (1966, p. 199), "the April 1964 coup was dominated by the idea of security and by the planning of national security. This was the new clothing worn by the current Brazilian government, a natural child of the National War College".

The geopolitical ideas of Couto e Silva (1967, 1981) were grounded in conceptions of national security. The perception was that in the historical moment of the Cold War, national security would only be guaranteed by strengthening national power. In his (1967, p. 75) view, "the strengthening of national prestige in the external ambit, based on the principle of the legal equality between states and the country's growing projection abroad to safeguard its interests effectively and to the benefit of international peace itself" were among the nation's permanent objectives. In contrast to the PEI, the idea of "strengthening national prestige in the external ambit" brought with it the aim of projecting Brazilian singularity internationally in the context of emerging countries, particularly South American ones. Couto e Silva (1967, p. 1981) did not have a bellicose perspective on Brazil's continental or regional projections. However, his ideas about strengthening national power and the country's greater projection in the region contained a destabilizing politico-strategic potential, with consequences regarded as negative by elites of other

South American countries (Miyamoto, 1995), though these concerns could only be resolved through sectoral cooperation.

For Couto e Silva, the best path to acquire power in the international system was through stronger bonds with the West. US hegemony in the South Atlantic was accepted, with the provision that Brazil had an "inalienable right" to exercise its own in the future. Once the "common threat" of Soviet expansionism was eliminated, Couto e Silva (1981) believed the US should voluntarily cease to exert its hegemony in the region, with Brazil taking on that right, given the geopolitical unity of South America (Cavagnari Filho, 2000). Although American hegemony was recognized, this did not imply subordination to US positions. For Couto e Silva (1981), the bilateral relationship was one of equally shared interests. In policy terms, the expectation was that Brazil would play a leading role in the region, as a strategic US ally, and due to its participation in the Western defence system against international communism. The alliance would yield benefits for the country, including a strengthening of its position. Even in other historical periods, ruling groups in charge of the state believed in this possibility, which, however, was not realized.

Regarding integration with neighboring countries, Couto e Silva (1967, pp. 134–135) held the view that greater physical integration could increase Brazil's specific weight. He saw such integration as making "Brazilian participation much more effective in the vital and decisive field of welding together the continent, whose natural instability may always constitute a hazard demanding swift remediation". He stressed the instability of neighboring countries and the consequent idea of Brazilian singularity. For him, the issue of integration was important and strategic. In discussions about regional integration in the 1960s, he thus adopted a favorable position. Couto e Silva (1967, p. 135) considered that "the common market currently being established, a great step designed in the direction of enhanced continental unity and faster and more coherent economic development, demands for its realization, above all, the physical base of an adequate transit system in the whole of South America. Brazil should not delay its cooperation, decidedly, in the creation of this indispensable base" (Couto e Silva 1967, p. 135). It is noticeable that tactical and strategic thinking dominates this perspective. Social actors' interest, even those of business, are not very visible.

Since the 1920s, most Brazilian geopolitical schemes that touched upon regional integration highlighted the geographic potential of the national territory and discussed the question of the physical control of the subcontinent and its sea access routes in line with the ambition to ensure Brazil's control of its vital areas. The essential idea was that if such control were achieved by peaceful means, conditions would be met for the formation of a powerful geopolitical unit under Brazilian hegemony or leadership, encompassing South America, the South American Pacific, and the South Atlantic. The implementation of this strategy would necessarily demand the integration and organization of the national space, the strengthening of border defenses, the exercise of politico-economic leadership in South America, the establishment of access to the Pacific, and the neutralization of hegemonic pretensions on the part of any other South American country (Cavagnari Filho, 2000).

As highlighted by Miyamoto (1995), within discussions of the ESG and Brazilian geopolitical thought, it is important to pay attention to the fact that the works of Couto e Silva, Mattos, Travassos and others were used by geopolitical thinkers of other countries in the region to show that Brazilian policy was grounded in the conceptions of these authors. Often, and even most of the time, however, this was not the case. The ideas of the ESG and Couto e Silva, like the theories of other Brazilian *geopolíticos*, saw the regional integration issue as based on the consideration that South America was a privileged area for the country's geopolitical projection. The concept of "projection of power" on the regional level and the perception of Brazil's destiny as a "world power", both strong within the ESG and among *geopolíticos*, caused distrust of Brazil's intentions in the region during the 1960s and 1970s. The geopolitical doctrine influenced ideas about regional integration, since it served to adapt relations between other countries to Brazilian needs. In the economic field, integration was again steered toward interests that could act as instruments to reinforce the country's trade position in the region. "We will do everything in favor of strengthening the ALALC, to increase Brazil's presence in the Latin American market" (Leitão da Cunha, 1965, p. 136).

3.5 CEPAL and the Dependency Theory

This section looks at the incorporation of CEPAL's ideas into the vision for Latin American and regional integration of some Brazilian thinkers, particularly in the 1960s. The main reference is Celso Furtado who influenced Brazilian economic thought within a national-developmentalist matrix. Furtado was one of the Brazilian authors most associated with CEPAL's theoretical formulations, having been amongst its founders. Dosman (2008, p. 279), underlines that "The most powerful of the CEPAL units was the Development Division, headed by Furtado [...] [and it] was the center of thinking on development theory and planning in the organization" in 1951. Furtado's contribution included structuring the body of concepts and fundamentals that gave rise to CEPAL's Structuralist Theory of Economic Development. One of the key ideas that drove the emergence of CEPAL was the belief that underdeveloped countries needed an independent theoretical formulation, or at least an adapted theoretical formulation, as they functioned differently from developed countries in certain aspects. Furtado played a fundamental role in this agenda of CEPAL studies initiated by Raúl Prebisch (1965). In Furtado's (1961) view, underdevelopment was an autonomous historical process and not a stage necessarily already experienced by the economies that had achieved a higher level of development. Underdevelopment was a particular process, resulting from the penetration of archaic social structures by modern capitalist enterprises. There was a phenomenon of homogenization of these hybrid structures starting with the process of industrialization. This line of thinking had affinities with other intellectuals and schools of thought.

In the following sections, we will discuss the ideas of Brazilian intellectuals linked to the Dependency Theory, which tackled some of the questions present in CEPAL's reflections, but from a different perspective. An idea emphasized by CEPAL was the importance of the state for the industrialization of the countries in the region. The authors of the theory sought to understand the limitations to and possibilities for development and industrialization in the region. We shall analyze Fernando Henrique Cardoso and Ruy Mauro Marini due to their importance and representativeness.

CEPAL's ideas provided the rationale for a nationalist and state-centric position that preceded the existence of this institution and had been present in Brazilian thought since 1930. Sola (1998) identifies a connection between economic development and a certain conception of political development in the way in which CEPAL's ideas were absorbed in Brazil. Hence, growth and integration of the domestic market in Brazil—the main engine of development in CEPAL's approach—were thought of as inseparable from a politico-ideological position. This was because the goal of molding and diversifying the domestic market—the "displacement of the dynamic center of growth"—took the form of a political category as well, that is, a process of internalization of decision-making centers. From the international point of view, this idea strengthened the perspective of independent external engagement, not conditioned by bilateral, regional, or multilateral ties.

For Bielschowsky (2004), Furtado's view had three main characteristics. Firstly, he advocated for the leadership of the state in promoting development through investments in strategic sectors and economic planning. The state would coordinate industrialization efforts to bring together conditions necessary to overcome structural obstacles that hindered development. Secondly, Furtado's work contained a defence of the structuralist thesis on the submission of monetary and exchange rate policies to the development policy. This was the basis of the nationalist line of argument in contrast to the stabilization programmes that had influential backers like Eugenio Gudin (Malan et al., 1980). Furtado believed that the success of Brazil's industrialization largely depended on the control that national agents had over fundamental decisions regarding the country's economy. Thirdly, over time, his work revealed an increasing commitment to social reforms, including land reform. There was a strong perception of the importance of the domestic market in adding dynamism to production and income generation. Furtado tended towards a historical analysis of the dynamic possibilities for overcoming dependence on foreign trade and of underdevelopment itself through economic growth spurred by a stronger domestic market (Bielschowsky, 2004). In the 1950s and 1960s, foreign capital originating in central countries was seen as a negative factor for development by Furtado. At the same time, because it was a factor for the integration of the economies of peripheral countries within the international economy, it was also seen to be compatible with the specific modalities of regional integration which were open to foreign capital. Consequently, there was no possibility for development other than along the national path.

Furtado (1978, 2000) attributed an important role to regional integration, whilst still emphasizing the ideas of planning and national decision-making centers. The theme of regional integration was not the main object of his reflection but was present in some of his works. "The theory of integration constitutes a higher stage of the theory of development and the policy of integration constitutes an advanced form of development policy. The planning of integration, therefore, emerges as the most complex form of this technique of coordination of economic decisions" (Furtado, 2000, p. 331). In another text, though in the same line of thought, Furtado (1978, pp. 267–268) stated, "far from being a simple question of trade liberalization, the real problem consists in promoting the gradual creation of a regional economic system, which will not be a small task, due to the previous orientation of development, to the risks of further geographic concentration both of economic activities and of the appropriation of the fruits of development [...] The most important decision-making centers, those that are political in nature and have the capacity to interpret collective aspirations, will continue to exist for a long time at the domestic level". It is important to note that regional integration thereby was thought of in terms of strengthening national capacities. This was not only a Brazilian view but also a Latin American one, since for example in European formulations on this issue, regional integration was more often than not seen as a process of partial abdication of sovereignty, albeit a slow one, or of change in focus of the national capacities from the level of the nation-state to the regional-community sphere (Haas, 1964). This could be summarized as supranationality.

In CEPAL's framework, industrialization in the 1950s and 1960s was seen as the long-term solution to the problem of external vulnerability—an intrinsic characteristic of peripheral industrialization processes. Regional integration was considered a possible solution to this problem. CEPAL was directly involved in the creation of the ALALC and took the view that this new regional agreement could start a process of diversification of the region's exports through regional states' own efforts, through the "theoretically" easier route of intra-regional trade. The Latin American common market would enlarge the market for industrial sectors that demanded scale, thus facilitating the import-substitution process (Bielschowsky, 2000). However, the major impulse to the 1960 Treaty of Montevideo was a reaction against the reduced exports and deteriorating terms of trade of the main countries—Argentina, Brazil, and Mexico.

CEPAL's goals *vis-à-vis* integration and other ambitious steps were difficult to achieve, as assumptions of national policies relating to development did not place them high on the agenda. As argued by Cervo (2008, p. 155) CEPAL's thinking, built around concepts like domestic markets, employment, industry, protection, and self-sufficiency, gained expression in political practices, which unintentionally constrained integration processes. As a formulator, Celso Furtado inspired a strong current based on the national perception of interests to be promoted. He broke with Prebisch in 1955, remaining loyal to the assumptions he had formulated. By conceiving the Office of the Superintendent for the Development of the Northeast (SUDENE) and becoming a pioneer in planning, he consolidated the idea that national integration was the central axis of development.

The Dependency Theory appeared in the same intellectual context as CEPAL, that is, amid attempts by thinkers of the region to analyze the local and regional economies in autonomous and particular fashions. The theory set out to understand how the reproduction of the capitalist system of production occurred in the periphery. Its starting point was the idea that the system created differentiation in economic, political and social terms between countries and regions, conditioning the economic performance of some countries on the development and expansion of others (dos Santos, 1970).

In a way different from CEPAL's formulations, among dependency theorists (*dependentistas*) there was a strong relationship between underdevelopment and global capitalist development. These intellectuals considered development a process that was a part of political and social disputes, that is, it had a dimension that was strictly political as well as economic. Cardoso and Faletto (2004) regarded politics as the means by which economic determination was made possible.

In other words, they started from the idea that referenced "historical situations" in which economic transformations took place as essential to understanding the meaning of these transformations, as well as in analyzing their structural limits and the conditions that made them possible (Cardoso & Faletto, 2004).

There are various interpretations within the framework of the Dependency Theory (Chilcote, 1974), which lead to difficulties in speaking of a homogenous theory. However, there is a convergent view among most authors who work within this perspective of a link between the paradigm of Latin American development and dependence. Part of the literature divides the theory into two currents: Weberian identified with the work of Cardoso and Falleto which accepts the possibility of dependent development, and Marxist, related to, amongst other, Marini, which is based on the idea of the hyper-exploitation of the labour force and discusses underdevelopment and the impossibility of dependent development. It may be claimed that the second version ascribes greater causal weight to external factors, though not disregarding internal issues in determining situations of dependency/underdevelopment. Cardoso and Faletto, on the other hand, relativize the weight of external determination, emphasizing the possibility of a situation of dependent associated development as a result of the actions of local agents in connection with external economic forces.

In Marini's understanding, the only way to confront and overcome the dependent situation experienced by the countries of the region, including Brazil, was through a socialist revolution. Underdeveloped countries were dependent because they reproduced a social system whose development was limited by both national and international economic and political relations. According to Marini (2000, p. 109), dependency had to be "understood as a relationship of subordination between formally independent nations, in whose environment the relations of production of the subordinated nations were modified or recreated to ensure the enhanced reproduction of dependency". The fundamental obstacle to any real development process was imperialism, responsible for extracting practically all the surplus produced by underdeveloped countries (Marini, 1978).

Within this view, the local bourgeoisie was largely subordinated to imperialism, in the sense that it lacked the freedom to create greater possibilities for autonomous development. In this interpretation, there were clear structural limits to national development projects, and for any form of regional integration. An approximation with other regional states implied a previous surmounting of these limits. Only a rupture with the international system would facilitate development along self-sufficient lines, thereby creating conditions to put integration on the agenda.

Marini (2000) also noted that in the case of post-coup Brazil with Castelo Branco's military government, after 1964, the bourgeoisie designed a foreign policy that resorted to sub-imperialism via the export of its manufactured products to even less developed countries, since the hyper-exploitation of labour-power prevented the formation of a domestic market. The concept of sub-imperialism refers to the bourgeoisies' need for dependent countries to project their accumulation abroad at the moment when they achieve a certain level of organic composition of capital with industrialization. In this sense, the weakness of Brazilian capitalism was that it reached the imperialist stage before achieving an overarching change in the national economy, as well as the situation of growing dependency in the face of international imperialism. The most important consequence of this state of affairs was that unlike central capitalist economies, Brazilian sub-imperialism could not convert the "plunder" it intended to conduct abroad into a factor for raising the domestic standard of living, thus mitigating the impetus of the class struggle. On the contrary, because of the need to supply extra surplus-value to its "major North American partner", it would have had to violently worsen the exploitation of labour in the framework of the national economy to reduce its production costs (Marini, 2000). Through sub-imperialism, Marini (2000) classified Brazil as entering the capitalist stage of exporting capital and manufactured goods, albeit in a dependent and subordinate fashion and explained the efforts to control raw materials and energy sources abroad. An important corollary of this situation was an "expansionist" and relatively autonomous foreign policy.

For Cardoso and Faletto (2004), the situation of dependency demanded an analysis of how underdeveloped economies were historically linked to the world market and how the internal social groups that defined the international relations intrinsic to underdevelopment were constituted. Depending on how the classes organized politically, there were different types of linkage with the center. According to Cardoso (2004, p. 23), while reviewing the Dependency Theory, these linkages had differentials. "It is one thing when one has, as in Brazil and Argentina, a local sector capable of producing accumulation—be it in agriculture, with coffee, or cattle. It creates capital here and later invests this capital, even in industry. Afterwards, it associates itself, but it has some dynamism. [...] Another thing is when you have an enclave when the capital comes from abroad, passes through the country and the profits are realized abroad [...] And there is a third way when external capital starts investing in the periphery [...] investment in the production of consumer goods and capital goods. Then you have another dynamic". Analyses of the different situations in Latin America influenced the ways of looking at integration. But in these three cases, the fundamental issue which would be intensely debated in subsequent phases, the role of technological autonomy, was not considered (Schumpeter, 1994).

According to this current of the Dependency Theory, development was a social process and it would not be correct to attribute full responsibility a priori to international imperialism for the weaknesses of dependent countries. Cardoso and Faletto (2004) considered economic development in peripheral countries as dependent on a strategy different from the idea of "inward development". Serra and Cardoso (1978) were critical of the idea of hyper-exploitation present in the work of Marini (2000) and indicated that development, even dependent development, could provide underdeveloped countries with productivity gains. There was a clear differentiation between the countries of the region, reflecting their varying levels of development and integration needed to take these into account. The perspective upon the region would thus depend on the varying levels of development. The integration process would thus need to contemplate these different levels.

The aim of Cardoso and Faletto's work (2004, p. 13) was "to clarify some controversial points about the conditions, possibilities, and forms of economic development in countries that have relations of dependency with the hegemonic centers of the capitalist system, but, at the same time, constitute nations and organized national states that aspire to sovereignty, like every state. On the other hand, as it has been sought implicitly demonstrated, to talk about Latin America not specifying the differences of structure and history within it, constitutes a theoretical mistake with practical and dangerous consequences".

Cardoso and Faletto (2004) took the view that from the moment the nation was established, the political center of Latin American countries' social forces tried to gain a certain amount of autonomy and overcome the situation of the market. However, the economic linkages continued to be defined objectively as a function of the external market and limited the possibilities for decision-making and autonomous agency. The development of Latin American societies was necessarily dependent. It was up to national political spheres to institute patterns that could oscillate between the binomials—development/dependency and stagnation/autonomy. Upon defining that the most adequate paradigm for Latin American development in the framework of dependency would be the binomial development/dependency, Cardoso and Faletto (2004) emphasized it as a limit to the expansion of the region and as the only possibility for development under known conditions. Reflecting upon the region—Latin America/South America—implied perceiving how the paradigm could be adjusted, so that countries with similar conditions could articulate themselves to maximize their relative advantages.

3.6 Analysis of Lafer and Guimarães: Contemporary Views

This section analyses ideas relating to the Brazilian view on the Latin American region in the works of Celso Lafer and Samuel Pinheiro Guimarães owing to their present importance, particularly for Brazilian foreign policy. Although these authors come from distinct theoretical backgrounds with differing views on the nature of the international system, they have an understanding that may be interpreted as being similar concerning the region and to Brazil's role in the world. Equally, they emphasize the importance of a strategic alliance with Argentina to optimize Brazil's insertion in the Southern Cone and South America. At the same time, part of the country's international insertion project present in their reflections raises challenges for the bilateral relationship with Argentina, owing to the stress put on Brazil's projection in the world. Lafer and Guimarães are important references of the liberal and national-developmentalist traditions of Brazilian international insertion.

Since the 1970s, Lafer (1973) has emphasized the importance of an understanding between Brazil and Argentina. The structural axis of his analysis present in a work published with Felix Peña (Lafer & Peña, 1973) was the idea of valuing the regional context—understood as the Latin American sub-system of nations—to formulate a strategy for autonomous participation in the international system. There was a recognition that, "in Latin America, national identification continues to prevail. The proof that the time has come to go beyond the nation-state (Hoffmann–Haas) is yet to be provided" (Lafer & Peña 1973, p. 30). Universalism was an important concept present in Lafer's (2004) reflections. It explained part of the contemporary view on the region and was associated with the country's cultural, ethnic and geographic characteristics. According to Lafer, the notion incorporated the plurality of the interests of state and society and historical and political affinities and symbolized the concern with diversifying the country's relations to the utmost, thus making the channels of dialogue with the world more plural, broad, and varied. On the economic front, the notion of universalism was manifest through the term "global trader", since Brazil conducted exchanges with an array of countries in various regions, thus not restricting its trade relations to specific and limited regions. On the political front, the idea permeating the notion of universalism was the project of making Brazil a relevant actor on the international stage through intense participation in diverse bilateral, regional, and multilateral fora, which had implications for the process of regional integration. The operationalization of universalist external activism with a national base required an essentially intergovernmental brand of regional integration, one that did not constrain Brazil's external projection in any way.

Lafer (2004) elaborated the concept of middle power to characterize Brazil's international insertion. Middle powers, he argued, were a specific group of countries in the international system, and had a particular kind of foreign policy, inasmuch as they differed from the great powers, but were also distinct from small countries of little significance in the system. In Brazil's case, the notion complemented the idea that the country should play a unique role in the world by virtue of its specific features. The increase in Brazilian influence in the international system would result in a broader scope of external engagement and a growing role for the country as an international mediator, thus projecting its power through its legitimacy rather than through confrontation or military capacity. Regarding regional integration, the characterization of the country as a middle power added to the concept of universalism, helping to understand part of the Brazilian difficulty in managing the issue of institutional deepening of integration in the Southern Cone. This could possibly restrict the autonomy or freedom desired for Brazilian policy in relation to the region and the world. Lafer (2004, p. 76) argued that while Brazil "by virtue of the limitation of its means was a middle power in the international system, at the same time, it was a middle power of a continental scale, a condition that naturally conferred it a role in the fabric of the world order". While emphasizing Brazil's multilateral insertion and issues relating to legitimacy and other forms of soft power, there was also a substantial regional component to the reflection (Lafer, 1973, 1993, 2004). "It seemed to me to be evident that Latin America in general, and the formation of the Common Southern Market (*Mercado Comum do Sul—Mercosul*) in particular, were our circumstance, our life, our destiny. Right from the start, I saw in the Mercosul a platform for Brazil's competitive insertion, which was important due to the opportunities it generated, and for what it represented in terms of interlocution at the world level. I was also very much aware that the existing tensions in the world made it clear that we should go from a notion of border separation to one of border-cooperation [...] I tried to conduct this kind of articulation between the internal and the external, and at the same time realized that a country with Brazil's dimensions has general interests" (Lafer, 1993, p. 279). In Lafer's reflections, the weight of regional integration for Brazil was always contextualized, while not failing to take into account the country's projection in other international arenas. Owing to the fact that Brazil had "general interests" in the workings of the international system, its insertion could not be restricted by the logic of the process of regional integration that tended to limit the autonomy of action of member-states.

Referring to Mercosul, Guimarães (2006, p. 359) stated, "Mercosul, not the programme of integration with Argentina, was imagined within a general neoliberal economic policy inside the countries [...] The myopia of the Brazilian strategy in abandoning the political model of Brazil-Argentina cooperation and exchanging it for the commercialist neoliberal model of integration professed by the Treaty of Asunción was notable" (Guimarães, 2006, p. 357). The early phase of integration with Argentina, (the Iguazú Declaration November 1985, the Economic Integration and Cooperation Programme (*Programa de Integração e Cooperação Econômica*) July 1986, the 24 resulting Protocols, and the Treaty of Integration, Cooperation and Development November 1988), corresponded to a developmentalist and protectionist logic that sought to stimulate business emulation with a view to the joint modernization and competitive insertion in the international economic system. Over time, as argued by Guimarães (2006), a gradual decline was observed in the importance of the development theme in the scope of integration. Simultaneously, trade issues took on growing significance. Consequently, the author discusses the need to restore the idea of economic development based on the (now regional) domestic market as the driving force. In Guimarães' view (2006), it was important to develop a gradual strategy to transform the Mercosul from a "neoliberal (scheme) of the open integration type" into a regional development scheme. Within the economic field, reducing external vulnerability and domestic social disparities were key factors as were recovering capacity to formulate and carry out policies autonomously (Guimarães, 2006).

Guimarães' (2006) arguments in favor of economic integration and political cooperation between Brazil and Argentina took a realist theoretical view of the global dynamic as their starting point. They presented the idea, that regional integration could not be exclusively commercial, but had to be part of a common development strategy, especially in the areas of industry and services. Regional commercial integration, as long as accompanied by a regional industrial policy, could contribute to higher and broader levels of industrialization. Guimarães (2007) considered the object of Brazilian foreign policy to be South America. In his view, the nucleus of Brazilian policy was the Mercosul and in it, the cornerstone was Argentina. His understanding was that any attempt to establish different priorities for Brazilian foreign policy, or even paying insufficient attention to these fundamentals, would have serious consequences and imply significant risks of failure (Guimarães, 2007, p. 1).

Guimarães (1999) used the notion of a "large peripheral state" to characterize Brazil's international insertion. In his perspective, this kind of state was faced with an international setting based on "hegemonic structures of power". Just like the strategic objective of the hegemonic structures of power was their own preservation and expansion, due to the benefits derived from them by the countries situated in their center, the final strategic objectives of large peripheral states was to participate in these hegemonic structures in a sovereign and non-subordinate fashion and to reduce their level of vulnerability in the face of the workings of these structures. Despite differences between Brazil and other large peripheral states, by virtue of sharing characteristics and interests, and being situated far from each other, so that their interests did not clash directly, common political projects could be built (Guimarães, 1999). The category "large peripheral state" set Brazilian foreign policy apart—even from other countries in the region. Guimarães identified the possibility of Brazil forming coalitions with other large peripheral states to play a more effective part in hegemonic structures, and to ensure the incorporation of its interests into the dynamics of international organizations. Guimarães (1999, p. 21) took the view that "despite notable differences, Brazil had similarities and common interests with certain states in the periphery precisely for being, like them, a 'large peripheral state', which radically distinguished them from medium and small countries of the periphery".

South American integration was present in the thought of both Lafer and Guimarães. They saw the integration of the Southern Cone as the first step towards a later, South America-wide integration. Furthermore, the reflections on South and Latin America were contextualized without leaving aside Brazil's insertion in other international arenas. This seems to be a permanent trait in Brazilian thought on regional integration.

3.7 Final Remarks

This discussion demonstrates that within important currents of Brazilian thought of the second half of the twentieth, and the beginning of the twenty-first century, the regional integration theme was not at the heart of the reflection—neither in the cultural, economic or political field. Although the theme of Latin America cropped up sporadically in the literature, the country's continental dimensions did not facilitate the inclusion of regional integration in national debates. There were many explanations for this. Nearly all other countries had Spanish colonial origins in common, which had its own weight. The changes sketched out in the 1970s and consolidated from 1985, were important. The currents of thought—the ISEB, PEI, PR, ESG and its geopolitical thought, CEPAL and the Dependency Theory, as well as the ideas of two representatives of contemporary Brazilian thought on foreign policy and regional integration—all emphasized national capacity and the need for the country to play an independent international role. Brazil's specificity, national development and national integration were stressed. The deeply rooted idea of strengthening the nation was the determinant of many domestic political battles. Since the emergence of a consistent debate in the 1980s, regional integration has been seen as a tool for strengthening the nation. This is not peculiar to Brazil. Every integration process starts with the assumption that it would be beneficial to the country, to all of society, and to the elites (Moravcsik, 2018). Among the authors and schools of thought studied here, the realist international relations theory predominated, that is, cooperation was seen as an instrument of national strengthening, which could take place within the perspective of the common interest. The core of the issue was development. As regards external projections, the debate focused on the role the country should play in the international system. Since the 1980s, regional integration has been seen as compatible with this aim, and even as a factor reinforcing the country's performance.

The concepts of nationalism and autonomy are strong. Brazil, like most countries in Latin America, was conditioned by relations with the US during the twentieth century; how to conduct this approximation, how to obtain benefits from this relationship, how to be autonomous, and bolster a nationalist project, etc. were permanent *leitmotifs*. Autonomy alluded to the idea of increased room of maneuver or freedom of choice for the state. The upshot was the non-urgency of a regional integration project. In some cases, the theme was not even an object of interest, while in others, as in Brazilian CEPAL-oriented thought, it was taken into consideration, but adjourned to a somewhat distant future. The economic and political changes of the 1970s brought about its transformation from an idealist formulation of integration to a concrete idea. The notion of development found common ground with the notion of integration, albeit with all the obstacles that remain at the end of the first decade of the twenty-first century. For this reason, this article shows that the ideas of Lafer and Guimarães, with all their differences, suggest the absorption of the theme by the Brazilian state and society or by the elites, at least. In the past, at the ISEB, during the PEI, in the realm of CEPAL-oriented ideas in Brazil, or among Brazilian dependency theorists there was no theorization contrary towards integration. This was only partly raised in the case of PR but not formulated, as the nation was the privileged topic, and within this, industrialization. The aspiration towards a more robust international role for the country was the consequence. During the 1950s and 1960s, the central theme that attracted the best minds together with development was understanding the causes of backwardness, the determinants for living conditions, and external projections. Understanding the mechanisms that regulated center-periphery relations was seen as decisive. Latin America thus became an important object of study because of this—as it belonged to the same pole.

References

Almeida, A. O. (2015). *PhD Thesis DCP – USP Alexandra Osorio de Almeida*. https://teses.usp.br/teses/disponiveis/8/8131/tde-04092015-172424/pt-br.php

Alves, W. C. (2007). *Da Itália à Coréia: decisões sobre ir ou não à Guerra*. UFMG.

Amado, R. (1982). *Ed. Araújo Castro*. Editora da Universidade de Brasília.

Amado, R. (1996). A política externa de João Goulart. In J. A. G. Albuquerque (Ed.), *Sessenta Anos de Política Externa Brasileira (1930-1990): crescimento, modernização e política externa*. NUPRI/USP.

Bielschowsky, R. (Org.). (2000). *Cinqüenta anos de pensamento na CEPAL*. Record.

Bielschowsky, R. (2004). *Pensamento Econômico Brasileiro: o ciclo ideológico do desenvolvimentismo*. Contraponto.

Cardoso, F. H. (1972). *Empresário Industrial e Desenvolvimento Econômico no Brasil* (2nd ed.). Ed. Difusão Européia do Livro.

Cardoso, F. H. (2004). *A dívida e sua hora*. Entrevista à Revista Primeira Leitura. Edição no. 29.

Cardoso, F. H., & Faletto, E. (2004). *Dependência e Desenvolvimento na América Latina*. Civilização Brasileira.

Castro, A. (1970). *Conferência no Colégio Interamericano de Defesa*. 11/12.

Cavagnari Filho, G. L. (1987). Brasil: Introdução ao Estudo de uma Potência Média. In E. R. Oliveira (Ed.), *Militares: Pensamento e Ação Política*. Editora Papirus.

Cavagnari Filho, G. L. (2000). Estratégia e Defesa (1960-1990). In J. A. G. Albuquerque (Ed.), *Sessenta Anos de Política Externa Brasileira (1930-1990): Prioridades, atores e política*. Annablume/NUPRI/USP.

Cervo, A. L. (2008). *Inserção Internacional: formação dos conceitos brasileiros*. Editora Saraiva.

Cervo, A. L., & Bueno, C. (2002). *História da Política Exterior do Brasil* (2nd ed.). Ed. UNB.

Chilcote, R. H. (1974). Dependency: A critical synthesis of the literature. *Latin American Perspectives, 1*(1), 4–29.

Corbisier, R. (1968). *Reforma ou Revolução*. Editora Civilização Brasileira.

Couto e Silva, G. D. (1967). *Geopolítica do Brasil* (2nd ed.). Livraria José Olympio Editora.

Couto e Silva, G. D. (1981). *Conjuntura política nacional: o Poder Executivo e geopolítica do Brasil*. José Olympio.

da Silveira, A. (1979). apud Magnoli; César E Yang, (2000, p. 43). Magnoli, Demétrio; César, Luís Fernando Panelli; Yang, Philip. 2000. Em busca do interesse nacional. Política Externa, Vol. 9, n. 1.

Dantas, F. C. D. S. T. (1962). *Política Externa Independente*. Editora Civilização Brasileira.

Dantas, F. C. D. S. T. (1964). Discurso de Paraninfo do Instituto Rio Branco. *Revista Brasileira de Política Internacional, ano VII, 27*, 482–485.

Dosman, E. J. (2008). *The life and times of Raúl Prebisch, 1901–1986*. McGill-Queen's University Press.

Dos Santos, T. (1970). The structure of dependence. *The American Economic Review, 60*(2), 231–236.

Dreyfuss, R. A. (1987). A noção de soberania na Escola Superior de Guerra. In E. R. Oliveira (Ed.), *Militares: Pensamento e Ação Política*. Editora Papirus.

Fausto, B., & Devoto, F. J. (2004). *Fernando J. Brasil e Argentina: um ensaio de história comparada (1850-2002)*. Editora 34.

Faverão, G. D. M. (2006). *Autonomia, universalismo e alinhamento na política externa brasileira do século XX e suas implicações nos processos de integração regional*. Dissertação de Mestrado, Programa de Pós-Graduação em Ciencias Sociais da UNESP-Marília.

Ferreira, O. (1975). Evolução da política internacional do Brasil. Texto da palestra proferida no dia 17/10/1975 na Comissão de Relações Exteriores da Câmara dos Deputados no Painel sobre Política Internacional.

Fonseca Júnior, G. (1996). Mundos diversos, argumentos afins: notas sobre aspectos doutrinários da política externa independente e do pragmatismo responsável. In J. A. G. Albuquerque (Ed.), *Sessenta Anos de Política Externa Brasileira (1930-1990): crescimento, modernização e política externa*. NUPRI/USP.

Fonseca Júnior, G. (1998). *A Legitimidade e Outras Questões Internacionais*. Paz e Terra.

Freyre, G. (1962). Idéias Errôneas sobre o Brasil. *Revista Brasileira de Política Internacional, ano V*, no. 18.

Furtado, C. (1961). *Desenvolvimento e Subdesenvolvimento*. Editora Fundo de Cultura.

Furtado, C. (1978). *A economia latino-americana (formação histórica e problemas contemporâneos)*. Companhia Editora Nacional.

Furtado, C. (2000). *Teoria e Política do Desenvolvimento Econômico*. Editora Paz e Terra.

Garcia, E. V. (1997). O pensamento dos militares em política internacional (1961-1989). *Revista Brasileira de Política Internacional, 40*(1), 18–40.

Gardini, G. L. (2011). *The origins of Mercosur: Democracy and regionalization in South America*. Palgrave Macmillan.

Gardini, G. L., & Almeida, M. H. T. (2016). *Foreign policy responses to the rise of Brazil: balancing power in emerging states*. Palgrave Macmillan.

Goldstein, J., & Keohane, R. (1993). *Ideas and foreign policy: Beliefs, institutions and political change*. Cornell University Press.

Guimarães, S. P. (1999). *Quinhentos anos de periferia: uma contribuição ao estudo da política internacional*. Ed. Da Universidade/UFRGS/Contraponto.

Guimarães, S. P. (2006). *Desafios brasileiros na era dos gigantes*. Ed. Contraponto.

Guimarães, S. P. (2007). *O Mundo Multipolar e a Integração Sul-Americana*. FUNCEB. 25/09. http://www.funceb.org.ar/pensamiento/mundomultipolar.pdf.

Haas, E. B. (1964). *Beyond the nation state*. Stanford University Press.

Jaguaribe, H. (1958). *O Nacionalismo na Atualidade Brasileira*. Instituto Superior de Estudos Brasileiros—ISEB.

Jaguaribe, H. (1972). *Desenvolvimento Econômico e Desenvolvimento Político*. São Paulo.

Lafer, C. (1973). Uma interpretação do sistema das relações internacionais do Brasil. In C. Lafer & F. Peña (Eds.), *Argentina e Brasil no Sistema das Relações Internacionais*. Editora Livraria Duas Cidades.

Lafer, C. (1993). Entrevista. *Estudos Históricos, Rio de Janeiro, 6*(12).

Lafer, C. (2004). *A Identidade Internacional do Brasil e a Política Externa Brasileira: passado, presente e futuro*. Editora Perspectiva.

Lafer, C., & Peña, F. (1973). *Argentina e Brasil no Sistema das Relações Internacionais*. Editora Livraria Duas Cidades.

Leitão Da Cunha, V. (1965). Palestra do ministro das Relações Exteriores na Associação Comercial do Rio de Janeiro, em 11 de novembro de 1964. *Revista Brasileira de Política Internacional. Ano VIII*, no. 29.

Magnoli, D., César, L. F. P., & Yang, P. (2000). Em busca do interesse nacional. *Política Externa, 9*(1).

Malan, P. S., Bonelli, R., Abreu, M. P., & Pereira, J. E. C. (1980). *Política Econômica Externa e Industrialização no Brasil (1939/52)*. IPEA/INPES.
Mariano, M. P. (2007). *A Política Externa Brasileira, o Itamaraty e o Mercosul. Tese de Doutorado*. Programa de Pós-Graduação em Sociologia. Faculdade de Ciências e Letras – UNESP – Araraquara – SP.
Marini, R. M. (1978). Lasrazonesdelneodesarrollismo (respuesta a F.H. Cardoso y J. Serra). *Revista Mexicana de Sociologia, 40*(special issue).
Marini, R. M. (2000). *Dialética da Dependência. Uma antologia da obra de Ruy Mauro Marini; organização e apresentação de Emir Sader*. Editora Vozes.
Martins, L. (1965). O Brasil e a América Latina na atual Conjuntura Mundial. In *Política Externa Independente. A invasão da República Dominicana*. Editora Civilização Brasileira. Ano I, no. 2, agosto 1965, 12–26.
Mattli, W. (1999). *The logic of regional integration: Europe and beyond*. Cambridge University Press.
McCann, J. F. D. (1973). *The Brazilian-American alliance*. Princeton University Press.
Mello, F. D. C. (2000). *Regionalismo e inserção internacional: continuidade e transformação da política externa brasileira nos anos 90. Tese de doutorado*. Departamento de Ciência Política da Faculdade de Filosofia, Letras e Ciências Humanas da Universidade de São Paulo.
Miyamoto, S. (1995). *Geopolítica e poder no Brasil*. Papirus.
Moravcsik, A. (2018). Preferences, power and institutions in 21st-century Europe. *Journal of Common Market Studies, 26*, 1648–1674.
Moura, G. (1996). O Brasil na Segunda Guerra Mundial: 1942-1945. In J. A. G. Albuquerque (Ed.), *Sessenta Anos de Política Externa Brasileira (1930-1990): crescimento, modernização e política externa*. NUPRI/USP.
Pécaut, D. (1990). *Os Intelectuais e a Política no Brasil. Entre o povo e a nação*. Editora Ática.
Pereira, L. C. B. (2004). O conceito de desenvolvimento do ISEB revisitado. *Dados, 47*(1), 49–84. Rio de Janeiro.
Pinheiro, L. (2000). Unidades de Decisão e Processo de Formulação de Política Externa durante o Regime Militar. In J. A. G. Albuquerque (Ed.), *Sessenta Anos de Política Externa Brasileira (1930-1990): Prioridades, atores e política*. Annablume/NUPRI/USP.
Pinheiro, L. (2004). *Política Externa Brasileira*. Jorge Zahar Ed.
Prebisch, R. (1965). Uma política de desenvolvimento econômico autônomo para a América Latina: os fundamentos doutrinários. In *Política Externa Independente*. Editora Civilização Brasileira. Ano I, no. 1, maio 1965.
Ramos, A. G. (1960). *O problema nacional do Brasil* (2ª ed.). Saga.
Rangel, I. (1962). A dinâmica da dualidade brasileira. *Revista Brasileira de Ciências Sociais, 2*(2), 215–235.
Ribeiro, D. (1996). *O povo brasileiro: a formação e o sentido do Brasil*. Companhia das Letras.
Ricupero, R. (2017). *A diplomacia na construção do Brasil (1750-2016)*. Versal.
Rodrigues, J. A. (1965). O Sistema Interamericano contra a América Latina. In *Política Externa Independente*. "A crise do Pan-Americanismo". Editora Civilização Brasileira. Ano I, no. 1, maio 1965.
Rodrigues, J. H. (1966). *Interesse Nacional e Política Externa*. Editora Civilização Brasileira.
Schumpeter, J. (1994). *Capitalism, socialism and democracy*. Taylor and Francis.
Serra, J., & Cardoso, F. H. (1978). Las desventuras de ladialéctica de ladependencia. *Revista Mexicana de Sociologia*. UNAM, Año XL, n. extraordinário.
Silveira, A. (1974). *Discurso de Posse. BRASIL/MRE. Resenha de política exterior do Brasil*. Departamento de comunicação e documentação do MRE. Ano I, no. I, p. 21.
Silveira, A. (1976). Silveira no Congresso expõe bases da diplomacia brasileira. In *BRASIL/MRE. Resenha de política exterior do Brasil*. Departamento de comunicação e documentação do MRE, no. 10.
Sodré, N. W. (1960). *Raízes Históricas do Nacionalismo Brasileiro. Textos de Formação Histórica do Brasil*. Instituto Superior de Estudos Brasileiros.

Sodré, N. W. (1967). *História da Burguesia Brasileira*. Civilização Brasileira.
Sola, L. (1998). *Idéias econômicas, decisões políticas: desenvolvimento, estabilidade e populismo*. Editora da Universidade de São Paulo, EDUSP.
Souto Maior, L. A. P. (1996). O "Pragmatismo Responsável". In J. A. G. Albuquerque (Ed.), *Sessenta Anos de Política Externa Brasileira (1930-1990): crescimento, modernização e política externa*. NUPRI/USP.
Spektor, M. (2004). Origens e direção do Pragmatismo Ecumênico e Responsável (1974-1979). *Revista Brasileira de Política Internacional, 47*(2), 191–222.
Stepan, A. (1975). *Os militares na política: as mudanças de padrões na vida brasileira*. Artenova.
Toledo, C. N. (2005). 50 anos de fundação do ISEB. *Jornal da Unicamp*, 8 a 14 de agosto de 2005.
Travassos, M. (1935). *Projeção continental do Brasil*. Editora Nacional.
Vizentini, P. G. F. (1994). O nacionalismo desenvolvimentista e a política externa independente (1951-1964). *Revista Brasileira de Política Internacional, 37*(1), 24–36.
Weffort, F. (1978). *O populismo na política brasileira*. Paz e Terra.

Chapter 4
The Grounding of Regional Integration for Brazil: Universalism, Sovereignty and Elite Perceptions

4.1 Introduction

Brazil's position within the process of regional integration, over time and at present, must be understood in the light of structural and historical foreign policy factors. This does not always imply rigidity and the impossibility of change, but these are aspects that must be taken into consideration in order to fully understand the difficulties that have become evident, even when governments are in favour of regional integration. Such difficulties cannot be seen—as is sometimes argued—as having originated only in economic issues or in non-convergent views of international affairs. There is tension between the structural needs of the integration process and the attitudes and positions of important social and governmental actors, and not just among diplomats. The origin lies in the positions of part of the elites and interest groups that contribute to the formation of the interests of the state.

Two very important concepts in Brazilian foreign policy formulation should be considered, namely autonomy and universalism, rooted in state and society. These concepts merge in the construction of a vision of regional insertion that complicates the deepening of the Mercosur. There are objective reasons to explain the difficulties experienced from 1991 to 2010. One refers to the challenge of integrating developing countries with significant asymmetries, low levels of interdependence, and histories of macroeconomic instability. The diplomatic and governmental argument in the Alfonsín, Sarney, Collor de Mello, Menem, Itamar Franco and Cardoso administrations was that the low level of institutionalization and the intergovernmental character of the process would ensure rapid progress, dispensing with heavy bureaucracies. The negative reference to the Brussels Euro-bureaucracy was evident. Brazil's defence of the principle of intergovernmentalism, not much different from the Argentinean position, relates to the conception of Mercosur's place within the full range of the country's international relations. Malamud (2011) accentuated that the Brazilian state made use of integration for the purpose of external projection. In

T. Vigevani, H. Ramanzini Junior, *The Challenges for Building Regional Integration in the Global South*, United Nations University Series on Regionalism 18,
https://doi.org/10.1007/978-3-030-93348-7_4

relation to Brazil, Danese (2017) developed the positive significance of the notion of presidential diplomacy, thus characterizing the direct involvement of the chief of state within foreign policy affairs. This notion was important within governments in which the presidency was exercised by individuals with a sense of the role of foreign relations for the national projects. This does not mean that the limits for the comprehension of regional integration have not been influential.

In the perception of some foreign policy-makers, the idea of universalism is associated with the country's geographical, ethnic and cultural characteristics. According to Lafer (2004), it represents the plurality of the interests of the state and society and historical and political affinities; it symbolizes the concern with maximum diversification of the country's foreign relations, i.e., enlarging, enhancing, and pluralizing the channels of dialogue with the world.

This chapter's hypothesis is that the structure of the Mercosur, as constructed from 1991 to 2010, is geared to the perceptions of part of the Brazilian elites, the interests of which the existing structure would serve. This model would be sufficient to provide the support considered possible, or the desired freedom, to the country's international engagement at the World Trade Organization (WTO), and in relations with the European Union (EU), the United States and China, making the country free from the constraints imposed by a customs union or a common market that rested on higher levels of institutionalization. Within this perspective, such higher levels of institutionalization condition the state-parties, even considering the power differential. To complement, we will argue that this model of integration would be compatible with the bloc's enlargement and make the inclusion of new members viable, which ends up strengthening the intergovernmental form and the low level of interaction between national policies in their various aspects.

In the mid-1980s, when Brazilian politics took the route of developing closer relations with Argentina, the idea of universalism was not abandoned but gained new meaning. There was an attempt to intertwine the national interest with the regional interest of the Southern Cone. In the Brazilian case, the idea prevailed that the national interest would be well managed in the context of a wide-ranging integration process. To this end, different perspectives came together, including from business and multinational groups, particularly the automotive industry (Vigevani & Veiga, 1997). Next to join were sectors of the labour movement and other groups, such as intellectuals. We will discuss how this intertwining seems to be running the risk of slow and incessant deterioration, both in Argentina and in Brazil, thus decisively limiting Mercosur's possibilities.

While there was a joining of the idea of national interest and regional interests within Mercosur, the concept of autonomy maintained a primordial character (Guimarães, 12/5/2006). We contend, that although in historical perspective autonomy is the objective of any nation-state, it has characteristics that transform throughout time. "The expressions of what autonomy is, vary historically and spatially, according to interests and positions of power" (Fonseca Jr., 1998, p. 361). The concept admits different approaches within certain historical periods, and according to the worldviews of the peoples and elites in question. The idea of autonomy in the second half of the 1980s, and for part of society and the high state bureaucracy in the

1990s and until the end of the Lula government, meant autonomy in relation to the outside world, and the capacity to make decisions in the face of the international centres of power, thus allowing Brazil to determine its choices. Mercosur was not seen as an autonomy-limiting factor. On the contrary, the sharing of interests would increase external capacities. Our goal is to discuss how the two concepts, autonomy and universalism, were treated. In our perspective, from Lula da Silva's second mandate, from 2007, there was a movement in the direction of establishing or reestablishing its significance, with point of departure in part of the business community, certain political forces, and also from parts of the initially minoritarian sectors of the high bureaucracy connected to the economic and diplomatic fields. This would result in the definition of a foreign policy through which the significance of Mercosur would be reduced, not least the relations with Argentina. This contributes to explaining the regional bloc's crisis and the difficulties associated with its affirmation.

4.2 Revision of the Paradigm for International Insertion: The Significance of Mercosur

In the 1980s, a rethinking of the country's model of economic development gained strength. This included the country's relationship with the outside world. Factors which contributed to this included the exhaustion of the import substitution model, the foreign debt crisis, high inflation, and economic stagnation. Added together, they weakened the foundations of the then predominant pattern of development, leading to divestment (Sallum Jr., 1999) and a fall in the domestic savings rate, in which the state had played an important role. This situation would persist until 2020, and probably transform the term "lost decade" to the "lost century" (Pereira, 2018).

While the world witnessed the rise of neoliberal values, in the last 2 years of the Sarney government several studies on international economic relations were conducted, chiefly by the Foreign Trade Agency of Banco do Brasil (FTABB—*CACEX*). This coincided with the development of the Uruguay Round GATT negotiations, above all from December 1988 when the Montreal Ministerial Conference was held (Mello, 2000; Pereira, 1992). In these studies, views critical of the national-developmentalism of the previous period prevailed. They also signalled a perspective of greater openness to the outside world. This perspective later guided the economic opening intensified during the Collor de Mello government.

Note that the beginning of the integration process with Argentina (The Iguaçu Declaration, November 1985; The Economic Integration and Cooperation Programme—PICE, July 1986; the 24 resulting Protocols; and the Integration, Cooperation and Development Treaty, November 1988) followed a developmentalist logic that aimed at stimulating business emulation, for the modernization and competitive insertion in the international economic system (Peña, 1991). The enlarged domestic market was a central pre-supposition. This phase strengthened the perception among part of the Brazilian elites, including business groups and state officials, that common interests would improve the international insertion, leading to greater self-esteem. Even at the moment of the signing of the Integration, Cooperation and Development Treaty, which provided the Mercosur with its design and gave a stable and strong character to the Brazil–Argentina alliance, the intergovernmentalist perspective still prevailed. To use the words of Moravcsik (2005, p. 276) when talking about the EU today, in Brazil–Argentina relations the idea was always present that "there is, moreover, an undeniable normative attraction to a system that preserves national democratic politics for those issues most salient in the minds of citizens". Certain authors consider that the concern with democratic stability played a fundamental role in the integration of the Southern Cone. One is dealing with a strong attraction to nationally-established political life, as indicated by Moravcsik. The design that the Mercosur gradually took on corresponded to the preferences manifested by national political and civil societies.

Within this process of revision taking place in bodies like the Ministry of Finance, *Banco do Brasil* and the Central Bank, and gradually absorbed by Brazilian diplomacy, the Brazil–Argentina approximation was seen as fundamental in international political terms. At the same time, it gained supporters among diplomats and was linked to the strategy of the universalist paradigm (Flecha de Lima, 1989, p. 30–31). This approximation seemed to strengthen the idea of an increased political and economic presence in the world, as well as to provide greater weight before international institutions and in the formulation of regimes. Hence the alliance was related to the ability to reform economic guidelines. For some, advancing the process of regional integration would increase capacities in relations with the larger power centres, particularly the United States (Amorim & Pimentel, 1996). These different perspectives made it possible for the alliance to be shared both by sectors connected with the nationalist tradition and by sectors that considered it inevitable that Brazil would join the liberal international order.

Thus the nexus between regional integration, the Mercosur, and the alliance with Argentina is hereby established, with the preservation of the values of universalism and autonomy. Regionalism would not diminish, but rather reinforce the Brazilian universalist paradigm of international insertion. The idea of "modernization via internationalization" (Przeworski, 1993) which would directly influence the paradigm of international insertion did not clash with regionalism during this phase, i.e., throughout the 1990s. The concept of open regionalism was part of this perspective of a comprehensive international insertion, seeking to benefit from a free trade area without creating the tools necessary for regional policies in the fields of development and complementarity, i.e., without policies directed at the sustainability of the integration. The value of autonomy remained rooted in the spheres of government and business, now under the aegis of an important, elaborate concept: autonomy through integration (Fonseca Jr., 1998).

The appreciation of autonomy, therefore, does not fade with the rise of Mercosur. Rather, it is reintroduced under other guises. There is a concern with the reaffirmation of the country's own, sovereign role in the world. Equally, it is manifested in relation to the rich countries, with which greater integration is sought, without abdicating from national interests considered fundamental (Cardoso, 2001). Paradoxically, in Brazil's relations with its immediate neighbours, the Mercosur and the rest of South America, the idea of autonomy is manifested in the form of an insistent revaluation of the potential for specific national action, not subject to the shackles that an institutionalized integration might imply (Pinheiro, 2000). From the economic viewpoint, regional production chains which demand investment and capacity in terms of R&D did not arise, at least not in more significant terms. On the contrary, the dependency in relation to the more advanced innovation systems of the central countries was consolidated, particularly regarding the United States, and later, China.

Brazil's traditional position of seeking a relevant role in the world—not essentially different from the Argentinian position under Menem—is reflected in the permanent drive for the country to gain a position of prominence. Lafer (1993) treats the need for Brazil to become more active within international affairs. We wish to stress that during a certain phase, roughly from 1985 and onwards, relations with Argentina gained an actual prominence for Brazil's international strategy. Albeit remaining highly significant during the 1990s, towards the late 1990s, these relations became infused with a strong universalist concern of a new kind. A significant manifestation of this evolution already appeared in the Itamar Franco government: the initiative of articulating a new project of South American integration. Presented as complementary rather than antagonistic in relation to the Mercosur, the proposed creation of the South American Free Trade Area (SAFTA) suggests that there would be space over the following years for the emergence of new initiatives, until the Rousseff government. These initiatives signal a relative attenuation of the strong initial desire to structure synergies focused on the Mercosur, creating complementarity and an integrated system of production with a view to a common market. It seems that the initial impulse towards common development had been diluted, but the search for possible economic advantages provided by a more substantive commercial exchange (and other factors), subsisted.

Seen retrospectively from the Brazilian foreign policy perspective, Mercosur emerges in a clearly ambiguous form, which is not essentially different on the Argentinian side. As a high international priority in the case of Brazil—where the strength of universalism remains—it is presented as a very important instrument, but always as an instrument. There is no clear specificity to the integration; it is not an end in itself. At the moment when the Mercosur was constituted, the governments made this explicit: "upon signing the Treaty of Asunción, the four presidents' starting point is the common perception that the deepening of the process of integration can be the key to their countries' more competitive insertion in a world in which large economic spaces are being consolidated and where technological-industrial advance becomes more and more crucial for national economies" (The Ministry of Foreign Affairs, 1991, p.279). The instrumental logic gradually asserts itself and prevails. "Mercosur is a process essentially open to the outside. In Brazil's case, the development of the Mercosur is part of a broad effort of economic opening, trade liberalization, and a more beneficial insertion in the world economy. The integration process is not conceived as an end in itself, but as an instrument for more wide-ranging participation in the global market (Lampreia, 1995, p. 135)".

The critique of liberal-intergovernmentalism has produced important ideas regarding the interpretation of the instrumental logic of integration. Sandholtz and Sweet (1998, p. 26) state that the analysis of European integration requires consideration of variables that do not underestimate relations that produce results that in turn can accelerate the integration process. In their perspective , integration interferes in political variables. When this does not happen, it is necessary to look for explanations. In other words, integration is not a static phenomenon; it has self-propelling aspects, called the "bicycle phenomena", or "spillover" by functionalists.

Nardin (1987) develops useful concepts for our objective. When discussing the forms of international association, he summarizes the possibilities respectively as: practical association and purposive association. Practical association is that in which relations between states are not necessarily engaged in any common aspiration, but in spite of this, have to coexist with one another. This coincides with Bull (1977) with regards to the compatibilization of anarchy and order. Therefore, the association is instrumental. For its part, purposive association is that in which states cooperate to ensure that certain beliefs, values and shared interests thrive, with common objectives in mind. On a normative level, that would be the idea of an international civil society (Archibugi et al., 1998). Nardin himself is sceptical as to the possibility of finding purposive association in the international system. As we have seen, within the field of Mercosur, on behalf of Brazil, Argentina, as well as Uruguay and Paraguay at certain moments, mutually shared aims prevailed. Including important coincidences with regards to political leaders.

The development of the Mercosur does not appear uniform. In 2021, four distinct phases can be pointed out. The first, which precedes Cardoso's first term, last from 1991 to 1994: from the Treaty of Asunción to the Ouro Preto Protocol. It is during this period that the institutional design is consolidated. Next, from 1995 to 1998, one notes the continuity of the intra-bloc commercial expansion, which had reached its apex. In the third, from 1999, with the Brazilian currency (*real*) crisis, leading to devaluation, and then the recession in Argentina, beginning in 2001, the Mercosur experiences a crisis, the effects of which were, and remain, unclear. The devaluation of the real was not negotiated with the other members of the bloc. The fourth phase begins in the Dilma Rousseff government with institutional stagnation between 2011 and 2016. Afterwards, with Temer, and more radically with Bolsonaro, the integration process entered a crisis, and even a possible setback. This in spite of business and social interests maintaining their support for the project. As we will argue, beyond the conjunctural elements, which become expressed through successive commercial and political disputes, structural questions, related to the economies of the involved countries, to the perception of their changing global insertion, and to values rooted within states and societies, should be considered in the search for consistent explanations. The instability and radical change of the internal relations in Brazil after 2016 make the pendulum of the Brazilian policy swing back towards the central economies, particularly the United States, but also to China and the European Union.

The economic crises, of different hues, experienced by Mercosur countries express this logic. The domestic crises were not moments of adjustment in the integration process, occasions used for searching for opportunities. They eventually weakened the integration and reduced the effort of complementarity.

The difficulties within the national economies can explain certain positions and contributed to the attitude of business groups and elite sectors, which in large measure evolve towards a lack of interest, or towards the instrumentalization of the integration as a consequence of internal political struggles. Our view is that material elements alone cannot explain the process fully. The fact that Brazil and Argentina have shifting trade deficits between them has contributed to the perception that regional integration could be harmful to local economies. Every time this takes place, in one direction or another, protectionist positions once again appear. In the Brazilian case, the Argentine crisis of 2001 reignited the always latent and deeply rooted conception that the Mercosur represents a narrow perspective for Brazil's economic and political potential. Conversely, the Brazilian trade surplus after the January 1999 devaluation of the *real* is highlighted in Argentina as one of the main causes of the latter country's own crisis of late 2001. The subsequent devaluation of the *peso*, after having been pegged to the US dollar from 1991 to 2001, generated a 10.9% fall in the Argentinian GDP (Kume & Piani, 2005). On the Brazilian side, this strengthened the belief that the macroeconomic instability meant there was no long-term basis for integration.

The experience of the Mercosur indicates that the economic benefits of integration are necessary elements, but not enough to ensure the continuity and deepening of the process. Equally, this experience demonstrates the limits of an integration process grounded only in utilitarian aspects. These are insufficient to guarantee the dynamic, even though they are *sine qua non* conditions. Integration cannot be thought of merely as a foreign policy project; it demands a strong intersection with a domestic policy project (Bueno de Mesquita, 2005). The perception that the partner is in a situation of advantage in terms of the benefits obtained from the integration process, as realist readings would suggest, has always been harmful to the continuity of efforts to consolidate the Mercosur. If this can be said of Argentina and Brazil, it is also true for Paraguay and Uruguay. Hence, one may state that elements from the realist perspective of international relations—that historically prevailed in Southern Cone relations—have not disappeared entirely. In other words, within the state apparatus and certain sectors of society remains a concern with the need for increases in benefits that do not alter pre-existing relations.

4.3 Theoretical Expectations for Regional Integration and the Case of Mercosur

In order to understand regional integration, the neofunctionalist and the intergovernmentalist contributions stand out in the field of theory. We seek to conduct a critical dialogue with these theories and, at the same time, to demonstrate the particularities of the integration process of the Southern Cone. This establishes a tension between the central variables of these theories, formulated during the European integration process.

Haas (1964), who had a key role in the consolidation of studies and the research agenda on regional integration, in particular the European, reconsidered some functionalist assumptions, conditioning them to the political impulses of the decision-making centres. He pointed out that regional integration is essentially a process of transfer of functions and loyalties from states to supranational institutions. In his perception, after an initial bureaucratic/state impulse—of major importance for the beginning of the European Common Market, before and right after the Treaty of Rome (1957)—the integration process would spill over to society as a whole, which, in turn, sought ways to intervene and participate more in the process. At a certain stage, integration would take on a dynamic of its own, less dependent on the political will of governments and more related to the expectations of gains and losses of the main domestic groups in the countries involved.

At the same time, Haas (1964) incorporates the functionalist assumption that political loyalties are related to the efficiency of a given agency, whether national or regional. In the case of the Mercosur, despite the bloc's reasonable efficiency level brought about by more intense relations from 1991, no agencies were developed around which relations of loyalty could emerge. At the same time, the dynamic remained strongly linked to the initiatives of governments and presidents, which gradually attenuated agents' expectations of gain. The strong role played by the Executive as the principal-agent of the process is confirmed by the fact that the body centralizing the decisions—upon which all the expectations converge—is the twice-yearly meeting of presidents, the Mercosur Council. In spite of being recognizably positive for integration (Malamud, 2000), this situation became a problem in the late 1990s and early twenty-first century, above all if one thinks—as the functionalists do—that the parameter for success is the capacity to change the reality in existence prior to the constitution of a regional bloc, thus producing new behaviours.

The authors who developed the neofunctionalist theoretical matrix highlight the fact that, for the purposes of integration, the social and economic actors must take an active part in the process, intervening from a certain point after the initial takeoff with the aim of pressing and convincing the national elites to transfer (or not) shares of sovereignty to the regional sphere. An important aspect is participation, the mobilizing effect of integration, which, in turn, is linked to the satisfaction of interests. This situation would allow for the deepening of the process and facilitate its propagation and maintenance. An enhancement in the action of social and economic actors, and of the elites, would lead to an increase in demands for the common management of interests, precisely the "spillover". The growing spiral of intervention and integration to regulate these interests constitutes the engine that ensures the continuity of integration. In the eyes of this approach—that implies expansion—if the impulse stops, i.e., if the self-enforcing momentum is lost, the whole process may be put at risk. This view of integration does not necessarily mean an absence of conflicts and difficulties, but conveys the idea of continuity that some refer to as the "bicycle theory". In other words, this analysis is fundamentally dynamic. The levels of regional integration are very different from free trade areas and political union, to federal or confederative forms. On all of the levels of integration, the idea of the growing spiral is important. This can attribute continuity to processes, as in the case of the North American Free Trade Area (NAFTA), renewed in the new United States-Mexico-Canada Agreement (USMCA) in 2019, or lead them towards crisis, as in the case of Brexit in 2016.

From a certain moment, even before 1998, the level of interest in integration on behalf of society and enterprises declined. This was particularly visible in the automotive sector. Since 1986, and especially in the early 1990s, multinationals such as General Motors, Volkswagen, Fiat, Ford had planned integrated production and investments. These plans aimed at using the Mercosur as a possible global export platform for part of their products, above all trucks and small and medium cars. From the mid-1990s and especially after 1997, with the commercial and political difficulties, the prospect of regional action became more remote, thus leading to a worsening of the crisis in the bloc. Faced with protectionist risks, many companies prioritized the biggest market: Brazil. The interests of public opinion and politicians were also attenuated. With some changes, in 2020 we can now say about the commercial differences that since the end of the 1990s there has been a slow and continuous reversal in business expectations. As we have seen, this raises the interest for deeper relations with the central countries.

If, as stated by Kratochwil (2006), the way ideas are constructed domestically is related to the normative framework that establishes the guidelines of external action, then it becomes necessary to analyse the norms and rules that orient a country's choices in order to understand its external agency. Perceptions and values justify and define the acceptability of certain courses of action. In other words, one way of measuring the dynamics of regional integration lies in checking whether issues related to the partner become problems of one's own domestic politics.

According to neofunctionalist authors, from Haas (1964, 1975) to Schmitter (2003), regional integration only occurs effectively when the interests of the main elites are attended. If the expectations of these sectors converge with integration, there would emerge a mobilization that could sustain the process. On the other hand, if this does not occur, regression becomes likely. Therefore, the deepening and expansion of integration are related to governments' ability to ensure the continuity of the material and symbolic gains for the elites, given their role as guarantors of integration. Equally, implementation of policies that aim at containing the pressures of groups adversely affected by the integration process is very important, as the groups and elites hurt by this process have large capacities for exercising pressures, proportionately greater than those of the beneficiaries. The latter generally present

Table 4.1 Annual flow of intra and extra-Mercosur trade

Year	Total trade 2018 US$ (billions)	(Δ%)	Mercosur trade 2018 US$ (billions)	(Δ%)	Outside Mercosur trade 2018 US$ (billions)	(Δ%)
1994	210.659	–	41.398	–	169.261	–
1998	277.608	31.78	63.583	53.59	214.025	26.45
2002	209.678	–24.47	30.623	–51.84	179.055	–16.34
2006	407.161	94.18	66.038	115.65	341.123	90.51
2010	622.479	52.88	100.372	51.99	522.107	53.06
2014	668.376	7.37	88.728	–11.60	579.648	11.02
2018	586.885	–12.19	80.422	–9.36	506.463	–12.63
Δ% 2018–1994		178.59		94.26		199.22

Source: Comtrade. Author's elaboration

themselves in the form of diffuse interests (Pastor & Wise, 1994). This perspective is fundamental to our analysis, as our hypothesis refers precisely to the fact that the worldview of the Brazilian political, economic and social elites has a very meaningful role in explaining the structural difficulties of the Mercosur in the twenty-first century.

The use of this analytical framework to interpret the integration of the Southern Cone demands reflection. Moravcsik (2005) accentuates that this approach yields little knowledge about the origins of states' preferences and the results of the intersate bargains. Mercosur has obtained relative success in terms of growth of its extra-bloc exchanges, as is illustrated in Table 4.1. This is expressed within the numbers of the trade balance, when the evolution of the bloc's total foreign trade was reasonably positive, changing from close to US$169 billion in 1994 and reaching nearly US$580 billion in 2014, and falling to little more than US$506 billion in 2018.

The Mercosur countries have been relatively successful in terms of the growth in their extra-bloc trade flows, despite the crisis in 2001–2002 (Kume & Piani, 2005). According to Table 4.1, the intra-Mercosur trade went from 41 billion in 1994 to close to US$63 billion in 1998, a growth of 53% in 4 years. In 2002, there was a noticeable setback, and in 2010 an important threshold of more than US$100 billion was reached, with a fall to US$88 billion in 2014 and US$80 billion in 2018, pointing to significant oscillations as a consequence of the economic and political crises of Argentina and Brazil. Mercosur gained a significance which spanned beyond trade, which until 2016 drew attention to themes related to this bloc. Albeit in a limited manner, the integration process reached groups within different spheres: labour unions, universities, culture, politicians, clerks, etc.

The evolution of the Mercosur remained undefined over the course of the 1990s. Even the events of 1999 and 2001 did not bring about an unbearable deepening of the crisis. However, interest in integration did not grow to the point of creating an inherent dynamic, as the neofunctionalist analysis suggests. No significant impact became evident within society. The dynamic of the bloc did not lead to an effective process of institutionalization, even though the 2000s saw some partial and embryonic initiatives, such as the Asunción-based Permanent Review Court, created in August 2004, and thereafter the Mercosur Structural Convergence Fund (MSCF—Port. *FOCEM*) and finally the Mercosur Parliament project. In 2006 the Mercosur Council approved the Constitutive Protocol for the Mercosur Parliament (Parlasul) (2006), establishing the date of December 2014 as a goal for its plain functioning with representatives elected by a direct vote within their countries, after a complex debate about the number of chairs for each member state. The bloc's predominantly political crisis made its effectivization impossible, in spite of Argentina and Paraguay having held direct elections. Their non-realization in Brazil and Uruguay made the Parlasul—which also was composed by representatives indicated by national parliaments—propose the Council a deadline of December 2020 for the member states to elect their representatives.

The intergovernmental logic, associated with an important role of the governments and presidencies, has made possible the maintenance of a certain equilibrium that ends up ensuring low-intensity integration levels. Figuratively, the bicycle seems to be balanced, but immovable. In the eyes of Brazilian diplomacy—and this is a consolidated idea in the analyses of officials, whether from the liberal or nationalist perspective—confidence prevailed regarding the possibility of contacts between the state-parties with minimum bureaucratization, prioritizing the non-institutionalized way, rather than procedures and rules of any given nature.

The low-intensity logic goes for relations between governments and between spheres of civil society. It was applied to the Mercosur bodies, i.e., the Council, the Mercosur Group, the Forums, the Committees, the Working Groups etc. The mediations and the solutions to problems followed this path. Conditions were gradually created for issues common in integration processes—conflicts between sectors, between production chains, or even between companies—to be taken to the arbitration of those instances considered most reliable and best able to solve or arbitrate problems, i.e., the presidencies (Malamud, 2000). The crisis of the *papeleras* (paper mills), from 2005, between Uruguay and Argentina, finally solved through a decision from the International Court of Justice in 2010, demonstrates the weakness of regional mechanisms, through the resort to extra-regional mechanisms. The establishment of a fabric of relations which could make integration operational has not advanced. This has allowed sectoral, corporate, and regional interests to gain much visibility, leading to the emergence of a new spiral that would strengthen the national perspectives, as became clear towards the end of the Menem and Cardoso governments, in the De La Rua government, and also later in the presidencies of Nestor Kirchner and Lula da Silva. Vaz (2002) considers that since the 1992 Las Leñas Schedule, assumptions have been made (which have shown themselves to be definitive) about the intergovernmental nature of Mercosur's negotiations and concerning the Mercosur itself.

In the theories of regional integration, the role of states and the elites is intertwined with the general inclinations of society. In a sense, the Mercosur has specific characteristics. This does not invalidate the statement about intertwining but accentuates a fact that is hard to find in other integration processes. The Mercosur was pushed forward by the heads of state and, in the case of Brazil, was helped along by the diplomats, in certain cases with support from groups within the Ministry of Finance. There was an absence of strong pressures or demands for cooperation on the part of the elites and interest groups. Some business sectors came onboard at the dawn of Argentina–Brazil cooperation, from 1986, but did not keep up the momentum over time.

At the heart of the Brazilian state, the implications of the intergovernmental format of integration are not unknown. Signs of worry are emerging as to the limits set since the low level of institutionalization seems to have been the natural result of a view that did not place the regional dynamic fully at the centre of domestic policy. Cardoso wrote: "I believe we are reaching the limit of what is possible to do before taking a bigger step towards institutionalization" (Cardoso & Soares, 1998, p. 266). The awareness of the limits and the important implications for Brazil's international strategy are not unknown. Lima (2007) shows that there is a real erosion of the domestic coalition in relation to what she terms the patrimony of Brazilian foreign policy, the strategic alliance with Argentina and the Mercosur. At the same time, she demonstrates how this policy had been the result of the convergence of sectors favourable to economic opening and developmentalist sectors. After a 35-year trajectory, from 1985 to 2020, it is possibly to conclude that the sectors that made up the coalition have not been capable of producing sufficient integration policies—today we know that they were never capable of delivering such results. On the contrary, due to economic and political interests, they have chosen not to provide the necessary support. The scarcity of resources invested, including symbolic ones, confirms this conclusion. For example, in 2006, 15 years after the Treaty of Asunción, the *FOCEM* (Structural Convergence Fund) was implemented, with resources totalling just US$100 million, to attenuate the unfavourable consequences of integration for the smaller states, Paraguay and Uruguay. The contributions are distributed between Brazil, which is responsible for 70% of the resources, Argentina, with 27%, Uruguay representing 2%, and Paraguay 1%. Inversely, the beneficiaries are Paraguay, which receives 48%, Uruguay 32%, Argentina 10%, and Brazil 10%.[1] In the following years, these recourses increased, although they remained scarce considering the dimension of the asymmetries. At the beginning of the second Rousseff mandate, in 2015 the Brazilian economic difficulties obstructed the payment of the debts bound in the Fund. Until 2014, these had reached 97.07 million. That year, the country omitted the payment of US$24.5 million (*O Estado de S. Paulo*, July 16, 2015).

According to Mariano and Ribeiro (2019, p. 185) "the first budget of the Fund was drawn up in 2006 for the financial year 2007. The contribution to *FOCEM* was in force for 10 years between 2005 and 2015. DEC/CMC 22/15 proposed to renew the Fund for another 10 years. To date, only Paraguay and Uruguay have legally incorporated this resolution; Argentina and Brazil have yet to take a position on the matter. As these data show, the member states did not make ordinary contributions

[1] https://sistemas.mre.gov.br/kitweb/datafiles/Brasaladi/pt-br/file/Folheto-Focem.pdf Accessed on: 03/06/2020

between the years 2016 and 2018. This is due to the aforementioned fact that the regulations governing the implementation of Focem II for another ten years had not yet been ratified". In Argentina and Brazil, economic and political crises increasingly obstructed ratification, a problem which persisted, thus hindering new allocations to the Fund.

In the face of this, the signs of worry over the limits set by the format of integration are recurring, but do not seem sufficient to overcome the structural weaknesses. President Lula da Silva seems to be approaching the issue: "Mercosur has before it the challenge of reinventing itself and meeting the expectations of all its members. We must design mechanisms that equate the asymmetries definitively, and this includes the provision of fresh resources" (Silva, 2006). Within Brazilian society, this view is not only far from consensual, but faces real resistance. In 2005, the Legislative Assembly of the state of Rio Grande do Sul, in a clearly unconstitutional act, voted for a blockade of rice imported from Uruguay, due to the losses caused to the state's producers.

According to Moravcsik (1994), political coordination negotiated on a case-by-case basis, i.e., the organizational structure based on a low level of institutionalization and on direct negotiations between the governments involved, serves as a mechanism of control for the participants of a regional integration process. This would be an incentive for the smaller countries to accept taking part in an asymmetrical bloc and, at the same time, for the larger countries to accept the idea of cooperation, inasmuch as the risks of integration would be smaller, given the minimal loss of sovereignty. In the case of the Mercosur, given the asymmetries in terms of power, liberal intergovernmentalism may seem like the explanatory instrument for the limits we are discussing. This explanation is important—we would even say, decisive—as we have seen for the Brazilian part, to explain the integration between Argentina and Brazil, but also to explain Uruguay's adhesion right after the Treaty in November 1988, and of Paraguay, in 1990.

However, a paradox that emerges from its application to the analysis of the Mercosur results from the historical tendency of integration processes. These processes, even when they are free trade areas or other low-intensity forms, tend to create some kind of institutionalization to coordinate their operation or for other purposes, as happens with any international organization. A regional integration process tends to overtake the initial objective by unleashing changes in participant states due to its own movement (Matlary, 1994). In the case of Brazil, the embedding of the concepts of autonomy and universalism counteracts this tendency. The difficulty in analysing the Mercosur according to consolidated theories is thus explained.

The liberal intergovernmentalism considers interdependence as a necessary and motivating condition for integration. Even with the development of integration, the constraints resulting from the increasing interdependence would not affect states' conditions for controlling the main decisions regarding integration and other international actions. In the case of Mercosur, the relation between interdependence and integration did not evolve in the ways liberal intergovernmentalism authors (Moravcsik, 1994) defend.

The initial political motivation, with the economic knock-on effects, lacked the steam that both intergovernmentalism and functionalism present as the inevitable consequence of integration. Also, the idea of collecting contracts, thus contributing to an increase in interdependence between the members and reinforcing the legitimacy of the process, is not entirely confirmed. Hence, neither of the two theoretical schools is fully applicable, nor can they be completely refuted based on the concrete data from the integration process of the Southern Cone.

In the case of Brazil, there seems to have been a deliberate wish to avoid going beyond the initial commitments or even the following ones, which remained within a cautious path. At the same time, regional integration was considered necessary to attain regional and international credibility. Integration was utilized selectively: partly useful in the resistance to the Free Trade Area of the Americas (FTAA/ALCA) and in the negotiations with the EU; not totally necessary for negotiations at the WTO or even at the UN. Or, when economically liberal governments reached office in Brazil and Argentina, Mercosur was used to stimulate a framework for the creation of a free trade area with the European Union.

4.4 Autonomy, Universalism, and the Brazilian Position in the Mercosur

Over the years, Brazilian diplomacy has played a significant role in building the integration model, characterized by a low level of institutionalization and by a fundamentally intergovernmental essence; a central role, but not the only one. In Brazil, the low level of institutionalization was an idea shared—even if passively—by the whole of the national government during various administrations, in the political and bureaucratic spheres, by business, by Congress, state governors etc. As stated by Vaz (2002, p. 223), if this was Brazil's position, Argentina's was not essentially different. "For Brazil, given its majority weight within the bloc, there was no interest in giving up any sovereignty to a supranational instance, in which it would see its capacity to forge decisions diluted and preserve its interests in relation to the bloc, whose importance for the country went beyond the commercial domain. For Argentina, giving up sovereignty in matters of economic and trade policy implied definitively losing the capacity to exert some degree of freedom in the conduct of trade policy, which was precisely what the Argentinian government was seeking to safeguard at that moment." For Mariano (2007, p. 194), in Brazil's case, one was dealing with a pattern of behaviour "based on the search for autonomy as a fundamental principle and for development as a central objective." As we shall see in the conclusions, the question was reverted only with the Bolsonaro administration and the plain acceptance of the North American centrality from 2019.

Existing research (CEDEC & PUC/SP, 2002; CEDEC, UNESP, PUC/SP & FGV/SP, 2004) has allowed us to measure the low level of adaptation and sensitivity of state and municipal governments in Brazil to international and integration questions. We have ascertained that the regional political and administrative elites do not consider these questions as pertaining to their government's sphere of agency. This has strong implications for national politics, being reflected in parliamentary representation, leading to the non-intertwining between themes with clear repercussions for regional integration and national issues, such as for example fiscal reform. This strengthens the tendency according to which Brazil always seeks intergovernmental routes to integration, thus maintaining a high level of autonomy.

Pinheiro (2000, p. 326–327) considers that the degree of commitment that the Brazilian state assumes regarding international matters varies according to its power resources. Brazil's posture in its geographical surroundings would thus be guided by a logic of gains, of benefiting from the advantages provided by the relative asymmetry, whereas multilateral engagement would be grounded in a logic of absolute gains. Multilateral engagement would thereby be guided by a logic of absolute gains in the aspiration towards the maintenance of autonomy and the possibility for the exercise of universalism. Hence, "pragmatic institutionalism assumes that—and works towards—the greater the Brazilian presence in the international system through institutions, the greater the access to development and to autonomy of action. It so happens that, since the search for autonomy has greater weight for Brazilian diplomacy than the search for justice, it is admitted that the former may be sought as much through cooperation arrangements with a high level of institutionalization as through other arrangements, whose level of institutionalization is kept deliberately low so as to guarantee the country's leadership position". For Pinheiro, this permits a conciliation of the Hobbesian and Grotian natures, reinforcing institutionalism, and spurring the adhesion to norms and rules. The graded and variable approach has instrumental ends. Hence, within the framework of a sub-system of power, it is possible to attain greater autonomy and, at the same time, reinforce one's voice in the global system through multilateral action.

From the minutes of the meetings of the Common Market Group in the early years, signs emerge that these, although without actual consequences, should be interpreted as being geared to favouring modes of integration where there is a superimposition of national interest, "national project", and integration, permitting autonomy, but without privileged status. For example, in 1992, the Group approved an agenda for economy ministers and central bank presidents dealing with "the economic situation and the analysis of the convergence of national economic policies" (Grupo Mercado Comum, 1992, p. 18). However, from 1996/7, a period combining specific trade problems with significant mismatches regarding international insertion, those sectors of the São Paulo State Federation of Industry (SPSFI—Port. *FIESP*), of the National Confederation of Industry, of the agribusiness representative bodies, of high-level officialdom, and of the media that had the perception that the Mercosur would narrow the country's universalist capacity, gained ground. Objective reasons—outside the scope of our analysis—contributed to this inflection: the progress of negotiations for the creation of the FTAA, the negotiations for the start of a new round at the WTO, and the start of the discussion on the role of the BRIC countries (Brazil, Russia, India and China). These negotiations or orientations needed not necessarily weaken the Mercosur. This nonetheless ended up happening, as the idea of integration never was properly embraced among the whole range of Brazilian elites, as we have seen.

The potential prospect of gains of scale in economic and trade terms stimulated the concentration of efforts in the search for access to the larger markets and meant that the themes of autonomy and universalism (that had never been abandoned) were resumed, but now in a more restricted sense in relation to the Mercosur. During the Worker's Party governments, this permitted some convergence between the political leaders within the state and the majority of the economic elite. The broader argument used was the need to ensure freedom of action in the international system. Only relations with the European Union evolved in a different direction, given the EU's decision to negotiate with the Mercosur, and not with each country separately, in relation to which the strategic partnership agreement signed with Brazil in 2007 is highly relevant.

At the beginning of the twenty-first century, the Cristina Kirchner and Lula da Silva governments did not display very different ideological signs, but this did not permit a deepening of the Mercosur, even though some common policies have materialized in specific cases. The two governments' agreement on certain issues demonstrates some identities, but not enough to permit the implementation of integration forms with cooperative actions that could deepen the process irreversibly. This concern is present within the Brazilian state's conceptual frame of reference, but its materialization has been complicated. "The touchstone [of regional integration] is the bilateral relationship with Argentina. The great convergence between the viewpoints of Presidents Lula and Kirchner on the most urgent questions we face was expressed in the 'Buenos Aires Consensus' adopted in October 2003. This document reflects our common aspiration to economic growth tied to social justice and manifests our determination to transform the Mercosur trade bloc (...) into a catalyst for the construction of a shared future" (Amorim, 2004, p. 158). In specific situations, the conceptual references produce common results. At the Mar del Plata Heads of State Summit of the Americas, held in 2005, there was agreement over delaying the FTAA negotiations *sine die*, contrary to what seemed to be the interest of at least part of the US administration.

In the Brazilian case, the difficulties of integration cannot be attributed exclusively to the government. Society's interest in the Mercosur and its possible deepening is scarce, and in some cases, openly negative. For example, a meeting held in November 2004, bringing together business people from various sectors and organizations like *FIESP*, *Abicalçados* (Brazilian Association of Shoe Manufacturers), *Eletros* (National Association of Manufacturers of Electro-electronic Products) and *AEB* (Foreign Trade Association of Brazil) demonstrated that there was a reasonable level of opposition to the regional bloc. The discussions revolved around the idea of taking a step back in relation to the Mercosur. Among business people, there is an intense discussion going on about the need to move from an imperfect customs union, full of holes, to a free trade area. According to representatives from those bodies, the Mercosur is the deadweight for Brazil in international negotiations, thus making it difficult to reach bilateral agreements with the United States and European Union (*Valor Econômico*, 16/11/2004).

The analyses that result from the concerns of business confirm this pressure for a reduction in the meaning of integration for Brazil. It becomes possible to notice an interest amongst these groups in reducing the role that the Mercosur plays in foreign policy and as a reference for part of the international economic and trade strategy. The values of autonomy and universalism stand out.

Studying regional integration policy from the Brazilian point of view implies understanding the role of the Ministry of Foreign Affairs and its officials' formulations. This explains the continuity of the country's position in relation to the Mercosur and the reasonable level of stability in the conduct of the process, together with the stumbling blocks that emerge in parallel with the foreign policy pattern and the interest (or lack thereof) of civil society and of the political forces. The sum of these factors has apparently paradoxical consequences. On the one hand, it permits a certain stability; on the other, in conjunction with the consequences of presidential prevalence, it complicates triggering the "spillover" phenomenon, considered by the functionalists a determinant in the affirmation of integration. At the same time, intergovernmental links are not sufficiently strengthened. In the Brazilian case, the low level of intervention on the part of Congress, generally approving government bills, laws, and projects, without much discussion, eventually obstructs the free flow of ideas, also those related to regional integration. Foreign Policy nonetheless became highly polarized when the Senate debated Venezuela's entry into Mercosur in December 2009, with 35 votes in favour and 27 contrary. From that moment and onwards, Congress has intervened effectively in these questions, which have become part of the general process of polarization. When other interests and positions develop within society, these are presented not in the form of proposals but of resistance. In the case of the Mercosur, the government's position, aiming at continuity with low intensity, seems to meet the average expectations and needs of the Brazilian elites, within and outside the state.

4.5 Motivations of the Brazilian Policy Regarding Supranationality

It is important to keep in mind that the concepts of autonomy and universalism present among part of the elites and the institutional memory of the Ministry of Foreign Affairs lead to questionings regarding the Mercosur. Wendt (1994, p. 386), picking up on ideas by Ruggie, states that, "collective identity is neither essential nor equivalent to such a multilateral institution but provides an important foundation for it by increasing the willingness to act on generalized principles of conduct and diffuse reciprocity". It is therefore fitting to state that the weakness of the pro-integration epistemic groups spurred the strengthening of others that, though not opposed to it, began valuing ideas, projects, and interests that did not converge towards, and neither strengthen it. The perception—which is true—that a greater deepening of the bloc would lead to a loss of sovereignty and of autonomy in

Brazil's relations with the world, has never disappeared and has eventually become an important component of the action of the state and society. Consequently, an option that may limit Brazil's international agency space and be contrary to universalism is rejected. The resulting position established limits to the Mercosur. Lima (1994, 2003) states that the Brazilian pattern in relation to the Mercosur has been similar in other aspects of foreign policy, i.e., opposed to a deepening of institutionalization, with a prevalence of the aspiration to convert the country into a relevant international actor, and the belief—especially present in Argentina—in its exceptional nature in relation to the other Latin American countries. The Brazilian elites have been educated in this political culture.

For our purpose, i.e., discussing the structural reasons for the Brazilian integration policy, it is interesting to show the rationality, from a certain point of view, of the position in defence of the principles of autonomy and sovereignty. Pierson (1998) holds the view that when national governments delegate certain functions to regional institutions or community agencies, over time they tend to lose control of the integration process to these institutions. The regional institutions or agencies would open the way for new domestic actors to participate in the decision-making process without the intermediation of governments, a fact that would tend to strengthen them and provide them with new sources of legitimacy. Once this institution or agency has achieved a certain level of authority in the integration process, it becomes difficult for governments to make them retreat, thus permitting the state-parties to recover their original power. The cost of this recovery would, in a way, make its concretization unfeasible. Gradually, the decision-making dynamics within the integration project tend to acquire more autonomy in relation to the nation-states. Hence, it becomes possible to understand Brazil's lack of inclination to the bloc's institutional strengthening, which gets translated into the constant defence of intergovernmentalism, since the state, for the abovementioned reasons, seems not to conceive of the possibility of losing control over the process. As analysed by Schmitter (2003) for the EU, the level of convincement and consensus required to change deeply rooted convictions is complex, not just time-consuming.

The bloc's structure, defined by the Treaty of Asunción in 1991, concentrates decision-making power and governability in the *CMC* (Common Market Council), made up of the presidents and ministers of foreign affairs and of the economy. The *GMC* (Common Market Group), made up of the deputy ministers or under-secretaries of foreign affairs, has the attribute of the executive direction of integration. This institutional engineering has shown itself to be effective, on the one hand, but on the other, inadequate in allowing the development of a body that could inspire affinities.

It seems that a more institutionalized Mercosur does not represent the interests of a considerable part of the elites, of social, economic and regional groups, and of political sectors, which feel their needs are met by the current structure. With the objectives re-defined, there remains the interest in increasing trade and, in certain cases, in cross-border investments, as exemplified by Petrobrás, Banco Itaú, Bunge, Gerdau, AmBev and other companies. These interests became evident in the liberal-democratic and the developmentalist and distribution-oriented periods. At the same time, the bloc continues having meaning in some circumstances. It is useful for a part of the relations with the USA; it is important in relations with the EU; and it has partial importance in the case of the WTO and in some negotiations with emerging countries, particularly in cases of bloc-to-bloc dialogue. However, there is an avoidance of positions that for some would limit the possibilities provided by greater autonomy and universalism. Consequently, say Gonçalves and Lyra (2003 p. 14), "the great obstacle, in Brazil and Argentina, to an effective 'investment' in the Mercosur project, beyond the rhetoric of the pro-integration discourse, is the ambiguity with which several sectors of the two societies and of the two governments evaluate the bloc".

4.6 Final Remarks

In our attempt to extract conclusions from the analysis we have conducted on the reasons for the Brazilian position before the Mercosur, we must take into account the fact that the natural protagonist and universalist aspirations of the country's elites lead them to believe in the need to be free to act with nimbleness on the international stage, without restrictive agreements at the regional level or the conditioning that would derive from the necessary concessions to the less powerful partners. Regional integration is not rejected. On the contrary, it is considered beneficial, but only as it does not imply costs of what Burges (2005, p. 450) calls "cooperative economic growth". Our analysis clearly suggests that adequate density to stimulate the deepening of integration does not exist within Brazilian society. We believe that albeit Mercosur figures within the priorities of the state, the government, and the Ministry of Foreign Affairs etc. there is a hesitation in bearing the costs and facing the existing asymmetries. Brazil's political system, parliamentary representation, and poverty in many regions and localities, all contribute to this. In the words of Mariano, "The expansion, combined with the low level of government commitment, in the sense of working on the existing asymmetries, has led to an integration that cannot be very ambitious as to its depth. At the same time, the limits constituted by a customs union that does not consolidate and the difficulties inherent to the management of the new demands resulting from this situation may make integration unattractive to governments and important domestic sectors involved, thus creating a situation of stalemate that would lead to the strengthening of disintegrating forces, which, incidentally, seems to be the current stage of the bloc" (Mariano, 2007, p. 194).

In Brazil, there is a low level of sensitivity to regional issues, which is explained by the attraction that domestic questions exert in a continental country. "In Argentina, for better or for worse, Brazil is an issue: it is a subject of everyday life, a matter permanently in the press. In Brazil, on the other hand, Argentina arouses much less interest, except in moments of deep crisis" (Gonçalves & Lyra, 2003, p. 21).

For Brazilian society, and for its elites, understanding the perspectives of the Mercosur has to do with the debate on the future of Brazil's global position. As we have discussed, the need to define better whether integration should be considered useful and important is on the agenda. If the answer is affirmative, the next point is checking whether there is a willingness to take on its costs. Assuming there is a need for a paymaster (Mattli, 1999) in the integration process, then the role would belong to Brazil. This would lead to a new question: is the country capable of playing this role or not? For developing countries there are objective limits; assuming the costs may be beyond their capacities. Mattli (1999) states that the role of paymaster is not related simply with the economy, but also has to do with other parameters, such as the delegation of certain functions to community institutions, which means accepting and trusting regional integration, and considering it part of one's domestic politics. Some measures, such as the abovementioned creation of the *FOCEM* (Structural Convergence Fund) arguably converge with the perspective of strengthening integration, just like it is the case with the creation of the Mercosur Parliament (replacing the Joint Parliamentary Committee). But the small dimension of the actions, both economic and political, seems to confirm the analysis we have developed, in the sense that in the Southern Cone bloc, assumptions of integration do not emerge that both functionalists and intergovernmentalists with conflicting interpretations have identified in the European Union. Differently from Burges' analysis (2005), it probably does not concern a somewhat myopic Brazilian interest—envisaging a leadership role without compensation in relation to the countries involved—but rather underlying structural difficulties of an economic and political nature. And, as we have highlighted, likely also the lack of social adhesion to the integration process (Gardini & Almeida, 2016).

In our view, if the Mercosur were to recede towards a free trade area, which, as we have seen, is the position supported by significant social sectors in Brazil, this would mean a weakening in the bargaining power of the country and the bloc in the international system, contrary to what a certain reading of universalism supposes. Greater institutionalization of the bloc, as we have discussed, would bring costs to Brazil, but considering the cost of non-institutionalization is also fundamental, as well as the onus resulting from the undefined situation that has lasted at least since 1997—or that perhaps is inherent to the process.

From the normative point of view, there is a need for agreements to permit the adoption of measures committed to some degree of supranationality, i.e., actions, rules, norms that ensure the bloc's deepening. This implies a re-evaluation of foundational concepts within Brazilian policy, such as autonomy and universalism, so that they may be able to absorb the principles of integration, including the idea of purposive association (Nardin, 1987). This implies creating and stimulating a culture that values long-term gain and accepts some measure of short-term costs. If the Mercosur, as the documents state, is the basis of Brazil's strategy of international insertion, this basis must achieve reasonable levels of affirmation. This also counts for relations with Argentina, the first to be reciprocally defined as a strategy within the official documents.

Integrative industrial policies on a sectorial basis, initiatives in support of regional production chains, and the improvement of institutional instruments—all of which was conceived in the 1980s and contained in the 24 sector protocols signed in 1986 within the scope of the *PICE* (Economic Integration and Cooperation Programme)—

would permit an attenuation of asymmetries and a logic tending to favour the allocation of resources where there is greater market potential. This requires changing the decision-making system. Put differently, it requires increasing normative and regulatory strength through apt and legitimate agencies. In this chapter, we have discussed how difficult it is for these perspectives to take root in Brazilian society due to the interests and worldviews of the elites, society, and the state. This situation persisted until 2016, when the bicycle tilted over.

References

Amorim, C. (2004). Interview with Ambassador Celso Amorim with Revista Cni—Indústria Brasileira. Available from: http://www.mre.gov.br/portugues/politica_externa/discursos/discurso_detalhe.asp?id_discurso=2175. Accessed 10 Nov 2005.

Amorim, C., & Pimentel, R. (1996). Iniciativa Para As Américas: O Acordo Do Jardim Das Rosas. In J. A. G. Albuquerque (Ed.), *Sessenta Anos De Política Externa Brasileira (1930-1990)* (Vol. II). Cultura/nupri - Usp/fapesp.

Archibugi, D., Held, D., & Kohler, M. (1998). *Re-imagining political community: Studies in cosmopolitan democracy*. Stanford University Press.

Bueno De Mesquita, B. (2005). *Principles of international politics. People's, power, preferences and perceptions* (3rd.ed. ed.). CQ Press.

Bull, H. (1977). *The anarchical society: A study of order in world politics*. Springer.

Burges, S. W. (2005). Bounded by the reality of trade: Practical limits to a South American region. *Cambridge Review of International Affairs, 18*(3), 437–454.

Cardoso, F. H. (2001, April 20). Speech on behalf of the President of the Republic, Fernando Henrique Cardoso, On the occasion of the opening of the III Meeting at the Summit of the Americas, Québec.

Cardoso, F. H., & Soares, M. (1998). *O Mundo Em Português: Um Diálogo*. Paz E Terra.

CEDEC (Centro De Estudos De Cultura Contemporânea), PUC-SP (Pontifícia Universidade Católica De São Paulo). (2002). *Gestão Pública Estratégica De Governos Subnacionais Frente Aos Processos De Inserção Internacional E Integração Latino-americana*. CEDEC/PUC-SP, Dez. 2002, 568p. And anexes (Relatório Final Do Projeto Temático Fapesp) (Mimeo).

CEDEC (Centro De Estudos De Cultura Contemporânea); UNESP (Universidade Estadual Paulista); PUC-SP (Pontifícia Universidade Católica De São Paulo) E FGV/SP (Fundação Getúlio Vargas, São Paulo). (2004). *Gestão Pública E Inserção Internacional Das Cidades*. CEDEC/UNESP/PUC-SP/FGV-SP, 2004 (Projeto Temático Para A Fapesp) (Mimeo).

Danese, S. (2017). *Diplomacia Presidencial: História E Crítica* (2nd ed.). Brasília. 641p.

Flecha De Lima, P. T. (1989). Dados Para Uma Reflexão Sobre A Política Comercial Brasileira. In G. Fonseca Jr. & V. C. Leão (Eds.), *Temas De Política Externa Brasileira*. Fundação Alexandre De Gusmão/ipri/ed. Ática.

Fonseca, G., Jr. (1998). *Legitimidade E Outras Questões Internacionais: Política E Ética Entre As Nações*. Paz E Terra.

Gardini, G. L., & Almeida, M. H. T. (2016). *Foreign policy responses to the rise of Brazil: Balancing power in emerging states*. Palgrave Macmillan.

Gonçalves, J. B., & Lyra, M. C. (2003). *Aliança Estratégica Entre Brasil E Argentina: Antecedentes, Estado Atual E Perspectivas*. Centro Brasileiro De Relações Internacionais, Ano 2 2003 (Dossiê Cebri, Vol. 2). Available from www.cebri.org.br

Grupo Mercado Comum. (1992). *V Reunión. boletim De Integração Latino-americana*. Ministério Das Relações Exteriores, no. 4, Jan./Mar.

Guimarães, S. P. (2006). Los Tres Años Del Gobierno Del Presidente De Brasil Luiz Inácio Lula Da Silva. La Onda Digital. Disponível: http://www.uruguay2030.com/laonda/laonda/277/recuadro2.htm. Accessed 12 May 2006.

Haas, E. B. (1964). *Beyond the nation state*. Stanford University Press.

Haas, E. B. (1975). *The obsolescence of regional integration theory* (Research series, no. 25). University of California, Institute of International Studies.

Kratochwil, F. (2006). On legitimacy. *International Relations, 20*(3), 302–308.

Kume, J. A., & Piani, G. (2005). Mercosul: O Dilema Entre União Aduaneira E Área De Livre-comércio. *Revista De Economia Política, 25*(4 (100)), 370–390.

Lafer, C. (1993). A Política Externa Brasileira No Governo Collor. *Política Externa, São Paulo, 1*(4), 12–26.

Lafer, C. (2004). *A Identidade Internacional Do Brasil E A Política Externa Brasileira: Passado, Presente E Futuro*. Perspectiva.

Lampreia, L. F. (1995). Seminário Sobre Mercosul. *Resenha De Política Exterior Do Brasil. Brasília, Ano 21*(76), Set.

Lima, M. R. S. D. (1994). Ejes Analíticos Y Conflicto De Paradigmas En La Política Exterior Brasileña. *América Latina/Internacional, 1*(2), 27–47.

Lima, M. R. S. D. (2003). *Na Trilha De Uma Política Externa Afirmativa. Observatório Da Cidadania*. Ibase.

Lima, M. R. S. D. (2007). *Decisões E Indecisões: Um Balanço Da Política Externa No Primeiro Governo Do Presidente Lula*. Observatório Político Sul-americano. Available from http://observatorio.iuperj.br

Malamud, A. (2000). *Presidentialism and Mercosur: A hidden cause for a successful experience* (Mimeo).

Malamud, A. (2011). A leader without followers? The growing divergence between the regional and the global performance of Brazilian Foreign Policy. *Latin American Politics And Society, 53*(3), 1–24.

Mariano, K. L. P., & Ribeiro, C. (2019). The finances of the Southern Common Market (Mercosur). In U. Engel & F. Mattheis (Eds.), *The finances of regional organisations in the Global South* (1st ed.). Routledge.

Mariano, M. P. (2007). *A Política Externa Brasileira, O Itamaraty E O Mercosul. Unesp-araraquara: Post-graduate programme in sociology*. PhD Thesis.

Matlary, J. H. (1994, May 5–6). Integration theory and international relations: what does the elephant look like today and how should it be studied. In *2nd ECSA world conference, Brussels*. http://ecsanet.org.

Mattli, W. (1999). *The logic of regional integration: Europe and beyond*. Cambridge University Press.

Mello, F. D. C. (2000). *Regionalismo E Inserção Internacional: Continuidade E Transformação Da Política Externa Brasileira Nos Anos 90*. PhD Thesis. Faculdade De Filosofia, Letras E Ciências Humanas Da Universidade De São Paulo, 219p.

Moravcsik, A. (1994). *Why the European Union strengthens the state: Domestic politics and international cooperation* (Working Paper Series, no. 52). Center For European Studies, Harvard University.

Moravcsik, A. (2005). The European constitutional compromise and the neofunctionalist legacy. *Journal of European Public Policy, London, 12*(2), 349–386.

Nardin, T. (1987). *Lei, Moralidade E As Relações Entre Os Estados*. Forense-universitária.

O Estado De S. Paulo. (2015, July 16). Brasil Dá Calote Em Fundo Do Mercosul. 6/7, 2015. https://economia.estadao.com.br/noticias/geral,brasil-da-calote-em-fundo-do-mercosul%2D%2Dimp-,1726070.

Pastor, M., & Wise, C. (1994). The origins and sustainability of Mexico's free trade policy. *International Organization, 48*(3), 459–489.

Peña, F. (1991). *O Mercosul E Suas Perspectivas: Uma Opção Pela Inserção Competitiva Na Economia Mundial* (Mimeo).

Pereira, L. C. B. (1992). Contra A Corrente No Ministério Da Fazenda. *Revista Brasileira De Ciências Sociais, São Paulo*, no. 19.

Pereira, L. C. B. (2018). *Em Busca Do Desenvolvimento Perdido* (Vol. 1, 1st ed.). Fgv Editora. 168p.

Pierson, P. (1998). The path to European integration: a historical-institutionalist analysis. In W. Sandholtz & A. S. Sweet (Eds.), *European integration and supranational governance*. Oxford University Press.

Pinheiro, L. (2000). Traídos Pelo Desejo: Um Ensaio Sobre A Teoria E A Prática Da Política Externa Brasileira Contemporânea. *Contexto Internacional, Iri-puc/rj, 22*(2), 305–335.

Protocolo Constitutivo Do Parlamento Do Mercosul. (2006). https://www.bcb.gov.br/rex/sgt4/ftp/cd%20fluxograma/tratados%20e%20protocolos/protocolo%20do%20parlamento.pdf.

Przeworski, A. (1993). A Falácia Neoliberal. *Lua Nova, 28/29*. CEDEC.

Sallum, B., Jr. (1999). O Brasil Sob Cardoso: Neoliberalismo E Desenvolvimentismo. *Tempo Social. São Paulo, 11*(2), 26–51.

Sandholtz, W., & Sweet, A. S. (1998). *European integration and supranational governance*. Oxford University Press.

Schmitter, P. C. (2003). Neo-neo-functionalism. In A. Wiener & T. Diez (Eds.), *European integration theory*. Oxford University Press.

Silva, L. I. L. D. (2006). *Declaração De Lula Da Silva Na Reunião De Cúpula De Córdoba*.

The Ministry of Foreign Affairs. (1991). *Ministerio das Relações Exteriores, Brasil, Argentina, Uruguai e Paraguai criam Mercado Comum do Sul* (p. 279). Resenha de Política Exterior do Brasil: . No. 68.

Valor Econômico. (2004, November 16). Empresários Defendem Um Passo Atrás No Mercosul.

Vaz, A. C. (2002). *Cooperação, Integração E Processo Negociador: A Construção Do Mercosul*. IBRI.

Vigevani, T., & Veiga, J. P. C. (1997). A Integração Industrial No Mercosul. In G. Arbix & M. Zilbovicius (Eds.), *De Jk A Fhc: A Reinvenção Dos Carros* (pp. 329–355). Scritta. ISBN: 8586567043; 9788586567049.

Wendt, A. (1994). Collective identity formation and the international state. *American Political Science Review, 88*(2), 384–396.

Chapter 5
The Social Mercosur Within a Brazilian Foreign Policy Perspective

5.1 Introduction

During the 2000s, social participation in the different structures of Mercosur was broadened. The Joint Parliamentary Commission (JPC—Port. *CPCM*) was created in 1991 and in 1994 became a formal part of Mercosur's institutional framework. The Consultative Economic and Social Forum (CESF—Port. *FCES*) was created in 1994. The SGT-11, Labor Relations, Employment and Social Security, along with eight commissions, were instituted by the Common Market Group (CMG—Port. *GMC*), shortly after the Treaty of Asunción. With the Ouro Preto Protocol, in 1994, its functions were broadened and its name was changed to SGT-10. The social summits and the Mercosur Parliament were created in 2006, and hereafter underwent the implementation of the Strategic Social Action Plan (*Peas*), in 2007, by the Social Institute, the Institute for Public Policies and Human Rights (IPPHR—Port. *IPPDH*), and the Mercosur Social and Solidaric Programme, as well as the Social Participation Unit (SPU—Port. *UPS*). In the 2000s, there was a strengthening and increasing recognition that integration and regional cooperation depended on societal involvement and on initiatives which market forces alone cannot provide. This thematic broadening and increased social participation in Mercosur leads to some reflection regarding its motivations and impacts on the structures of the bloc.

If we take our point of departure in the idea that the density of a regional integration process relates to the degree of societal adhesion to the integration dynamic, it becomes of fundamental importance to seek a more precise understanding of the way that the involvement of domestic actors has occurred regarding the issues concerning Mercosur. The aim of the present chapter is thereby to engage with the changes that have occurred in Mercosur since the 2000s, particularly those concerned with the reduction of inequality and with the broadening of the space for participation and for the social issues within the block. We similarly seek to analyze how social participation in relation to the issues related to Mercosur took

T. Vigevani, H. Ramanzini Junior, *The Challenges for Building Regional Integration in the Global South*, United Nations University Series on Regionalism 18,
https://doi.org/10.1007/978-3-030-93348-7_5

place in Brazil, with focus on the analysis of the Mercosur Programme for Social Participation (*PMSP*).

Based on a Brazilian foreign policy perspective, this chapter's focus is to highlight the connection between social participation within the domestic field and the broadening of the space for social issues in the Mercosur sphere, with a point of departure in the idea that these processes are interconnected and possibly mutually enforcing, and with our attention focused on the Workers' Party (PT) governments. In this regard, the political participation strategy of the domestic actors involved with Mercosur impacts—and is itself influenced by—the dynamics associated with the bloc's development. The inclusion of social issues and the initiatives to broaden participation has its origin in the domestic political changes in members countries with the emergence of new political leaders in the 2000s (Ayerbe, 2008). In spite of their diversity, these were more closely connected to social actors. At the same time, the evolution towards a more social Mercosur has to do with the recognition of the difficulties confronted by the block and the intent to construct a more positive agenda with the involvement of domestic actors relatively more favorable towards integration.

Persistent problems from within the economic sphere, including obstacles to economic liberalization, influenced the general environment for the integration process, encumbering its advancement. Albeit only partially, leading governments incorporated the underlying idea that although Mercosur might be faced with problems related to trade and productive integration, it could still advance within other issue areas such as health (Riggirozzi, 2016), education (Botto, 2016; Perrotta, 2016), migration, and culture, etc.

The chapter is organized in the following way. In the second section, we analyze the relation between social participation and regionalism. In the third, we discuss the spaces for social participation in Mercosur and the changes in the integration process in the direction of broadening social themes. In the fourth section, we analyze the Mercosur Social and Participatory Programme (*PMSP*) in a Brazilian context. In the fifth section, we conclude, demonstrating the significance of the intensification of the debate about social policies within regional integration.

5.2 Social Participation and Regionalism

In the first decade of the 2000s, South America was confronted with a relatively new situation. With the consolidation of the democratic regime, the notion of delegative democracy underwent a clear evolution towards forms of participatory democracy as a necessary stage towards maturity and stabilization of regional politics (O'Donnell, 1994, 2001). The study of democracy in South America would thereby have to consider not only the formal aspects of the democratic regime—press freedom, election, the separation of powers—but also the institutional framework which connects the citizens' preferences and public policies, particularly the "new modes of institutionalized participation" (Córdova, 2015, p. 155). Such was the debate at that moment. In this context, it became increasingly questionable whether bureaucratization, in terms of isolation of state agencies, would be a necessary factor for the formulation of efficient public policies. The arguments which we presented in the previous chapter, with regards to the positive role of the presidents, began to display certain insufficiencies. The debates about economic complementarities, trade, and production chains, as well as deficiencies in institutional frameworks, did not proceed easily. Resistance towards Mercosur and the expansion of regional cooperation already began to arise in Brazil from Lula da Silva's second term. On the other hand, regional governments' positive disposition paved the way for a post-hegemonic regionalism (Riggirozzi & Tussie, 2012a), as this would later be termed.

The predominant politically significant trend was to strengthen different political actors' participation which contributed to the formulation, implementation, and evaluation of public policies. In some countries, social participation increasingly became an organizational principle for public management. This has consequences for the experiences of regionalism and regional integration, which also passed through a period of important transformation characterized by the creation of new institutions, such as the Bolivarian Alternative for the Americas (Alba), in 2004, the Union of South American Nations (*Unasul*), in 2008, the Community for Latin-American and Caribbean States (CLACS—Port. *CELAC*), 2010, and the modification of others, as is the case of Mercosur, which will be treated in the next chapter. A common point is the broadening of the relevant actors and of the issues related to cooperation and regional integration in order to expand social participation beyond trade-related issues.

The rise of new regional political leadership (Ayerbe, 2008), with center-left presidents, generally developmentalists inclined towards increased redistribution, notably Tabaré Vásquez and José Mujica, in Uruguay, Nestor and Cristina Kirchner, in Argentina, Luis Inácio Lula da Silva and Dilma Rousseff, in Brazil, and Fernando Lugo, in Paraguay, despite their differences led to a broadening of the opportunities for historically excluded groups to gain a voice, be this either through their participation in executive positions within the state, or in state, municipal or national councils, at the community level, in plebiscites, national conferences, referendums or in the participatory budget. Zaremberg (2014, p. 384) raises some relevant questions to help reflecting about the expansion of social participation within this new context: are these experiences of participations new ways to hide old political vices? Or, to the contrary, are they genuine innovations which open paths for new horizontal and inclusive processes? What influences the results of these experiences for them to evolve in any given direction, towards political control and the deepening of democracy? It is certainly not possible to generalize about these experiences. In Brazil, the understanding at the beginning of the 2010s was that the efficiency of the participatory frameworks for political management and the quality of democracy depends on factors such as: the presence of civil associations, the role of associative tradition in structuring the participatory practices, and the compatibility between political projects of the government and civil society and its institutional design (Carlos et al., 2014). The degree of successful incorporation of social actors' demands, in turn, appears to be directly linked with aspects such as organizational capacity, the degree of internalization, and the connection with relevant political actors.

Reflecting on the participatory experiences, it becomes necessary to adopt some caution when considering the relation between participation and social influence. In a seminal work, Arnstein (1969) points to the existence of eight different levels of citizen's participation in public policies: manipulating, therapy, informing, consultation, placation, partnership, delegated power, and citizen control. Albeit simplified, they constitute useful analytical artifices. In the first six, citizens are heard and express their opinions, but cannot guarantee that their viewpoints will be considered by the more powerful actors. As we shall see below, this was the predominant pattern in the Mercosur Social and Participatory Programme (*PMSP*). The levels of delegated power and citizen control would not be considered. Other authors follow in line with the same conceptual perspective. Lasker and Guidry (2008, p. 201) present a differentiation between opportunity, voice, and influence in the decision-making process: "Players have an opportunity to participate in the process when they are invited or when they initiate an opportunity on their own. They have a voice when the opportunity enables them to express their ideas to others. They have an influential voice when their ideas are used to make something happen (for example, when actions are taken to address issues they raise or when their ideas shape actions that are taken)". In the cases analyzed within this chapter, the predominant logic was that social actors gain a voice in so far as they have the opportunity to present their ideas.

It is possible to identify different paths through which the policy process can be influenced: "(1) provide written comments; (2) Participate in meetings; (3) Participate on advisory, regulatory negotiation, or other alternative dispute resolution committees; (4) communicate informally with agency personnel; (5) litigate; (6) use the Parliament; (7) use another agency; (8) mobilize membership and society; or (9) go to the president" (Dür & De Bièvre, 2007, p. 2). Various factors affect this influence: institutions, group characteristics, specific thematic factors, authority, and legal backing. Differences in resources mean that organizations have varying capacities of influence (Dahl, 1982). This initial caveat about the relevance of seeking to differentiate our notions of participation and influence in the analysis of social life becomes necessary, as sometimes there can be overlaps of the two ideas, which in fact, refer to two different processes. The first concerns the manner of interactions; the second, the result of this interaction. As we shall see in the following sections, this differentiation is relevant in order for us to understand the significance of the social agency in Mercosur and the Mercosur Social and Participatory Programme.

Within the domestic level of the countries, there was a broadening of social participation, even though this also had diverse consequences, concerning the deepening of democracy or the expansion of societal influence in defining political strategies. Yet, it is a fact that as the 2010s came to an end, it becomes important to keep in mind that this broadening led to a reaction on behalf of elites in the opposite direction, in the case of Mercosur, against the integration, as they believed that this could harm their interests. Beyond this, when one reflects on the role of society in Mercosur countries regarding public policies, including foreign policy, there are enormous challenges. One of these is that what was understood with social participation at the beginning of the 2010s in these countries is not exactly the same thing. This has consequences regarding the understanding of how social participation can be identified within the regional bloc.

The very logic and objective of social participation may differ according to the policy in question. Beyond this, as Bruera (2015) highlights, social participation is inserted within a complex political game in which electoral questions and the need for governability plays a central role. This also applies to social participation within Mercosur. In this perspective, it becomes possible to think that the broadening of the participation and the social issues was aimed at balancing the movements of those contrary to the bloc and favorable to the setback towards a free trade area. In the same way, the political leaders sought to define new issues and questions for the integration agenda, in order to engage a larger number of domestic actors and try to garner new sources of support for the integration project. Opening channels for social participation within the structures of the bloc would make the integration process less prone to be identified with the preferences of political and economic elites (Martins, 2014).

Regarding governmental actors, Martins (2014, p. 106) considers that in recent years, expansion has occurred with regards to "the degree of participation of other fields of government beyond the Ministries for Foreign Affairs, Economy, and Trade, which always have been at the forefront of Mercosur. Nearly all Brazilian Ministries have some sort of interface with Mercosur". This was also evident with regards to social actors and movement. Since the 1990s, a process of mobilization of social actors concerning Mercosur becomes evident, not least regarding labor movements. In the 2000s until 2015, when the 18th and last Mercosur Social Summit was held, this mobilization was broadened significantly and began to include organizations such as the Brazilian Association of NGOs, the Articulation of Brazilian Women, and the Brazilian Centre for Solidarity with the Peoples and the Struggle for Peace, the Centre for Migrant Support, the National Confederation of Agricultural Workers (*Contag*), the Brazilian Network for the Integration of the Peoples (*Rebrip*), amongst others (Budini, 2015). This was a highly relevant effort, considering that in Brazil social movements and organizations related to labor, women, human rights, education, the environment, micro and small and medium-sized enterprises, solidaric economy, amongst others, are generally important points of support within society for policies favorable to Mercosur and for the implementation of sectoral policies within the bloc. This became evident within a context in which skeptical visions began to arise in relation to the bloc's importance for Brazil's foreign and trade policy. These perspectives were strengthened from the Dilma Rousseff's second term in 2014 and onwards.

In the first decade of the 2000s, the notion of participatory regionalism (Acharya, 2003) gained ground, both in relation to a higher degree of connectedness between the societies and states regarding the promotion of issues related to the Mercosur agenda, but also concerning the broadening of the possibilities for social participation in the bloc's structures, albeit operationally limited, as we shall see in the following section. According to Acharya (2003, p. 382)

> The term 'participatory regionalism' as used here is distinguished by two key features. The first, at the level of official regionalism, is the acceptance by governments of a more relaxed view of state sovereignty and the attendant norm of non-interference in the internal affairs of states. This allows for more open discussion of, and action on, problems facing a region and creates more space for non-governmental actors in the decision-making process. A second feature of participatory regionalism is the development of a close nexus between governments and civil society in managing regional and transnational issues. This means not just greater cooperation among the social movements leading to the emergence of a regional civil society, but also closer and positive interaction between the latter and the official regionalism of states.

In this book, we use the notion of participatory regionalism to express the increased degree of connectedness between states and societies in the promotion of some of the questions related to the Mercosur agenda and also to characterize the very institutional changes within the bloc, aimed towards the broadening of social participation. We do not adopt the first part of Acharya's (2003) definition, as it is not possible to observe a decrease in the emphasis and the centrality that the idea of state sovereignty holds for the Mercosur member states, particularly Brazil (Desiderá Neto, 2014; Lazarou & Luciano, 2015; Mariano, 2007).

The modifications in Mercosur in the 2000s are rooted in domestic changes within its member countries. As Acharya (2003, p. 388) affirms "the emergence and role of regional institutions are often the product of domestic political institutions and structures". The central point is that changes within the bloc can indeed wield a spillover effect onto the internal level within states, thus, possibly consolidating the process of integration but at the same time generating new forms of resistance. The broadening of the modes of integration in Mercosur beyond the contacts between state actors and, mainly, the inter-presidential relations (Malamud, 2005) impact the agency of social actors within the domestic sphere and can favor pressures for encountering regional solutions for endogenous and transnational challenges for the region, such as migration, the environment, drug trafficking, and human rights. The very promotion of these issues implies the involvement of social actors, with knowledge and capacity to articulate demands, even if, in some cases, these are contrary to state policies.

Beyond this, with the broadening of the channels through which citizens can participate in the agenda and, to a lesser degree, in the decision-making in relation to the bloc, the possibilities to influence the trajectory of the integration process are broadened. Social participation within the domestic sphere can generate a culture of participation which tends to extend towards the regional arena, with favorable results in terms of integration. It thus increases the space for decentralized bonds to form between member states. In the same way, the regional and international interactions between social actors is a way to compensate for the eventually limited capacity to exercise influence at the domestic level. Keck and Sikkink (1998, p. 12) work with this idea from the notion of a "boomerang pattern" meaning that "when channels between the state and its domestic actors are blocked, the boomerang pattern of influence characteristic of transnational networks may occur: domestic NGOs bypass their state and directly search out international allies to try to bring pressure on their states from outside".

In some cases, the linking of specific social groups within societies in Mercosur member countries antecedes the creation of institutional spaces within the bloc, making it possible to think of situations in which the formation of an institutional space also is the fruit of previous work of defining common demands and of bonding between social actors. In the case of labor movements, the coordinator of the Central Unions of the Southern Cone (CUSS—Port. *CCSCS*) was created in 1986, and thereby before the emergence of Mercosur and the creation of the Subgroup for Labor Relations, Employment, and Social Security, before the Subgroup for Work (SW—Port. *SGT*) n° 11, created in 1991 (Mariano, 2001), after 1994, SGT-10. The bodies of Mercosur engaged with social issues played an important role in terms of presenting these movements' demands.

5.3 The Spaces for Social Participation in Mercosur and the Changes in the Integration Process

In the 2000s, a broadening took place in the social participation within the institutional structure of Mercosur. Characterizing the changes in the block in the first decade of the 2000s compared to the 1990s, some authors use the notion of "post-regional liberalism" (Serbin, 2013) or post-hegemonic regionalism (Riggirozzi & Tussie, 2012a). According to this notion, the focus of the new accords in relation to regional integration, from that point and onwards became more intensely related to the perspectives for development, social justice and national and regional autonomy. On the other hand, it became less associated with trade liberalization and productive integration, which were prevalent in the 1990s. In this context, there was a strengthening of a social agenda which sought to broaden both participation and the scope of integration themes.

The opening of institutional spaces for social participation in Mercosur would broaden the bloc's legitimacy (Riggirozzi & Tussie, 2012a; Serbin, 2013). This could make the integration process less dependent or vulnerable in relation to personal or idiosyncratic preferences of political leaders. In this perspective, the realization of the Mercosur Social Summit, created during Brazil's *pro tempore* presidency in 2006, is considered as a landmark with regards to social participation. The Final Declaration of the Mercosur First Social Summit, on December 13, 2006, highlights that "we propose that governments support and stimulate the direct participation of the civil society organizations and of all of the Working Subgroups and the Specialized Meetings of Mercosur and that mechanisms be created to incorporate them as observers in the Common Market Group (*GMC*) and the Common Market Council".[1] This illustrates the demands by social actors for conditions for effective and direct participation in Mercosur.

[1] Available from: http://www.secretariageral.gov.br/.arquivos/imagens-publicacoes/decfinalport.pdf. Accessed on August 23, 2015.

In line with the goal of this chapter, the study of social participation in Mercosur should be considered both from the perspective of the state's agency to promote participation, as well as the perspectives related to the demands and initiatives from social actors in favor of a higher degree of opening of institutional spaces. Analyzing the final declarations from the Mercosur Social Summits, it is possible to notice a constant support for the bloc and its deepening on behalf of social entities interacting within this. In the final declaration of the XVIII Social Summit of Mercosur, which took place in July 2015, this support also becomes clearly evident "it is essential that we affirm that the problems and limitations of the present Mercosur process should be resolved through more rights, more participation, and more integration, and not through the negation or retrocession which the free trade agreements represent".[2]

In Lula da Silva's evaluation at the end of 2010:

> (...) we all desire a higher degree of participation of the societies in the construction of an even more democratic, civic and solidaric Mercosur. It would not be possible to maintain the spirit of integration solely with a basis in the actions of states and governments, however convergent and motivated they may be. We therefore significantly emphasize the social participation within the Mercosur Summit, with emphasis on the Costa do Saufpe Summit, in Bahia, when we two years ago created the Commission for the Coordination of the Ministries for Social Affairs and the Mercosur Social Institute. On that occasion, for the first time, ministers from the social field participated in the meeting of the Common Market Council, in order to take the first steps in the direction of a Strategic Plan for Social Action for Mercosur. In line with this Plan, we established regional development goals which were more ambitions than the United Nations' Millennium Development Objectives. To give continuation to this Plan, common social policies will be adopted between the four members of Mercosur representing a hitherto unseen effort of coordination. It is with these values that we build a new Mercosur, a Mercosur of the peoples.[3]

With the idea of a "Mercosur of the Peoples"—an idea which became evermore present towards the end of the first decade of the 2000s—it becomes necessary to include issues such as social policies, culture, education, health, labor issues, migration, amongst others within the bloc's agenda. These issues coincide with the logic of participatory regionalism, as they refer to objectives which tend to lend themselves more towards social participation. A corollary of this dynamic is reaching agreements, rules, and regulations which favor ways of social cooperation, such as the Strategic Social Action Plan (Peas), which was devised in 2010, the High Level Employment Group (2004), the Social Institute (2007), the Participatory Social Unit (2010), the Action Plan for the Creation of a Statute for Citizenship in Mercosur (2010) and the Meeting of Ministers and High Authorities for Women in Mercosur (2011).

---

[2]Available from: http://www.decidamos.org.py/www/index.php?option=com_k2&view=item&id=1808:declara%C3%A7%C3%A3o-final-%E2%80%93-c%C3%BApula-social-do-mercosul-bras%C3%ADlia-14-16-de-julho-de-2015&Itemid=1. Accessed on August 24. 2015.

[3]Speech by the President of the Republic, Luiz Inácio Lula da Silva, during the closure session of the Mercosur Social Summit in Foz do Iguaçu-PR, December 16th, 2010.

The realization of the social summit and the different ways of social participation in the bloc tend to spread out towards the domestic level within member states and towards the integration process. In this regard, according to Martins (2014, p. 113) "it was the Social Summit in Cordoba, in 2006, in which the idea of the elaboration of a Social Action Plan was discussed for the first time. Brought before the bloc's presidents, the proposal was approved and officially incorporated into the official agenda, thus, giving birth to Peas". In this same perspective, as we shall see in the next section, the need to organize the Brazilian participation in the Mercosur Social Summit was a relevant factor behind the creation of the Mercosur Social Participatory Programme, in 2008. These provide evidence of events that strengthened the social participation which occurred with a basis in incentive structures nurtured by the bloc.

Mercosur priorities within the field of regional social development under the Peas defined by the governments at the time, comprise of:, (1) the eradication of hunger, poverty and the combatting of social inequality; (2) guaranteeing human rights, humanitarian assistance and ethnic, racial, and gender equality; (3) universalizing public health; (4) universalizing education and eradicating illiteracy; (5) appreciation and promotion of cultural diversity; (6) guaranteeing productive inclusion; (7) guaranteeing access to decent work and pension rights; (8) promoting environmental sustainability; (9) assuring social dialogue; (10) establishing regional cooperation mechanisms for the execution of financing of public policies (Peas, 2010).[4] Referring to the conditioned income transfer programmes of the countries in the Andean Community, (Bolivia, Ecuador, Colombia and Peru), Romão (2014, p. 184) considers this as a sort of "non-coordinated regional strategy for fighting transgenerational hunger". Based on Peas and thinking with a point of departure in Mercosur, this effort appears to have been aimed exactly at defining a manner of coordinated action to combat hunger.

In 2004, the Specialized Meeting for Family Agriculture (Reaf) was created, which permitted an agreement about the bases for the recognition and identification of family agriculture in Mercosur, beyond the implementation of national registers for family agriculture (Ferreira, 2017). In line with an agreement with the Ministry for Agrarian Development (MAD—Port. *MDA*) "throughout the process of consolidation of the REAF the functioning of the National Sections has been managed by the national coordinators, and there is a salient participation from civil society through the organizations for family agriculture".[5] As one of the effects of Reaf's engagement, the Mercosur Family Agriculture Fund (FFA—Port. *FAF*) was created in 2008. In this field, civil society and regional organizations, such as the Confederation of Organizations for Family Producers in Mercosur (*Coprofam*), contributed significantly to *Reaf's* work. This occurred through the knowledge and the planning efforts of these member organizations, which also participate in the national sections of *Reaf* (Ferreira, 2017; Martins, 2014). It becomes evident that the treatment of the

[4] Available from: http://www.mda.gov.br/reaf/pt-br/brasil. Accessed on October 14, 2015.

[5] Available from: http://www.mda.gov.br/reaf/pt-br/brasil. Accessed on August 24, 2015.

issue of family agriculture within the Mercosur sphere contributed to the strengthening of the instances of participation within the domestic sphere.

With regards to the incorporation of social demands within the block, the creation of the Mercosur Parliament in 2006 can be viewed as a means towards the institutional strengthening of these demands. The parliament could become a relevant political actor by incorporating the bloc's social demands, by contributing to the definition of a proprietary agenda for the region, thus, spurring discussions or the formation of new bodies to treat these issues through a regional perspective. Universal suffrage could, according to an institutionalist reading, consolidate the democratic values in the region, by incentivizing voters, parliaments and political parties to discuss regional issues. The Constitutive Protocol (2005) established the Parliament's main functions as: (1) the strengthening of inter-parliamentary cooperation; (2) increasing the flexibility of the incorporation of the internal juridical orders of the Mercosur legislation; (3) contributing to an adequate representation of the interests of citizens in member states; and (4) supporting Mercosur's democratic commitment. As the immediate successor of the Joint Parliamentary Commission (*CPC*), it is also the parliament's role to make recommendations to the Common Market Council (*CMC*). In the case of the approval by the *CMC* these should be passed on to the respective national congresses for internalization.

The Constitutive Protocol (2005) of the Mercosur Parliament does not imply the decisive participation of the organ for regional legislative participation processes, or the possibility for a higher degree of control of the bloc's decision-making bodies, including its major instance, the Common Market Council. This way, the bloc's intergovernmental character was strictly maintained and supranational concepts were not incorporated. From the Brazilian point of view, it is worth highlighting that the government at the time remained faithful to the principles of autonomy and of sovereignty, which historically had guided the Brazilian foreign policy, as we saw in previous chapters. The idea of holding direct elections to guarantee representativity and a communitarian parliament contrasts with the fact that this institution was attributed an essentially consultative function, in relation to the bodies which retain decision-making power (Mariano, 2011).

Article 4 of the Constitutive Protocol (2005), referring to competences, indicates that the Parliament's main function is consultative and to provide information, and not the communitarian legislative production. The consolidation of the Mercosur Parliament is nonetheless related to certain effective, and not merely consultative powers, such as decision-making capacity in the distribution of communitarian resources, which is the case with the Mercosur Foundation for Structural Convergence (*FOCEM*), in so far as its original rules are maintained. If the prerogatives of members states are respected, this distribution could be decided by the parliament. With this diversity in mind, the parliament's main competence relates to voting about the budget proposed by the Commission.

With a point of departure in the analysis of the changes of Mercosur towards the broadening of the participation and social issues with which the bloc engaged during the 2000s, it becomes evident that there was a certain distance between the political will to broaden the social aspect and the limitations of means for the bloc's institutions and agreements to operate effectively. In other cases, there was a lack of information about the concrete possibilities for action towards social participation, which limits the potential impact of the existing agreements and institutions. This was related to the importance of the integration project for the public opinion in each country. Of the four countries which constituted Mercosur, Brazil was the one in which the bloc had the lowest degree of salience, which should not be confounded with opposition (Gardini & Almeida, 2016). This can be explained by Brazil's larger economic and demographic weight and by the bloc's relatively lower incidence on political life. In any case, it must be concluded that amongst the bloc's leaders in these years, there was a clear intent of broadening of the spaces and the opportunities for social participation. According to institutionalist authors (Pierson, 1998), in this case, the metaphor of the bicycle can be applied, through which an elected parliament creates a momentum of acceleration, based on its representative legitimacy. This approximates Arnstein's (1969) notion of delegated power.

In the 1990s, civil society representation was concentrated on the actors with the most economic power, particularly enterprises. These have the highest capacity to influence the Mercosur Economic and Social Forum, and, above all, the decision-making instances of each state, ministry, and presidency. The social and popular movements did not feel adequately represented in the Forum, (Martins, 2014). In the first decade of the 2000s, there was a change in this perception, which was the fruit of the advances in regional trade and the possibilities offered by new center-left governments. Despite these changes, there were also difficulties, which eventually hindered the materialization of the goals stated within the very documents about participatory regionalism in Mercosur. The continuity of decisional power within the decision-making structures of the Common Market Group and the Common Market Council, as defined by the Treaty of Asunción, is evident. The same was the case with the operational difficulties of the Mercosur Parliament and its consultative function. To this should be added the low incorporation of the recommendations approved by the Social Summit on behalf of part of the regional bodies and member-states.

The question of the decision-making process in every regional integration project is always highly complex (Hoffmann & Hoffmann, 1998). It involves state sovereignty. The Brazilian foreign policy concerning regional integration maintained its focus on the principles of sovereignty and autonomy. Therefore, the continuity of the defence of the intergovernmental institutional design, which privileges national positions above integration, had the limitation of the implementation of social policies as one of its consequences. This is one of the aspects to be considered *a-posteriori* to explain the involution from the second half of the 2010s.

5.4 The Spaces for National Participation in Mercosur Issues: The Case of the Mercosur Programme for Social Participation[6]

In Brazil, a space for social participation in the questions related to Mercosur was Mercosur Programme for Social Participation (*PMSP*). The *PMSP* has as its aim to brand governmental initiatives related to Mercosur, debate issues concerning the bloc, and transmit suggestions from civil society. The programme was established by "representatives for the Ministries which are active in the bloc and leaders of social organizations engaged with sectors such as family agriculture, small and medium enterprises, women, the environment, juvenile policies, urban and rural workers, human rights, solidaric economy, health, education, cooperativism, culture, and indigenous populations, amongst others" (Brasil, 2014). The involvement of governmental and social actors was integrated into its basic structures. Martins (2014, p. 122), who himself occupied the post as Secretary-General for the President of the Republic (2006–2010), evaluates that "the Mercosur Programme for Social Participation in practice functions as a council, informally known as *Conselho Brasileiro do Mercosul Social e Participativo*". Therefore, the *PMSP* fits within what Córdova (2015, p. 155) refers to as "the new forms of institutionalized participation". In fact, the Council did not only play a consultative role, but also depended on the government for its convocation, and also for defining its participants.

Some basic questions are common within the different works that analyze councils[7] for public policies (Pires, 2011). To what degree do these spaces offer possibilities to influence public policies? Do people who are active within these councils represent civil society organizations? Which organizations occupy chairs within these councils? What are their composition and the criteria according to which they were included within participants? What is the relation between participation and the strategic lines of actions of civil society actors involved in public policies? Are councils seen as appropriate instances to promote the interests of the organizations formally represented? In the same way, considering the conceptual discussion within the first section of this chapter about the difference between participation and influence, it becomes important to consider questions such as: who decides who participates in the decision-making or consultative process? How are participants selected? Does participatory practice change policies? Who has the final say regarding decisions? Is it possible for other actors to alter the viewpoints

---

[6]This section is based on Ramanzini Júnior and Farias (2014).

[7]According to the definition by the Brazilian federal government's transparency portal "councils are public spaces of a plural and party-based composition between the state and civil society, of a deliberative and consultative nature, which function it is to formulate and control the execution of sectorial public policies. Councils are the main channel for popular participation within the three governmental instances (federal, state, and municipal) available from: http://www.portaltransparencia.gov.br/controleSocial/ConselhosMunicipaiseControleSocial.asp. Accessed on August 20, 2015.

and positions of those who conduct the consultative process? Are there informal channels of interaction? What is their role? The empirical observation, and above all, the research on the effective transformations regarding the measures related to the issues discussed and the proposals approved, suggest strong limitations to this process, as we shall see below. Discussing the different forms of social participation, Sousa Santos (2017, p. 256) recognizes that a great variety exists: "We should also develop the law of deep democratic pluralism a new constitutional law from below. For example, Article 11 of the Bolivian Constitution establishes three kinds of democracy to be equally respected by the citizens: representative democracy, participatory democracy, and communitarian democracy—democracy by consensus, which is typical of indigenous peoples [...] In a participatory democracy, we would make decisions in citizen councils instead of electing the decision-makers. The idea of participatory budgeting in Brazil and in Latin America is now being copied in Europe". The author shows how forms of participation can be both diverse and complementary. The events within Mercosur countries—and more generally in Latin America—show that the difficulties of grasping the diversity of experiences are rooted in processes defined by different elites. The logic of participation in the 2010s in Mercosur, occurring according to Arnstein's (1969) classification on the level of consultation, therefore encounters its roots in the limits of the state and in class relations.

According to the Decree nº 6.594, of October 6th, 2008, from the Presidency of the Republic which instituted the Mercosur Social and Participatory Programme,[8] this has the following ends: (1) publicize the policies, priorities, negotiation proposals, and other initiatives of the Brazilian government related to Mercosur; (2) support discussions within the political, social, cultural, economic, financial, and trade-related fields that involve aspects concerned with Mercosur; (3) transmit proposals and suggestions with the capacity to generate consensus within the discussions undertaken with civil society organizations, to the Common Market Council and the Mercosur Common Market Group.

As can be seen from these aims, their nature is fundamentally consultative, and there are no mechanisms to guarantee their influence.[9] The decree presumed that civil society participation would be defined in terms of a joint ordinance form the General-Secretary of the Presidency of the Republic and the Ministry of Foreign Relations. The criteria for participation, according to the General-Secretary was that

[8] Available from: http://www.planalto.gov.br/ccivil_03/_Ato2007-2010/2008/Decreto/D6594.htm. Accessed on August 25, 2014.

[9] Also according to the Decree, in its article 3o "the Mercosur Social and Participatory Programme will be coordinated by the Chief of Staff of the Secretary General of the Presidency of the Republic and by the Ministry of Foreign Relations or by the substitutes designated to this end". Finally, item 1 of the Article 3o indicates that "participation in the Mercosur Social and Participatory programme and the bodies and entities of the federal public administration, in accordance with their competences, and the civil society organizations invited, in the terms and the modalities defined in the joint ordinance of the General-Secretary of the Presidency of the Republic and the Ministry of Foreign Relations".

"the entities invited to compose the *PMSP* have a national projection—through the presence of diverse federal states or through distinguished conduction of specific thematic agendas—and are dedicated to the issue of integration, specifically to following the diverse initiatives within Mercosur".[10]

The idea that it would function as a space for permanent dialogue between the government and society regarding the definition of proprietary themes and policies between Brazil and Mercosur is clearly present within the governmental authorities' declarations about the *PMSP*. According to Luiz Dulci, then minister of the Secretary-General of the Presidency of the Republic, at the moment of the *PMSP's* launch, "we hope that this council can express not only civil society's viewpoints, but also enrich the proposals that the Lula government presents to the decision-making bodies within Mercosur".[11]

In accordance with this book's goal—to analyze Mercosur's development through a Brazilian foreign policy perspective—it is important to mention that the forms of participation maintained a very low-profile character, and mainly aimed towards consensus. Shifting Brazilian governments considered social participation over a long period, from 1991 to 2016, to be of some relevance. The intergovernmental perspective obstructed the deepening and extension of the integration issue in broader social spheres. Neither did the expected spillover materialize within this field. The participation and incorporation of the idea of integration as an important concern thus weakened in Brazil. On the contrary, as we shall see, this fragility also meant that those who mobilized against it did not encounter significant opposition.

From 2008 to 2014, the *PMSP* meetings did not occur with regularity. The programme never had an executive secretariat. When it was created, in October 2008, the expectation was that it would meet four times every year—always preceding the meetings in the Common Market Group—to publicize the government's policies and initiatives related to Mercosur, spur discussions about diverse integration issues, and forward suggestions emanating from civil society.[12] The meetings, though, occurred two or three times every year, and according to the Institute for Development and Human Rights, there were no meetings in the period from October 2010 to March 2012.[13] The idea of partial connection with the meetings in the Common Market Group also appears to have vanished.

[10]Mercosur Social and Participatory Programme, July 8th, 2015. Available from: http://www.secretariageral.gov.br/noticias/2015/julho/08-07-2015-programa-mercosul-social-e-participativo. Accessed on August 25, 2015.

[11]Brazilian Mercosur Social and Participatory Council was created during a ceremony in the Planalto Palace. Available from: http://www.secretariageral.gov.br/noticias/2008/10/Not_06102008. Accessed on August 20th, 2015.

[12]Available from: http://www.secretariageral.gov.br/noticias/2008/10/not_02102008. Accessed on August 20, 2015.

[13]Human Rights and Social Participation in Mercosur Report. Parallel document: report from meetings. Available from: http://www.iddh.org.br/v2//upload/282e25a4dac24e36cf84ac2f3be819b9.pdf. Accessed on August 20, 2015.

Through its trajectory, between 2008 and 2014, the *PMSP's* main activities were to prepare the Brazilian representation for the Mercosur Social Summit, define the Brazilian delegation during these summits, and reflect on forms of participation. The subject matter discussed during the last *PMSP*, on the Brazilian side, which took place on April 1st, 2015 confirms this analysis. The meeting's goal was to "initiate the process or organization and preparation of the 18th Mercosur Social Summit, which should take place towards the end of the Brazilian *Pro Tempere* Presidency in June of that year".[14] In a posterior report, the Secretary-General of the Presidency indicated that during the meeting, a more central role within the Summit and the increase in the number of represented entities was requested. According to Antônio Simões, Sub-Secretary General for South and Central America, and the Caribbean, of the Ministry of Foreign Affairs, during the *PMSP*, Brazilian efforts were concentrated on two aspects: "The first was the renovation of the Mercosur Structural Convergence Fund (*FOCEM*), which had its 10th anniversary in 2015 and comprises of 45 projects, with investments of US$1.4 billion. The second aspect is to discuss the excesses of the Common External Tariff'.[15] It becomes important to observe that the priorities defined by the Brazilian *Pro Tempore* Presidency in relation to the bloc did not arise from the interaction with *PMSP*. On the other hand, the role of the *PMSP* and the actors within Brazilian civil society in the organization of the XVIII Mercosur Social Summit, which took place in Brasília in July 2015, recognizes this Summit's final document.[16] We understand that this situation results from the transaction costs, both in relation to the member states, but also in relation to other relevant actors within Brazilian civil society, whatever the strong and growing opposition from the political level, as well as from other social actors, such as the business community. Towards the end of the chapter, we shall see how this phase is analyzed through the perspectives of post-hegemonic (Riggirozzi & Tussie, 2012b) or post-liberal regionalism (Serbin, 2013).

A merit of the *PMSP* was its involvement of social actors in the integration dynamics. This has an effect of socialization and information exchange regarding the issues of Mercosur. Yet, with regards to influencing the Brazilian government, especially the positions which Brazil assumed within the Common Market Group—the main instance of Mercosur—retrospectively, this exercise appears limited. Apparently, this was not its main goal. Even the inclusion of issues such as family agriculture, migration, health, education and the efforts to harmonize and coordinate social policies present within Brazil's agenda for Mercosur, appears more

---

[14] Secretary-General initiates the process of organization of the Mercosur Social Summit. Available from: http://www.secretariageral.gov.br/noticias/2015/abril/sg-da-inicio-ao-processo-de-organizacao-da-cupula-social-do-mercosul. Acessed on: June 19, 2015.

[15] Secretary-General initiates the process of organization of the Mercosur Social Summit. Available from: http://www.secretariageral.gov.br/noticias/2015/abril/sg-da-inicio-ao-processo-de-organizacao-da-cupula-social-do-mercosul. Accessed on June 19, 2015.

[16] Available from: http://www.decidamos.org.py/www/index.php?option=com_k2&view=item&id=1808:declara%C3%A7%C3%A3o-final-%E2%80%93-c%C3%BApula-social-do-mercosul-bras%C3%ADlia-14-16-de-julho-de-2015&Itemid=1. Accessed on August 24, 2015.

like the fruit of governments and sectorial ministries. It thus appears to be less of a result of pressures from social movements related to these issues and actively participating in the *PMSP*. This in spite of the agenda enjoying support from these actors, which in some cases extends to its very formulation.

Amongst the themes debated regarding the social issues within Mercosur, the question of social security was highlighted in the *FCES* and the *SGT*-11 (later known as the *SGT*-10). It related to the issue of migration. Therefore, the issue of social security has grown in importance and seen significant participation from social actors. Directly related to the issue of migration, given its possible expansion, in 2009, two agreements signed in 2002 went into effect: the Residence Agreement for the Nationals of the Mercosur State Parties and the Mercosur + Bolivia and Chile Agreement. These agreements permitted "the citizens of these countries to reside and work in Brazil for two years with provisional status, and thereafter apply for permanent status" (Pires, 2011, p. 57). Another instrument of significant importance for the migrants was the Mercosur Multilateral Social Security Accord, signed in 1997, which entered into force in 2005.[17] It determined that "the pension contributions made to the social security system by a worker in each one of the signatory countries will accumulate in the same way as if they had been made in one specific country" (Brasil, 2010, p. 19).

We observe that the *PMSP* was a relevant mechanism for interaction between the state and society in the discussions of issues related to Mercosur. It sought to broaden the density of regional integration through the inclusion of new actors. This took place within a broader opening of the state towards social participation, a movement which resulted from demands by civil society movements and organizations for an institutionalized space for participation—especially within Mercosur. The diffusion from existing structures within the European Union is highly evident, including as a stimulus to the emulation.

With regards to its agency, the *PMSP* had a very limited capacity to influence the paths for integration and Brazil's behavior in relation to Mercosur. There were no mechanisms for monitoring and accompanying the agreements reached in that sphere. The exercise seems to be more directed towards participation than guaranteeing the influence of various societal sectors within the country's international insertion. A potential risk which should be highlighted *a-posteriori* is that this situation leads to a process of loss of interest in the *PMSP* on behalf of the domestic actors involved, and to the bloc's normative exhaustion.

---

[17] Other important instruments are: The Internal Migration Regularization Agreement for Citizens of Mercosur State Parties (signed in 2002); The Asunción Declaration on human trafficking and illicit trafficking in migrants (signed in 2001); The Santiago Declaration on migratory principles (2004); The Declaration of Asunción against Trafficking and Exploitation of People in Mercosur and Associated States (2005).

5.5 Final Considerations

As we have seen throughout this chapter, the analysis of participatory regionalism through a Brazilian foreign policy perspective enhances our comprehension of the difficulties confronted by the Brazilian state in the construction and strengthening of the initiatives related to social issues within the regional sphere. We have discussed the interests of the social groups and the state, as well as the reasons for their difficulties which, finally, may aid our understanding of the distancing concerning regional integration, which became visible from 2016. Yet, the seeds of these difficulties reach further back in time. At the same time, in this chapter, we have discussed the reasons from which the social actors began to take an interest in regional integration. The significance of these actors within the integration process in terms of bargaining and national disputes hereby became evident.

Some aspects point to this perspective: The creation of the Mercosur Family Agriculture Fund (*REAF*), the Mercosur Parliament, the concretization of the Social Action Plan represented by the Peas and the creation of the *PMSP*, as a necessary aspect to organize the Brazilian participation in the social summits. Through a governmental perspective, these should also be viewed as intents to create new agendas and interactions ahead of the difficulties faced by the bloc. As we shall see in the next chapter, the acceleration of the debate about social participation began at a time which by some authors has been termed as the post-hegemonic or post-liberal period. This period implies the crisis of the growth of trade relations, as can be seen in Table 4.1. It also points to an increasingly evident failure of the construction of production chains. Considering the different theories of regional integration, doubt thus emerges, that if because of internal resistance within the societies of member states and due to preference for the cultivation of relations with central countries, the problems of integration of trade and development within the region are not resolved, the situation of impasse might be overcome through the institutional favoring of social policies. Would this not be a "*Salto in Avanti*"? Although Mercosur incorporates social agendas, such as the eradication of hunger, food security, and combatting of extreme poverty, and the improvement of public health quality, the question which arises relates to whether and how the bloc could contribute to the improvement of these challenges, and how much they relate to the dynamic of regional cooperation and integration between countries.

In the 2000s, the materialization of the instances for social participation in Mercosur yielded results. The interface between actors and national policies with dynamics within the bloc was broadened. Yet, they were still limited in terms of the goal of amplifying the influence of social actors within the integration process and within the organ's executive bodies. It is important to keep in mind that the consolidation of the bodies and the social issues within the bloc has to do with the ambition to reach certain pleaded objectives. As we saw, there is a discrepancy between the debate and the conditions for the realization of the goals. The Brazilian state seeks a defensive stance, and in the case of Mercosur, accepts and even spurs this participation, while it simultaneously contains it to the level of a consultative instance.

Writing this book in a context in which regionalism is undergoing a very different moment than that analyzed in this chapter, we cannot evade certain conceptual questions. It does not appear correct to affirm that the organizations created by Mercosur from 1991, not least those expanded in the 2000s, would be directly connected only to the interests of that period, which we define as the prevalence of center-left, developmentalist, and redistributionist governments. Neither would it be correct to affirm that their stability is conditioned by the permanence of this kind of government. Therefore, at least with regards to Brazilian politics, the organizations of the 2000s were adequate for post-hegemonic conditions (Riggirozzi & Tussie, 2012a). What would their opportunities for survival be in a context in which these same conditions would encounter difficulties to consolidate?

We can therefore characterize the Brazilian foreign policy in relation to Mercosur in the first decade of the 2000s as the result of more long-term public policies. Therefrom our interest in discussing these. What is important to notice is, that in the formulation of integration and cooperation policies of Brazilian governments crystalize certain lines of action with roots in processes of a longer duration. As we have seen, these encountered strong resistance from the elites. In the period referred to as post-hegemonic, this aversion resisted not only the deepening of the social demands but also reiterated preferences for relations with central countries. It thus appears important to consider a conclusion by Riggirozzi and Tussie (2012a, p. 184): "Post-neoliberalism, we suggest, is therefore not a rupture with the past, but an evolution, shaped by legacies of past development trajectories, pragmatism, ad hoc policy making and responses to global and regional politics". We could, therefore, conclude that if the phase of policies with an accentuated emphasis on distributive rationales move in the direction of a welfare state, then the inauguration of a period of radical rupture in relation to them stimulates their destruction without eliminating their normative positive significance.

References

Acharya, A. (2003). Democratisation and the prospects for participatory regionalism in Southeast Asia. *Third World Quarterly, 24*(2).

Arnstein, S. (1969). A ladder of citizen participation. *Journal of the American Institute of Planners, 35*(4), 216–224.

Ayerbe, L. F. (2008). *Novas Lideranças Políticas e Alternativas de Governo na América do Sul*. Editora Da Unesp.

Botto, M. (2016). Policy diffusion and higher education reforms: Between market and state regulation—Where does Mercosur stand? In A. Ribeiro Hoffmann & A. C. Bianculli (Eds.), *Regional organizations and social policy in Europe and Latin America: A space for social citizenship?* (1st ed.). Palgrave Macmillan.

Brasil. (2010). *Ministério Do Trabalho E Emprego (Mte). Como Trabalhar Nos Países Do Mercosul: Guia Dirigido Aos Nacionais Dos Estados Parte Do Mercosul*. Mte.

Brasil. (2014). Secretaria-geral Da Presidência Da República. Antecedentes Mercosul e Unsasul. In *Debate Sobre a Participação Social Nos Processos de Integração Regional, 2014, Brasília.* Anais.

Bruera, H. G. (2015). Participation under Lula: Between electoral politics and governability. *Latin American Politics and Society, 57*(2), 1–20.

Budini, T. (2015). *Encontros Com O Mercosul: A Atuação De Organizações Da Sociedade Civil Brasileira Na Integração Regional.* Doutorado (Tese)—departamento De Ciência Política Da Universidade De São Paulo.

Carlos, E., Oliveira, O. P., & Romao, W. (2014). *Sociedade Civil e Políticas Públicas: Atores e Instituições No Brasil Contemporâneo* (1st ed.). Argos Editora Universitária.

Constitutive Protocol. (2005). *Protocolo Constitutivo do Parlamento do Mercosul.* https://www.bcb.gov.br/rex/sgt4/Ftp/CD%20Fluxograma/Tratados%20e%20Protocolos/Protocolo%20do%20Parlamento.pdf

Córdova, A. (2015). Old and new forms of civic engagement. *Latin American Politics and Society, 57*(2), 154–161.

Dahl, R. (1982). *Dilemmas of pluralist democracy.* Yale University Press.

Desiderá Neto, W. (2014). Relações Do Brasil Com A América Do Sul Após A Guerra Fria: Política Externa, Integração, Segurança E Energia. In W.A. Desiderá Neto (Org.) *O Brasil E As Novas Dimensões Da Integração Regional.* Ipea.

Dür, A., & De Bièvre, D. (2007). The question of interest group influence. *Journal of Public Policy, 27*(1), 1–12.

Ferreira, G. A. G. (2017). *Governos, Organizações Sociais do Campo e Integração Regional: Um Estudo da Reunião Especializada Sobre Agricultura Familiar do Mercosul (Reaf).* Dissertação de Mestrado. PPGRI—San Tiago Dantas.

Gardini, G. L., & Almeida, M. H. T. (2016). *Foreign policy responses to the rise of Brazil: Balancing power in emerging states.* Palgrave Macmillan.

Hoffmann, J., & Hoffmann, R. (1998). Globalização. Riscos e Oportunidades Para a Política Trabalhista na Europa. In T. Vigevani & J. Lorenzetti (Eds.), *Globalização E Integração Regional: Atitudes Sindicais E Impactos Sociais* (Vol. 1). Ltr/fapesp/cedec/escola Sul-cut. 342p.

Keck, M. E., & Sikkink, K. (1998). *Activists beyond borders: Advocacy networks in international politics.* Cornell University.

Lasker, R. D., & Guidry, J. A. (2008). *Engaging the community in decision making: Case studies tracking participation, voice and influence.* Mcfarland.

Lazarou, E., & Luciano, B. T. (2015). Regionalism as an instrument: Assessing Brazil's relations with its neighbourhood. *Global Society, 29*(3), 390–408.

Malamud, A. (2005). Presidential diplomacy and the institutional underpinnings of Mercosur. *Latin American Research Review, 40*(1), 138–164.

Mariano, K. L. P. (2001). *Integração Regional do Cone Sul: Os Partidos Políticos e as Centrais Sindicais do Brasil. 2001.* Doutorado (Tese Em Ciências Sociais)—Universidade Estadual De Campinas (Unicamp).

Mariano, K. L. P. (2011). A Eleição Parlamentar no Mercosul. *Revista Brasileira de Política Internacional, 54*(2), 138–157.

Mariano, M. (2007). *A Política Externa Brasileira, O Itamaraty eo Mercosul. 2007.* Doutorado (Tese Em Sociologia)—Universidade Estadual Paulista (Unesp).

Martins, J. R. V. (2014). Mercosul: A Dimensão Social e Participativa Da Integração Regional. In W. A. Desiderá Neto (Ed.), *O Brasil E As Novas Dimensões Da Integração Regional.* IPEA.

O'Donnell, G. (1994). Delegative democracy. *Journal of Democracy, 5*(1), 55–69.

O'Donnell, G. (2001). Reflections on contemporary South American democracies. *Journal of Latin American Studies, 33*(3), 599–609.

Peas. (2010). *Plano Estratégico de Ação Social do MERCOSUL (PEAS)* [online] https://www.mercosur.int/documento/planoestrategico-de-acao-social-do-mercosul-peas/. Accessed 29 Sept 2022.

Perrotta, D. (2016). Mercosur's regional policies in higher education: The diffusion of accreditation and quality assurance policies. In A. Ribeiro Hoffmann & A. C. Bianculli (Eds.), *Regional organizations and social policy in Europe and Latin America. A space for social citizenship?* (1st ed.). Palgrave Macmillan.

Pierson, P. (1998). The path to European integration: A historical-institutionalist analysis. In W. Sandholtz & A. S. Sweet (Eds.), *European integration and supranational governance*. Oxford University Press.

Pires, R. R. (2011). *Efetividade Das Instituições Participativas No Brasil: Estratégias De Avaliação* (Diálogos para o Desenvolvimento) (Vol. 7). IPEA.

Ramanzini Júnior, H., & Farias, R. D. S. (2014). Missão Impossível? Mercosul, Participação Social e Política Externa no Brasil. *Pensamento Próprio, 40*(19), 355–374.

Riggirozzi, P. (2016). Regionalism and health policy in South America: Tackling germs, brokering norms and contesting power. In A. Ribeiro Hoffmann & A. C. Bianculli (Eds.), *Regional organizations and social policy in Europe and Latin America. A space for social citizenship?* (1st ed.). Palgrave Macmillan.

Riggirozzi, P., & Tussie, D. (2012a). Postlude. In P. Riggirozzi & D. Tussie (Eds.), *Post-hegemonic regionalism. The case of Latin America*. Springer.

Riggirozzi, P., & Tussie, D. (2012b). *The rise of post-hegemonic regionalism: The case of Latin America*. Springer.

Romão, W. M. (2014). Os Programas De Transferência Condicionada Nos Países Andinos: Características, Avaliações E Integração Regional. In W. A. Desiderá Neto (Ed.), *O Brasil E As Novas Dimensões Da Integração Regional*. IPEA.

Santos, B. D. S. (2017). The resilience of abyssal exclusions in our societies: Toward a post-abyssal law—Montesquieu lecture. *Tilburg Law Review, 22*, 237–258.

Serbin, A. (2013). Atuando Sozinho? Governos, Sociedade Civil E Regionalismo Na América Do Sul. *Lua Nova, 90*, 297–327.

Zaremberg, G. (2014). Força, Projeto, Palavra E Povo: Circuitos De Representação em Conselhos de Desenvolvimento Municipal na América Latina (Nicarágua, Venezuela, México E Brasil). In E. Carlos, O. P. Oliveira, & W. Romao (Eds.), *Sociedade Civil e Políticas Públicas: Atores e Instituições no Brasil Contemporâneo* (1st ed.). Argos Editora Universitária.

Chapter 6
The Brazilian Economic Interests in Regional Integration: Mercosur and Latin America

6.1 Introduction

This chapter's goal is to analyze the economic aspects within the context of international transformations which influenced the Brazilian positions in relation to the regional integration processes in South America, mainly Mercosur, from the late 1980s and until 2020. From 1985, the integration of the Southern Cone took place within different external environments. Evolving from developmentalist attempts to forms of open regionalism, which were inserted within an international climate of liberal regimes. Hereafter, with the advent of developmentalist-distributivist governments, in the so-called post-hegemonic period, Latin American countries sought to enhance the different instances of integration, cooperation, and regional articulation as part of the aspirations to strengthen multilateralism, though without resorting to protectionism. From 2016, the inauguration of the Mauricio Macri government and Rousseff's impeachment eventually strengthened the movements opposed to integration, particularly in Brazil. This tendency has intensified at previously unimaginable levels with the Jair Bolsonaro administration from 2019. In 2020, a developmentalist-distributivist government returned to power in Argentina under Alberto Fernandez. In Uruguay, with the elections in November 2019, the liberal-conservative government of Luis Lacalle Pou, from the *Partido Blanco,* took office after 15 years of dominance by the *Frente Amplio.* In Paraguay, the Mario Abdo Benitez government of the *Partido Colorado* ended a period of crisis in 2018.

In this chapter, we identify the elements of continuity and change in the Brazilian behavior—encompassing the government, business sector, and civil society—in relation to Mercosur and regional integration, and how the transformations of the global environment have influenced these actors' positions. We analyze not only the economic transformations but also the political weakening of multilateralism and the accentuation of the political/economic/strategic tensions. With reference to the Alfonsín-Sarney period, particularly the years from 1985 to 1988, Carmargo

T. Vigevani, H. Ramanzini Junior, *The Challenges for Building Regional Integration in the Global South*, United Nations University Series on Regionalism 18,
https://doi.org/10.1007/978-3-030-93348-7_6

highlights that "with regards to the Brazilian business community, a relative indifference can be observed, as the commercial success of the anteceding years allowed for hopes for the increased marketing of their products within developed economies, mainly the United States" (Camargo, 2000, p. 160).

From the very beginnings of Mercosur, we can thereby see how issues which in the following decades would interfere negatively have deep roots, as would be seen in 1999 and 2001. Not least from 2016, these decisively hindered the spillover phenomenon of regional integration. These issues were also accentuated due to the influence of business sectors seeking relations with more powerful traditional partners (Araujo, 2004). The state's positions concerning the Southern Cone integration process were marked by a real interest in integration, but this interest cannot be detached from the objective of guaranteeing improved conditions for the insertion within other international arenas. To a certain degree, some of the Brazilian ambiguities in relation to Mercosur are related to the dilemmas and contradictions of the post-Cold War world, and are marked by attempts to reach hegemony and movements of systemic decompression. In contrast to the developed countries, whose economic, military, and technological power-resources guarantee them international influence,—even considering the potential risks of overextension,—the Brazilian external projection was pursued through intense participation within the political and economic, regional and multilateral forums, albeit on basis of different strategies. These were the policies of autonomy through distance, participation (Fonseca Júnior, 1998), and diversification. They were in effect until 2016 but were not completely changed during the Temer administration. This projection was based on a concern for the preservation of the country, implying on the one hand the risks of vulnerability, and on the other, the intent to increase its power, through what Pinheiro (2004) calls "institutional pragmatism". As this aspiration is common amongst all states, in the Brazilian case, it implies a positioning within diverse global and/or regional playing fields, with different positions.

We will argue that the transformations which took place within the international system,—which until the early 1980s did not present themselves as predictable scenarios,—from 1985 influenced the Brazilian perception of regional integration. Amongst them, it is worth highlighting: (1) the process of intensification of North American unilateralism during the first decade of the XXI Century; (2) the impact of the rise of China; (3) the appreciation of agricultural commodities from 2003, at least until the financial and economic crisis beginning in the second semester of 2008; (4) the restructuring of the axis of global development, particularly the role of India, Russia, and South Africa; (5) the growth in trade flows to countries which until 1990 were not relevant to Brazil; and (6) the role attributed to multilateral economic negotiations by Brazil, including during the phase immediately after the 2008 crisis, which became evident with its active participation in the financial G-20.

In the post-Cold War world until 2018, Brazil's international engagement was not,—as it until then had been—structured within the context of a polarized articulation within the international system; it took place despite the uncertainty within the contemporary international environment, seeking to attenuate the vulnerabilities and strengthen the country's opportunities. These objectives make it possible to understand, for example, the evolution of the idea of the broadening of Mercosur, and of the *União das Nações Sul-Americanas* (Unasur). Concretizing in a strategy which has been present since the last part of the 1980s, at the beginning of the 1990s, Brazil redirected its international engagement towards seeking to strengthen its position ahead of the new challenges, particularly those defined by the tendency towards the formation of regional blocs. From the point of its inception, Mercosur has been considered as the basis for the strategy of Brazilian international insertion. Despite this, as we shall see, there appears to be a certain tension between the structural needs for integration and the attitudes and positions of important social and governmental actors in Brazil. On the other hand, with the objective of avoiding the adherence to arrangements which could limit future options for the country, it is possible to observe a certain convergence,—albeit still based on different motives—between sectors adhering to a national developmentalist perspective and those connected to the liberal tradition. This understanding has a direct impact on the Brazilian positions in relation to integration.

Mercosur's institutional architecture as it was constituted in 1991 is effective, at least in a formal sense, until today (2020), and appears to attend the Brazilian elite's interests, as we saw in Chap. 4. This format is adequate to provide the support considered possible, or the desired freedom, for the country's international actions within the World Trade Organization (WTO), in the relations with the United States and with the European Union, and the commercial and financial G-20. This format permitted the country a degree of relative independence in relation to the constraints provided by a Customs Union and a Common Market, marked by a higher degree of institutionalization. An important variable which defines the Brazilian positioning regarding regional integration is the change within the global economic geography.

The difficulties related to the relative growth of trade and regional integration, in Mercosur and South America—despite some advances which took place within energy cooperation, albeit still facing certain contrasts—show that structural economic reasons persisted, which compromised this process. Paradoxically, this continued to be the case, even in moments of a higher degree of political convergence between the governments that we classify as developmentalist-distributivist.

There were nonetheless significant changes in the external environment, of which the Brazilian governments and elites appear to have been mindful. This has been evident to such a degree that these changes, as well as the country's commercial insertion, continue to weigh even within the Bolsonaro administration, whose" North", within its central core, is constituted by the complete alignment with the sphere of influence of the United States under the Trump presidency. One of the changes within the external environment was the growth of the world economy from 2001 until 2008, with special emphasis on China's role, which made business sectors and important groups within government reorient their interests. Although the political emphasis on integration was still maintained, its significance has been proportionately reduced. In the first years of the twenty-first Century, the rise in commodity prices, including oil and gas, as well as the liquidity of the financial system, together led to increases in exports, not only in Brazil but also in other countries in the region. Although it has not contributed to the efforts to reach productive and commercial regional complementarity, this positive international moment was important for regional states to maintain their economies reasonably stable.

Even the recession in central countries, which began in 2008, could suggest that a new favorable cycle to Latin American integration was about to materialize, exactly because of the contraction of the markets in central countries. The international crisis, brought about by the crash of Lehman Brothers, had been partially overcome by 2010, with the undeterred growth of the North-American and Chinese economies, which lasted until the Covid-19 pandemic. As there were no internal forces within the Mercosur countries decidedly in favor of economic integration, the international context, of either crisis or growth was not prone to productive integration. As we have mentioned, this was the case although, paradoxically, there was in fact agreement amongst political leaders with respect to its importance. In Chap. 5, we showed that the paradox was partially overcome by the accentuation of the idea of a social, participative, and cultural Mercosur. We refer to this as a "*salto in avanti*".

The relations between Argentina and Brazil,—the history of which we reviewed in Chap. 2—from 1985 to 2016 played a central role for these two countries in sustaining the integration dynamics. The strategic alliance Argentina-Brazil was signed by the Presidents Fernando Henrique Cardoso and Carlos Menem in April 1997 (Gonçalves & Lyrio, 2003). The economic crises in the relations within Mercosur, which were rooted in the non-negotiated devaluation of the Brazilian Real in 1999 and the end of the peso-dollar parity in Argentina in 2001, although still determined by serious internal financial and political crises, were significant setbacks and spurred mutual distrust which would persist. As we shall see, the economic relations between Brazil and Argentina continue to be highly important throughout time, even during the Temer period, and also during the troubled Bolsonaro administration. But they have been increasingly viewed as being of lesser relative significance. Brazilian ministers and chiefs of state have increasingly been diminishing their importance.

The capacity of actors negatively affected by foreign trade to exercise pressure is larger than that of those whom it benefits, because these generally tend to obtain diffuse and less focalized gains (Wise, 2009), as different currents within international trade theory defend. The production structures of the bloc's two most important countries did not advance towards effective forms of complementarity, in spite of what had been agreed upon within the Programme for Integration and Economic Cooperation (PICE) aiming towards productive integration, signed in July 1986 by Alfonsin and Sarney. This agreement included 14 protocols, followed by another 10 signed shortly thereafter (Brazil-Argentina ACE 14, 1990). As we have discussed in Chap. 4, the area within which perhaps the greatest progress was made was the automotive sector, to some degree even as a consequence of the initial push by developed country producers. The Treaty of Asunción, which was signed during a liberal phase, did not spur these economies to actively,—and through public stimulus,—seek complementarity; the weight which primary commodities continue to have within these two countries and the role which national political elites project for their own international insertion are elements which provide significant obstacles for the bilateral articulation. The years of developmentalist-distributivist governments were not sufficient to reestablish instruments for productive integration.

A regional integration project demands initiatives which the market by itself does not undertake. As we shall see, the history of regional integration, particularly in Argentina and Brazil, but also in Paraguay and Uruguay, shows that the behavior of the states continue to be directed towards fragmented solutions instead of integrated approaches. For example, the use of common energy resources did not lead to a strengthening of coordination. In some cases, they even paved the ground for new contentious issues: the Itaipu and Bolivian gas. On the other hand, the conflict between Argentina and Uruguay regarding the cellulose company, Botnia, can be highlighted, in which highly conflicting interests became evident concerning environmental preservation and development. Beginning in 2004, this reached its conclusion in 2010 with an arbitral decision from the International Tribunal in Hague. The financial crisis from 2010 appeared to provide opportunities for the strengthening of economic complementarities, which nevertheless did not occur. This is demonstrated by data of inter-regional trade—also understood as indices of complementarity.

The initiatives focusing on integration and cooperation do not appear to be sufficient to overcome the structural weaknesses of the countries or to insert the regional dynamics within the domestic political agendas. It is difficult to devise compensatory policies which facilitate the social adhesion to a regional bloc within processes of regional integration between developing countries. The generic affinities between governments like those of the first decade of the 2000s, have not been sufficient to deepen the integration policies. In the second part of the 2010s, the ascent of conservative governments, strictly rooted in pro-market perspectives, resulted in the deconfiguration of the regional bodies of Unasur and the weakening of Mercosur. The growing regional instability also had other consequences, such as the inability to provide support for legitimate governments (Paraguay, Bolivia, and Brazil) or to mediate in cases of strong radicalization, such as Venezuela. This happened without any new institutions arising. The *Foro para el Progreso de América del Sur* (Prosur or Fórum Prosul), a Chilean initiative of President Sebastián Piñera, which was constituted in March 2019, was created within this context (Sanahuja, 2019), with 8 South American countries. In contrast to Unasur, which englobed all the region, the Prosur is a fragmented initiative which emphasizes elements differentiating the countries (Barros & Gonçalves, 2019). It contributes to raising the regional vulnerability, particularly in relation to external actors, not least the United States, thus, making certain countries the center stage of geopolitical disputes (Bolton, 2020). The Prosur does not even contemplate any proposal for the articulation of regional capacities.

The intensification of North-American unilateralism under the Bush administration (2001–2008) did not result in the strengthening of Southern Cone integration. The agreement between the countries to oppose the FTAA initiative in Mar del Plata in 2005 was a signal of resistance, but it cannot be viewed as a regional advance. In the Brazilian case, the governments of Cardoso and Lula, particularly the last, sought to react to this unilateralism by adopting policies through international articulation focused on the large emerging countries. In the case of China, as we shall see, the existing commercial potential was highly significant, and benefitted Brazil for more than a decade as the most important anchor for trade, and hereafter, investment. The same happened to Argentina, Chile, and other countries within the region. In the cases of Russia, India, and South Africa, apart from the efforts made towards economic and trade cooperation, quintessentially political factors were also highly relevant. Great efforts were directed towards the European Union, Japan, the Middle East, and Africa. Mercosur, even as it was considered a fundamental pillar within the country's external engagement,—being a tariff union—was not adequately directed towards the objective of contributing to multilateralism. According to the Brazilian perception, which was expressed within international forums such as the UN, the WTO, the commercial G-20, the national capacity is considered as the most decisive and apt to produce results that help overcome unilateralism.

6.2 Changes and Continuity within Brazilian Positions in Relation to Mercosur

In the twenty-first century, Brazil's international insertion took place within a context in which the parameters constantly changed; this movement affected all states, and the reaction in relation to it is marked by some specific features. The North American centrality was put into question (Waltz, 2000), and this situation has had implications for the Brazilian policy, also concerning Brazil's and Mercosur's positions (Amorim, 2015), but not exclusively so. In this section of the chapter, we briefly review Mercosur's development and discuss the changes and continuity within the Brazilian position in relation to the bloc, considering domestic and international factors which molded their positions.

During a large part of the period of the so-called "defined polarities", or rather, the Cold War (1946–1989), Brazil's international positions generally resisted the consolidation of international institutions and regimes, based on the consideration that these would lock in the existing power relations. One of the formulators of this position was Araújo Castro (1982), as we saw in Chap. 3. From the 1980s, at the height of the external debt crisis, the elevated inflation, and the economic stagnation, the debate within parts of the Brazilian elites about rethinking the country's development model was accentuated. In the late 1980s and early 1990s, the perception that Brazil should assume a more participative position regarding the large international questions gained ground. The pathway chosen by Brazilian foreign policy formulators to guarantee a more dense international insertion in the post-Cold War world was the aspiration towards a higher degree of participation within international organizations and regimes, and the adoption of initiatives aiming towards international integration (Fonseca Júnior, 1998).

At the time of the approximation between Brazil and Argentina in the middle of the 1980s, there was an overlap between the idea of regional integration, the alliance

Table 6.1 Geographic, social, demographic and economic data of Mercosur members in 2018

Country	Area (sq km)	HDI (#189)	Population (million)	Nominal GDP (billions of USD)
Argentina	2,780,400	0.83 (#48)	44.560	519.49
Brazil	8,515,770	0.761 (#79)	208.495	1867.82
Paraguay	406,752	0.724 (#98)	7.053	41.85
Uruguay	176,215	0.808 (#57)	3.506	59.65
Country	GDP PPP (billions of USD)	Nominal GDP PC (USD correntes)	GDP PC PPP (USD internacionais)	
Argentina	915.75	11,658.22	20,551.04	
Brazil	3366.38	8958.58	16,146.09	
Paraguay	94.51	5934.18	13,399.77	
Uruguay	81.19	17,014.13	23,157.97	

Source: CIA (2019); UN (2019); IMP (2019). Author's elaboration

with Argentina, and the preservation of the values of universalism and autonomy. Regionalism would not diminish, but rather strengthen the universalist paradigm for Brazil's international insertion. This was important for the integration process between Brazil and Argentina, and hereafter, for the insertion of Paraguay and Uruguay, and the perception of the risk of isolation as a consequence of the end of the Cold War (Moreira, 1989) and the recognition that the country's internal weaknesses would constrain their external positions. In this regard, Onuki (1996) argues that the creation of Mercosur represents an attempt to reformulate the strategic interests of the countries in the Southern Cone within a changing international environment.

An initial relevant question when we analyze Mercosur and the Brazilian foreign policy relates to the fact that the regional integration process involves four countries with very distinct characteristics, despite all of them being developing countries. As we can observe from Table 6.1 below, Brazil is by far the country with the largest territorial dimension. The same is the case with regards to the population size. Yet, if we observe the indicators for human development, or the GDP/purchasing power parity, within this perspective, Uruguay and Argentina are richer than Brazil. This presents a very delicate structural situation for Mercosur, as the expectations of assuming a part of the costs of integration and contributing to the development of the other members of the bloc which the neighboring countries manifest concerning Brazil encounter certain difficulties in materializing. In other words, as it repeatedly would prove to be the case already from the Itamar Franco and Cardoso governments from 1993 and onwards, and after the creation of Unasur in 2008, the expectation of Brazil becoming a regional paymaster (Mattli, 1999; Mariano, 2015) was frustrated. This is also due to the fact that domestically in Brazil, this is a sensitive political question for governments to justify the allocation of resources to the Mercosur countries when these states score higher than Brazil on important indicators.

In the 1990s, even as governments in this period maintained their commitments to regional integration, the issue of development within the integration agenda lost some importance due to the corporate and sub-regional domestic resistance. The data in Table 6.1 clearly show the radical differences between the national GDP, and the GDP PC PPP. This refers to the weight of each country's economy and the living standards of its citizens, which helps to explain the weakening of the so-called bicycle movement, which, viewed through a strictly functionalist perspective, results in a low spillover effect,—not least for Brazil.

The discrediting of the neoliberal development models within the countries in the region which became visible from 2000, and more accentuated with the financial and economic crisis of 2008, presented the possibility for this trend to change,—a situation which is analyzed in Chap. 4. In the case of Brazil until 2016, it becomes possible to think of the resurgence—albeit somewhat complicated,—of the perspective that development is favored by the integration process. At the seventh extraordinary Mercosur Council Meeting, which did not produce concrete results due to the financial crisis of 2008, Foreign Minister Celso Amorim declared that "the solution to the crisis is more integration, more trade, fewer subsidies, and less distortion" (Gazeta Mercantil, 28/10/2008).

With the devaluation of the Real in 1999 and the following recession in Argentina in 2001, the Mercosur underwent a crisis, the repercussions of which were not immediately evident. Beyond the conjunctural elements, which were expressed through recurrent commercial and political disputes, as well as the absence of regional institutional mechanisms which could guarantee the continuance of the integration dynamic, structural questions, related to the economies of the developed countries and the values embedded within the states and societies should also be considered in the search for consistent explanations. Concerning Brazil, we discussed the country's historical relation to its neighbors, not least in the *Rio de la Plata* basin, in Chaps. 2 and 3.

From 1996 to 1997, a period in which specific commercial problems combined with significant misunderstandings about international insertion, the sectors which believed that Mercosur would narrow Brazil's universalist vocation gained traction, such as the Federation of Industries of the State of São Paulo (FIESP), the National Confederation of Industries (CNI), different sectorial entities representing agribusiness, and high-ranking officials as well as individuals from the press. At that moment, the apparent advances of the negotiations for the initiation of the creation of the Free Trade Areas of the Americas (FTAA), the negotiations for the beginning of a new round of in the WTO, which concretized in the Doha Conference in November 2001, and the beginning of discussions—which later would gain momentum—about the role of large non-central countries, which later would be known as the BRICS (Brazil, Russia, India, China and South Africa) all jointly worked to spur a redefinition of the role of regional integration. All of these negotiations or orientations should not necessarily weaken Mercosur, but this eventually did happen, because the idea of regional integration was not assimilated with the necessary depth by Brazilian elites at large.

In parts of Brazilian society, there was a reduced interest and, in some cases, an openly negative posture in relation to Mercosur and its possible deepening. It is important to keep in mind, for example, that the meeting which took place in November 2004, which brought together businessmen from different sectors and entities such as FIESP, Abicalçados (the Brazilian Association of Footwear Producers), Eletros (the National Association of Electrical Products Fabricants) and the Brazilian Association for Foreign Trade (AEB), proved to be somewhat negatively inclined towards this regional bloc. The discussions revolved around the idea of defending taking "a step backwards" in relation to Mercosur: within the business environment, discussions focused on the need to fall back from what was considered an imperfect customs union, towards a free trade area. According to the group, Mercosur would be an anchor which constrained Brazil within international negotiations, thus, obstructing bilateral agreements with the United States and the European Union (Valor Econômico, 16/11/2004). The analyses which result from the preoccupations of part of the business community confirm the tendency to reduce the significance of integration for Brazil and the role which Mercosur plays within the foreign policy as a reference for the international economic and commercial strategy. In general, these analyses reiterate how Mercosur and South American integration hindered a higher degree of external dynamism of Brazil. Even as the government supported regional integration,—a clear objective pursued by both the Lula government and later during the Rousseff period,—the commercial integration displayed increasing difficulties in advancing, as we shall see in the tables below. Through the universalist and the global trader perspectives, the main focal point should be the central countries, given their diversified economies and a strong import capacity for sophisticated goods and raw materials and agricultural products. Fonseca and Marconini (2006, p. 87) state that: "it would be highly recommendable if the Brazilian authorities in a near-future had the realistic audacity to change Mercosur, extinguishing the increasingly problematic regime of the customs union, in order to become a free-trade area".

The potential perspective of large-scale economic gains, which some believed could be strongly stimulated through the access to major markets, led to the reappreciation of issues related to autonomy and universalism, which never had been completely abandoned, and now had gained a more restrictive significance regarding Mercosur. For elites assuming that position at the time, this meant a stronger relationship with the United States, the European Union, and, with regards to agribusiness, also China. Still, during the Lula government, these interests and pressures explain Brazil's difficulties to position itself as a paymaster. This points to a clear gap between governmental interests and effectively pursued policies.

The overlap between the idea of regional integration, the alliance with Argentina, and the preservation of values of universalism and autonomy which, as we have highlighted, was significant concerning important actors in the second half of the 1980s and the beginning of the 1990s, did not disappear, but was reduced. The declaration which defined the partnership between the two states as a strategy, in 1997, has revealed an interest in this overlap. From 1999 to 2001, old and new arguments were resuscitated, at least in form of justifications: the small dimension of the regional market, the instability in the countries, the potential attraction of rich countries, particularly the United States, and a certain feeling, albeit diffuse, of distrust in relation to Brazil on behalf of the other three members of the bloc. Yet, the strongest argument, as we here emphasize, was the need to guarantee freedom for the government to act within the international system. On this level, only the relationship with the European Union appears to work in the opposite direction, considering the decision of this Union to negotiate with Mercosur as a bloc and not separately with each country. Even so, from July 2007, with the signature of the "Strategic Partnership" between the EU and Brazil, signals of potential autonomous advances on behalf of Brazil in relation to this interlocutor appeared to emerge (Saraiva, 2018).

Therefore, within the Brazilian foreign policy perspective, seen in retrospect, Mercosur surged and developed in a clearly ambiguous manner, which is not essentially different in the Argentinean case (Onuki, 1996). Within a Brazilian foreign policy perspective, at the top of international priorities, where universalism,—understood as multilateralism and the tightening of relations with all states, remains,—Mercosur was presented as a very important instrument, but still as an instrument. There was not any clear specificity of the integration, and it was not seen as a goal in itself. Yet, at the moment at which Mercosur was constituted, its respective governments explicated it. Resuming part of the analysis from Chap. 4, the predominant vision was that of competitive global insertion for which the bloc would constitute a highly interesting platform (Ministério das Relações Exteriores, 1991). That is, the bloc aimed towards international insertion; from the very beginning, the question of identity was secondary.

We can say that since the early 1990s, the idea of autonomy becomes manifest within Brazil's relations with its close proximity, Mercosur and South America, in form of an insistence upon the revaluation of the potential for specific national initiative, which is free from the constraints which institutionalized regional integration could entail. Almeida (1993, p. 138) considers that "common sense would recommend the implementation of a supranationality strictly limited to the functioning of a plain customs union. In any case, there is no reason to reproduce an enormous communitarian bureaucracy as it was constituted throughout many years within the European Community, in Mercosur, a truly interventionist 'eurocracy', usurping part of the national competency of member states".

The protagonist and universalist aspirations of the Brazilian elites, which vary according to the dynamics within the international system at any given moment, imply the need to be free to act resourcefully within the external environment, without conditioning or restrictive agreements, mainly from a regional platform. The worldviews and actions of a part of the elites, just as it is the case with the significance of concepts of autonomy and universalism, influence the dynamics of regional integration. It is true that throughout the past years, we have been able to observe positions focused upon the search for special advantages also within other countries, in Argentina (Escude, 2004), Uruguay, and Paraguay. As they gradually change, distancing themselves from Mercosur, they open the road for a deepening of special relations, mainly with the United States. Today, we know that this evolution took place mainly on basis of the destabilization of the Dilma Rousseff government upon her tight victory in the elections in October 2014. It was further deepened during the Temer administration, and not least during the policy of unconditional alignment under the Bolsonaro administration with the office of Minister of Foreign

Relations attributed to Ernesto Araujo (2017). The perception that the increased deepening of the bloc implies a reevaluation of sovereignty and autonomy, thus at least partially, Brazil's relation to the world has always been present and was an important motivating factor on behalf of the state and society. Limiting Mercosur, commitments that could obstruct Brazil's international room of maneuver, or contradict the desire for autonomy and universalist actions, were firmly rejected.

From the beginning of the 1990s until 2014, there was a strengthening of the universalist paradigm within Brazilian foreign policy, which is related to the understanding of the permissibilities of the international system for the country's international projection. In line with the concept of autonomy through participation, the initiatives aimed at reaching a higher degree of active international insertion of Brazil were intensified. This happened through the intense participation in various international organizations, in the Peace Missions organized by the United Nations,—as is exemplified by the case of Haiti—through the aspirations towards a permanent seat within the UN Security Council, within the articulation of multilateral coalitions like the commercial G-20 during the Doha Round within the WTO, within the group India, Brazil, South Africa (IBSA), and in the BRICS.

An aspect of Brazilian foreign policy during the developmentalist-distributivist period with anteceding roots was the attempt to guarantee a minimal cohesion within Mercosur to use the integration as a platform for its international insertion (Mariano, 2015). In the same way, as we shall see in Chap. 7, using Mercosur as a strategic basis for South American integration has also been an important component within the country's regional positioning, including the need to maintain an essentially intergovernmental institutional apparatus, which would guarantee the possibility for the entry of new members. The efforts of integration within South America demonstrated that there was a South American dimension to the Brazilian state; on the other hand, it encompassed the search for alternative solutions, although still presented as complementary to a profound regional integration process and a common market in the Southern Cone, with the consequences and the commitments which this would imply. The position of varying Brazilian governments from 1986 to 2016 of seeking a continuous and low-intensity engagement within regional integration, appears to attend the general expectations of elites, both within and outside the Brazilian state. Even with the radical changes introduced within the foreign policy from 2016, but mainly after 2019, the positioning of Brazilian business elites did not change completely, as we shall see from the postures of the Confederação Nacional de Indústria (CNI) (2020), which during the Bolsonaro administration defended the continuity of Mercosur due to the advantages which this would imply for certain Brazilian industrial sectors.

6.3 International Changes from 2008 and Their Consequences for Mercosur

Since the beginning of the 1990s, an understanding became increasingly consolidated amongst Brazilian foreign policy-makers and operators, that the maintenance of the Brazilian room of maneuver within the international system depended mainly on the country's capacity to project itself, and at the same time, be recognized as an influential actor in directing the main themes within the international agenda. This understanding encompasses both liberal as well as national developmental sectors (Barbosa, 1996; Cervo, 2006). In contrast to the developed countries, whose economic and military power resources already guarantee them international influence, the Brazilian external projection and the country's capacity to pursue its preferences within international decision-making forums could only be reasonably guaranteed through the participation in diverse political, economic, regional, and multilateral forums (Narlikar, 2003). Within this context, the establishment of coalitions that increase the country's capacity to project influence within the international system and strengthen the universalist character of Brazilian foreign policy was a central objective. Through an overview of the international agency of the first Lula government (2003–2006), Celso Amorim evaluates that this influence was effective. "Without any false modesty, I would say that Brazil changed the dynamic of the negotiations in the WTO. It was not only Brazil. But Brazil led the G-20 and it has been approached—I would even say courted—by the United States, the European Union, Japan, as well as other countries (Gazeta Mercantil, 19/10/2006).

The weight attributed to the multilateral negotiations within the WTO, just like the movements made by the United States, at least since the 1990s, in the direction of deepening the discussions about hemispherical integration, or effectuating bilateral agreements with countries within the region, in particular Mercosur, were important exogenous factors which defined the Brazilian positions in relation the regional bloc in the Southern Cone. As Mello (2000) argues, in the 1990s, the North American aim of advancing towards hemispheric integration resulted in the strengthening of the Brazilian commitment to Mercosur. This commitment, though, was not sufficient to sustain the deepening of the integration process. After the conference of chiefs of state and governments of the Americas in Mar del Plata in 2005, where there was a convergence around a postponement *sine die* of the FTAA negotiations, Mercosur saw a reduction in its significance as a bargaining instrument in relation to the United States. This can be proved by the difficulties of coordinating policies during the WTO negotiations, including in the important meeting in Geneve in July 2008. Referring to this, President Lula affirms that, "there was no divergence of concepts". Yet, he recognizes that often, at critical moments, the national interest prevails within the government's decisions: "try to understand, as much as you may work in favor of a process of regional integration, be this within the European Union or South America, or in Asia, at certain moments you have to consider your own nation's situation. In our circumstances, we should not see situations of conflict, but situations of differences; economic differences, and differences related to industrial potential" (Clarín, 7/9/2008).

In order to understand the evolution of the Brazilian position within the process of regional integration and regarding Mercosur, it becomes necessary to consider the grand international transformations that influence states. On one hand, as it was made clearly evident by the financial crisis in 2008, there was a reduction in the North American economic capacity; on the other, the significance of other countries and regions grew, something which became evident regarding all the countries, including those in South America. The extraordinary growth of China and Asia was a factor of great significance, the dimensions of which were not completely visible at the beginning of the 1990s. Since 1985, when the approximation between Brazil and Argentina took place, or from 1991, with the creation of the Mercosur, the international political and economic geography has undergone profound changes. Waltz (2000, p. 30, 32) states that "Theory enables one to say that a new balance of power will form but not to say how long it will take [. . .] the all-but-inevitable movement from unipolarity to multipolarity is taking place not in Europe but in Asia."

The restructuring of world power (Valasco & Cruz, 2007) in the 2000s, with the development focused on non-central countries as, beyond China, the roles of India, Russia, and South Africa demonstrate, as well as the relative changes in the flows of Brazilian foreign trade, were events that contributed to the process of regional integration gaining a smaller relative weight within the projects of external insertion of the Brazilian elites and state. Both within the liberal as well as the national developmentalist perspective, Mercosur continues to be important as a base for the Brazilian policy, but the focus of interest was reoriented and the business and governmental initiatives concentrated on other matters. According to Guimarães (2006, p. 275) "it is highly necessary to work in a consistent and persistent manner towards the emergence of a multipolar world system in which South America would constitute one of the poles, by not merely being a sub-region of any other given economic or political pole".

One of the important factors that explain this reorientation can be clearly illustrated. It regards the changes that occurred within the country's foreign trade. In the period from 1994 to 1998, and from 2006 to 2010, as we saw in Chap. 4, the evolution of the intra-bloc trade was highly significant. On the Brazilian side, the exports to the countries that would constitute Mercosur, which in 1985 represented 3,86% of the total, would represent 17,37% in 1998. During the same period, imports evolved from 4,88% to 15,19% (ECLAC, 2003). Beyond the obvious importance of this evolution, the quality of the Brazilian intra-zone trade was favorable, as the presence of services and higher value-added products was highly beneficial, as we shall see below.

The (Figs. 6.1 and 6.2) and the (Tables 6.2 and 6.3) below demonstrate the changes occurring in the structure of the Brazilian foreign trade from 1991 to 2019; within these, we present the evolutions of the imports and exports and the percentage represented by Mercosur.

As it is possible to verify from the data above, in 1991, the Brazilian exports to other Mercosur countries represented 7.29% of the total. In 1998, this percentage

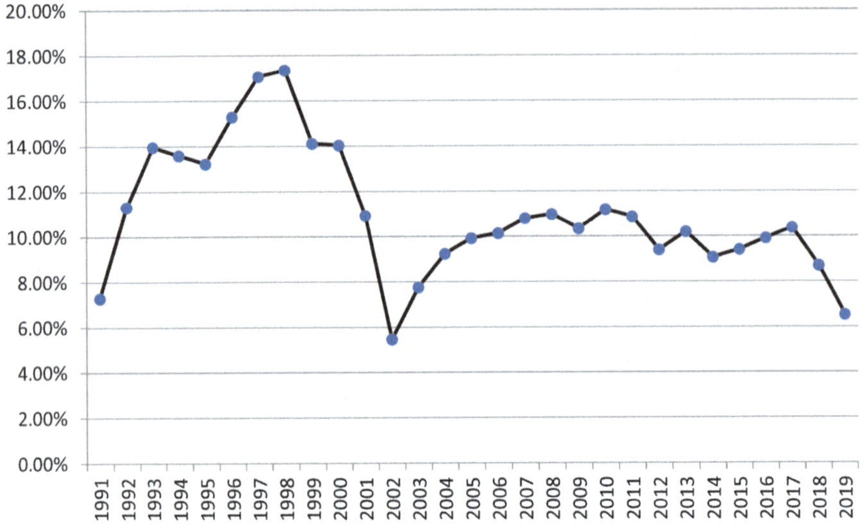

Fig. 6.1 Share of Mercosur in Brazilian exports. Source: MDIC (2020)

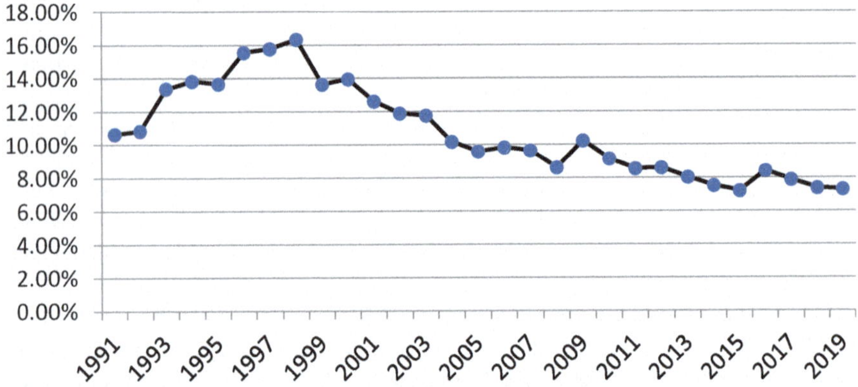

Fig. 6.2 Share of Mercosur within Brazilian imports. Source: MDIC (2020) and Central Bank of Brazil (2020)

reached 17.37%. In 2002, not least due to the crisis in Argentina in 2001, this percentage fell to 5.48%. In the following years, this growth was resumed, until reaching the level of 11.19% in 2010. In the second decade of the 2000s, the general tendency has been one of a decrease in the weight of Mercosur in the percentage of Brazilian exports. In 2011, the exports to the countries of Mercosur represented 10.88%. In 2019, this value had declined to 6.54% and thereby reached a lower level than that verified at the establishment of Mercosur.

With regards to imports, as we shall see below, in 1991, the Brazilian imports from Mercosur countries represented 10.66% of the total value of Brazilian imports.

Table 6.2 Share of Mercosur in Brazil's exports

Share of Mercosur in Brazilian's exports					
Year	Share	Year	Share	Year	Share
1991	7.29%	2001	10.93%	2011	10.88%
1992	11.32%	2002	5.48%	2012	9.41%
1993	13.97%	2003	7.77%	2013	10.20%
1994	13.60%	2004	9.25%	2014	9.07%
1995	13.23%	2005	9.93%	2015	9.42%
1996	15.30%	2006	10.15%	2016	9.92%
1997	17.08%	2007	10.81%	2017	10.39%
1998	17.37%	2008	10.99%	2018	8.71%
1999	14.13%	2009	10.35%	2019	6.54%
2000	14.05%	2010	11.19%		

Source: MDIC (2020). Author'selaboration

Table 6.3 Share of Mercosur within Brazilian imports

Year	Share	Year	Share	Year	Share
1991	10.66%	2001	12.63%	2011	8.56%
1992	10.84%	2002	11.90%	2012	8.61%
1993	13.38%	2003	11.78%	2013	8.04%
1994	13.86%	2004	10.18%	2014	7.54%
1995	13.70%	2005	9.60%	2015	7.22%
1996	15.56%	2006	9.83%	2016	8.43%
1997	15.79%	2007	9.65%	2017	7.89%
1998	16.34%	2008	8.63%	2018	7.38%
1999	13.66%	2009	10.26%	2019	7.31%
2000	13.97%	2010	9.14%		

Source: MDIC (2020) and Central Bank of Brazil (2020). Author's elaboration

In 1998, the percentage reached a level of 16.34%, the highest value during all of the period from 1991 to 2019. In 2002, the Brazilian imports from its Mercosur partners represented 11.90%, and in 2010, the last year of the Lula Government, these had fallen to 9.14%. In similarity to what had happened with exports, during the second decade of the 2000s, the imports from Mercosur countries present a general tendency of decline, although less accentuated than the trajectory of exports. In 2011, of the total value of Brazilian imports, 8.56% derived from Mercosur. In 2019, this percentage was reduced to 7.31%. In 1991, 10.66% of Brazilian imports had their origin in the other three Mercosur countries.

Analyzing the Brazilian foreign trade through a broader perspective, according to Fig. 6.3 and Table 6.4 below, strong changes can be observed, mainly spurred on by the role of China. In 1991, China represented 0.7% of total Brazilian exports. In 2000, this number reached 2.0%, and in 2010 increased to 15.2%, and in 2018 reached 26.8%. In 1991, the United States accounted for 20.2%, and for 9.6% in 2010. In 2018, the exports to the United States' represented 12.2% of total Brazilian exports. In 1991, Latin America, excluding the Mercosur countries represented 8.8%

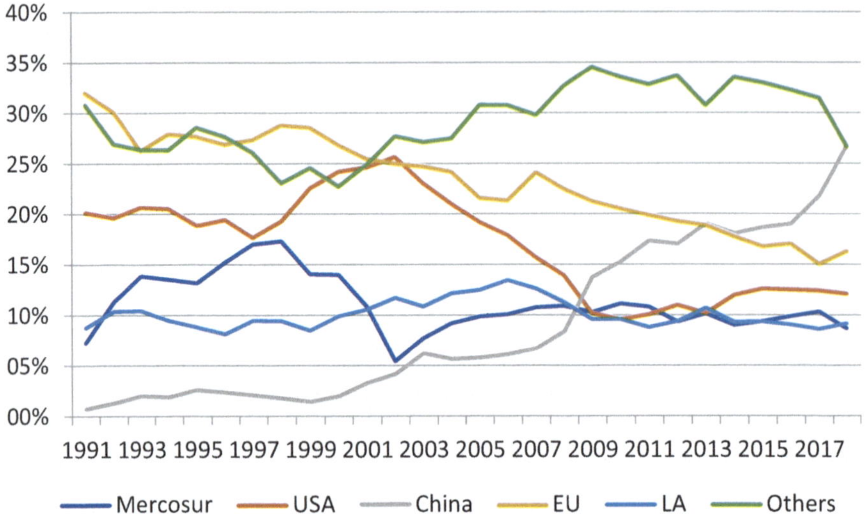

Fig. 6.3 Share of countries and blocs in Brazilian exports. Source: Comtrade (2022)

Table 6.4 Share of countries and blocs in Brazilian exports

Year	Mercosur	USA	China	EU	LA	Others
1991	7.3%	20.2%	0.7%	32.1%	8.8%	30.9%
1995	13.2%	18.9%	2.6%	27.8%	8.9%	28.6%
2000	14.0%	24.3%	2.0%	26.9%	10.0%	22.8%
2005	9.9%	19.2%	5.8%	21.7%	12.5%	30.8%
2010	11.2%	9.6%	15.2%	20.6%	9.7%	33.6%
2015	9.4%	12.7%	18.6%	16.9%	9.4%	33.0%
2018	8.7%	12.2%	26.8%	16.4%	9.2%	26.7%

Source: Comtrade (2022). Author's elaboration

of Brazilian exports. In 2010, these had reached 9.7% and in 2018 accounted for 9.2% of total Brazilian exports. The EU countries which represented 32.1% in 1991, rose to 26.9% in 2000 and in 2018 represented 16.4% of total Brazilian exports.

Of total Brazilian imports, as we shall see in Table 6.5 and Fig. 6.4, in 1991 the United States represented 23.5%, while China accounted for 0.3%. In 2000, the United States represented 23.3% of Brazilian imports and China some 2.2%. In 2010, the United States represented 15% and China 14.1%. Finally, in 2018, the United States represented 16.2% and China 19.2%. In other words, throughout time, even considering imports, China did also become the most important country of origin for Brazil. Latin America maintained a relatively similar position during all of the period, representing around 7% of total Brazilian imports.

The factors which define international insertion are many, with special emphasis on: flows of capital, technology, values, culture, and power relations. Trade is one of the factors of central importance, and the relatively diversified

Table 6.5 Share of countries and blocs in Brazilian imports

Year	Mercosur	USA	China	EU	LA	Others
1991	10.5%	23.5%	0.3%	23.5%	7.2%	34.9%
1995	13.5%	23.7%	0.8%	27.9%	6.9%	27.2%
2000	14.0%	23.3%	2.2%	25.2%	7.0%	28.3%
2005	9.6%	17.5%	7.3%	23.9%	6.3%	35.5%
2010	9.1%	15.0%	14.1%	20.6%	7.5%	33.7%
2015	7.2%	15.6%	17.9%	20.2%	8.0%	31.1%
2018	7.4%	16.2%	19.2%	18.1%	7.7%	31.5%

Source: Comtrade (2022). Author's elaboration

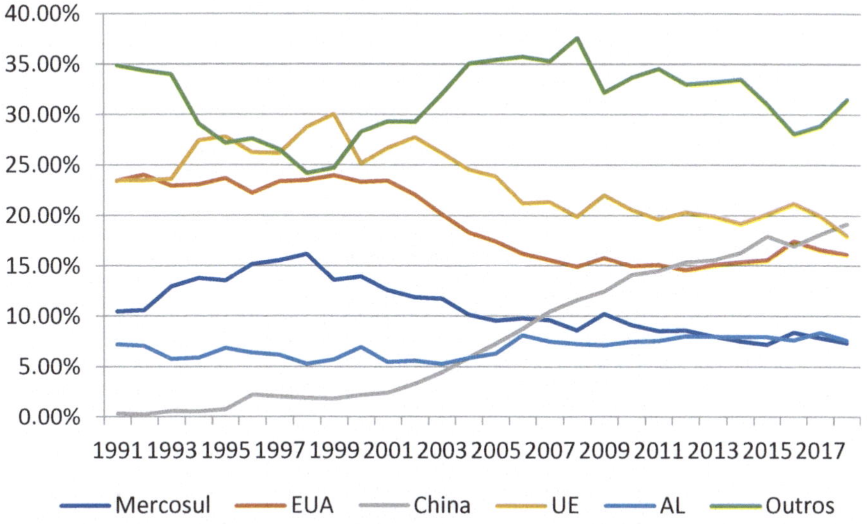

Fig. 6.4 Share of countries and blocs in Brazilian imports. Source: Comtrade (2022)

destinations and origins of Brazilian foreign trade tend to support the universalist arguments in relation to the country's foreign policy. This diversification also occurs in Argentina, where primary commodities have even more pronounced importance. Brazil's main trading partner in 2000 was the United States, accounting for 23.92% of exports and 23.09% of imports. The second partner was Argentina with 11.32% of exports and 12.26% of imports. As we can see below (Tables 6.6 and 6.7), China was not even in the top ten. Yet, by 2010, China became the main export destination and the second-largest origin of Brazilian imports, with Argentina as third. In 2019, China came in as first within the two rankings of both imports and exports with the United States as second.

The trade with Argentina, and more generally, with Mercosur, which was resumed after the urgent crisis between 1999 and 2002 did never reach its relative spike from 1998. As it can be seen in the Figs. 5.1 and 5.2, the trade relations with Mercosur were partially recovered after 2002, but their relative significance has not

Table 6.6 Top ten destinations of Brazilian exports in Brazilian exports in 2000, 2010 and 2019 in absolute values (US$) and relative share (%)

Top ten destinations of Brazilian exports in 2000, 2010 and 2019 in absolute values (US$) and relative share (%)											
	Country	2000 (USD)	%		Country	2010 (USD)	%		Country	2019 (USD)	%
1	USA	13,160,699,765	23.92	1	China	30,747,553,704	15.24	1	China	63,357,520,588	28.11
2	Argentina	6,229,543,769	11.32	2	USA	19,300,906,943	9.56	2	USA	29,715,863,527	13.18
3	Netherlands	2,794,779,576	5.08	3	Argentina	18,507,273,060	9.17	3	Netherlands	10,125,900,763	4.49
4	Germany	2,524,701,057	4.59	4	Netherlands	10,225,857,321	5.07	4	Argentina	9,791,474,547	4.34
5	Japan	2,471,254,287	4.49	5	Germany	8,134,386,646	4.03	5	Japan	5,431,769,382	2.41
6	Italy	2,142,988,525	3.90	6	Japan	7,140,402,276	3.54	6	Chile	5,162,879,630	2.29
7	Belgium	1,778,417,889	3.23	7	UK	4,625,093,694	2.29	7	Mexico	4,898,455,548	2.17
8	France	1,729,729,489	3.14	8	Chile	4,256,776,051	2.11	8	Germany	4,731,497,703	2.10
9	Mexico	1,709,783,257	3.11	9	Italy	4,232,361,792	2.10	9	Spain	4,042,567,106	1.79
10	UK	1,496,503,491	2.72	10	Russia	4,147,690,633	2.06	10	South Korea	3,449,684,302	1.53

Source: Samurio et al. (2019) for 2000 and 2010 and MDIC for 2019

Table 6.7 Top ten origins of Brazilian imports in 2000, 2010 and 2019 in absolute values (US$) and relative share (%)

	Country	2000 (USD)	%		Country	2010 (USD)	%		Country	2019 (USD)	%
1	USA	12,906,099,243	23.09	1	USA	27,038,687,487	15.24	1	China	35,270,816,762	19.89
2	Argentina	6,849,829,801	12.26	2	China	25,591,460,070	9.56	2	USA	30,090,157,711	16.97
3	Germany	4,445,211,380	7.95	3	Argentina	14,433,416,651	9.17	3	Argentina	10,552,232,182	5.95
4	Japan	2,970,860,904	5.32	4	Germany	12,553,495,025	5.07	4	Germany	10,280,263,597	5.80
5	Italy	2,171,362,283	3.88	5	South Korea	8,425,993,375	4.03	5	South Korea	4,705,681,345	2.65
6	France	1,858,380,051	3.33	6	Japan	6,979,711,623	3.54	6	India	4,257,612,842	2.40
7	Algeria	1,508,469,854	2.70	7	Nigeria	5,925,152,202	2.29	7	Mexico	4,196,694,599	2.37
8	South Korea	1,439,468,186	2.58	8	Italy	4,837,793,744	2.11	8	Japan	4,094,098,846	2.31
9	Venezuela	1,327,901,894	2.38	9	France	4,800,675,893	2.10	9	Italy	4,041,399,190	2.28
10	UK	1,223,307,927	2.19	10	India	4,243,145,061	2.06	10	Russia	3,680,499,839	2.08

Source: Samurio, Barros and Severo (2019) for 2000 and 2010 and MDIC for 2019

regained its importance from the 1990s. With this situation in mind, it becomes important to note, as we have already highlighted, that the region's contribution to the Brazilian trade surplus is significant. It is even more important to remember that this regards products of a higher added value. Even so, there is a decrease in the regional bloc's market share within Brazil's trade relations, as the main growth of Brazilian trade can be detected with regards to the countries which import commodities, with special emphasis on China. The internal debate regarding deindustrialization,—which in 2020 remains in a deadlock, without any viable answer at hand,—is strengthened by this situation.

The growth in the world economy from 2001—with special emphasis on the role of China and Asia-, the importance attributed to the WTO negotiations by Brazil, and the use of this organization to strengthen its positions, as well as the rise in commodity prices since 2003 (Prates, 2006) are all factors which made business sectors and important groups within government seek to reorient their focus and interests. The Brazilian behavior in relation to the financial and economic crisis of 2008 suggests that the emphasis on the aspiration towards a multipolar world system and the end of unilateralism rests in the perception that a maximization of capacities occurs through participation in diverse political and economic, regional and multilateral forums. This is demonstrated by the dynamism of the Brazilian engagement in the financial G-20, along with the difficulties of regional political coordination. Towards the end of the financial G-20 summit about the world economy and financial markets, which took place in Washington in November 2008, President Lula da Silva concluded that "the fact of the matter is, that through political strength, through the representation of the countries that were inserted within the G-20, I believe that there no longer is any sense in making decisions about economy and politics without considering this forum today (Gazeta Mercantil, 17/11/2008). The Brazilian government's expectations regarding international negotiations hereby become clearly evident.

The expectation was that the emphasis on universalism could generate positive externalities in terms of convergence of positions, both within multilateral and regional forums, but this was only partially fulfilled. Albuquerque (2007) observes that, in the transition from the Cold War towards an emerging global order, the decoupling between political and military supremacy and economic competitiveness changes the foreign policy options into a complex calculus, given that the trade and financial alliances do not necessarily coincide with the political convergences. Mercosur and Unasur, and the relations with the associated countries, would be strengthened as a consequence of the end of unilateralism and by the affirmation of multilateralism. The Brazilian policy maintained a strong regional interest until 2016, but its deepening, in particular with regards to Mercosur, is related to the global environment, which constitutes an important factor for its promotion. From that year, the global environment underwent a sharp shift towards unilateralism, which was accentuated with the inauguration of the Trump administration in January 2017, whose hemispheric orientation was based on the reinsertion of the countries considered as dissidents within the system led by the United States. From this point and onwards, the dominant trend was that of a weakening of the regional bodies. In the case of Unasur, this spelled its *de facto* termination, albeit not formally. The intertwinement between domestic and foreign policy became increasingly evident, even considering the asymmetry between states (Walt, 2020).

As we have now grasped the general lines and perceptions that structure Brazilian policy in relation to regional integration, it becomes important to explain the political significance of the relations with China, as these are both economically and commercially important for the entire region. According to Vadell (2008), this country's weight within South American investments and trade has changed national actors' expectations, which could be understood from the shifts in the orientation of Brazilian foreign trade. A similar phenomenon occurred in Argentina and other countries. León-Manríquez (2006) considers how all countries have created elevated expectations and begun to view China as an important alternative for national development. The type of economic relationship which has been practiced has also led to a certain perplexity. Vadell (2008) underscores the need to consider the risk of the consolidation of a productive specialization in the molds of Centre-Periphery relations. These risks can arise both in a situation of global growth, and particularly within China, due to its enormous need to acquire commodities, but can also materialize in a situation of global recession, as that which appeared from 2008. This negative development occurred in the United States only in 2008 and 2009, and in the European Union in 2009 and 2012. Anti-cyclical measures, part of which are internationally determined,—at a moment in which the financial G-20 gained a strong momentum—help to avert recession. This was possible due to the role of multilateralism. Important Brazilian business sectors, such as Abicalçados (the Brazilian Association of Footwear Producers), Furniture (Abimóvel), and Clothing (Sindivestuário) feared a movement from Asia in search of new markets for their products due to what was thought to result from a possible economic deacceleration and a fall in demand within developed countries (Gazeta Mercantil, 21/11/2008). A similar situation, which also could lead to a type of Centre-Periphery specialization,—as we had read in Table 6.8 occurred in Chile and Uruguay,—did also take place in Argentina, although on a much smaller scale, spurring protectionism with potential consequences for Mercosur. Although it did not become a systemic recession, like the one that took place in 1929, at this moment the reaction from the industrial sector did not lead to a push for modernization and a higher degree of competitiveness, but rather a search for protectionist solutions. Paradoxically, at the same time, these business sectors also sought a higher degree of insertion,—albeit subaltern—within the so-called global value chains.

Even faced with the risks of a reprimarization of the Brazilian economy, the opportunities which the relations with China provided for business or social groups fostered a dynamic which did not directly converge with regional integration, as its benefits did not depend on regional productive complementarity. In some cases, the surpluses from the trade with China, which according to Godio (2006) had become increasingly important for Argentina, could feed a phenomenon classified as modern forms of national-developmentalism. In the Brazilian case, the trade balance has displayed both favorable and unfavorable oscillations. By sustaining a rate of growth which cannot be compared to that of any other country, from the 1990s and until

Table 6.8 Share of exports of selected South American countries to China (%)

Year	Argentina	Bolivia	Brazil	Chile	Colombia	Ecuador	Guyana	Paraguay	Peru	Suriname	Venezuela	Uruguay
2000	3.03	0.38	1.97	4.95	0.22	1.20	0.18	0.27	6.99	**0.25**	0.31	**3.97**
2001	4.22	0.37	3.27	5.68	0.16	0.20	0.24	0.45	6.24	**0.75**	0.58	5.09
2002	4.25	0.56	4.17	7.03	0.23	0.29	0.33	0.81	7.80	**0.62**	0.60	5.57
2003	8.28	0.70	6.21	8.82	0.63	0.22	0.08	1.33	7.50	**0.21**	2.17	4.40
2004	7.61	1.04	5.65	10.42	0.82	0.65	0.23	1.44	9.78	**0.09**	1.85	3.91
2005	7.86	0.71	5.75	11.66	1.12	0.07	0.87	2.11	10.87	**0.16**	2.23	3.53
2006	7.47	0.84	6.10	8.67	1.85	1.53	2.38	0.55	9.55	**0.29**	4.30	4.23
2007	9.26	1.16	6.71	15.32	2.62	0.26	1.31	1.16	10.83	**0.47**	3.66	3.58
2008	9.08	1.88	8.35	13.21	1.18	2.06	1.50	1.51	11.94	**0.86**	11.61	2.92
2009	6.59	2.47	13.73	23.49	2.91	0.90	1.39	0.69	15.25	1.67	6.48	4.34
2010	8.51	3.00	15.24	24.36	4.98	1.88	0.81	0.53	15.18	0.72	7.35	5.54
2011	7.27	3.68	17.31	22.88	3.53	0.86	0.64	0.39	15.03	0.44	12.38	9.32
2012	6.34	2.68	17.02	23.17	5.55	1.64	0.94	0.58	16.92	0.36	16.53	11.62
2013	7.26	2.62	19.02	24.84	8.67	2.28	0.53	0.60	17.28	0.60	–	15.74
2014	6.52	3.38	18.05	24.23	10.50	1.89	1.96	0.51	18.22	1.79	–	16.47
2015	9.11	5.34	18.62	26.15	6.34	3.94	1.68	0.36	21.95	1.03	–	18.30
2016	7.66	6.68	18.97	28.64	3.63	3.91	1.24	0.25	23.39	0.93	–	16.12
2017	7.41	5.11	21.81	27.58	5.29	4.04	1.49	0.32	26.28	**0.96**	–	22.38
2018	**6.84**	**5.07**	26.76	33.50	**9.70**	6.92	1.49	0.29	**27.64**	**1.31**	–	21.64
2019	**10.47**	–	**28.36**	**32.39**	–	–	–	–	–	–	–	–

Note: datas in bold are not in Samurio, Barros and Severo (2019)
Source: Samurio, Barros and Severo (2019), Comtrade and MDIC

today, and even considering the slowdown of the international economy in 2020 because of the sanitary crisis provoked by the Coronavirus pandemic, China provoked a strategic reorientation, be this either in relation to advanced technology (for example Embraer, satellite launches), of within the commodity sector (for example Vale do Rio Doce). These reorientations led to a sectorial strengthening of the Brazilian economy, not least the production of commodities. The deactivation of the Embraer factory in Harbin[1] in 2016 signaled the difficulties of industrial cooperation between the two countries. In the case of Argentina, China conjecturally surpassed Brazil as the largest market for its exports in 2020 because of the productive difficulties in Brazil due to the sanitary crisis (BBC 2020).

6.4 The Emergence of Post-Hegemonic Forces in South America and the Brazilian Integration Policy During the First Fifteen Years of the Twenty-First Century

Due to its original social basis, the Lula government could represent a higher degree of openness to regional integration. The parties which sustained it, in particular the Workers Party, were favorably minded towards this process. The classical theory of regional integration (Haas, 1964) shows that this motivation does not demand a homogeneity of values. Although the country has been in favor of regional integration since 1985, the Brazilian interest in Mercosur and regional integration was not sufficient to guarantee the bloc's reinvigoration during the 2000s. If values were insufficient, then neither would interests permit a leap forward.

Argentina, as it had been the case with all the governments from 1985, was the first country which Lula visited after his election. This tradition would only be broken in 2019, after Bolsonaro's inauguration. For Lula, the idea of strengthening Mercosur and the strategic alliance was always present. At Lula's first meeting with the Argentinian president at the time, Eduardo Duhalde, in November 2002, the need to resume the PICE (Programme for the Trade and Economic Integration) signed by Sarney and Alfonsin in 1986 was discussed. On different occasions, the importance of a common trade and financial policy was reaffirmed. With the election of Néstor Kirchner in 2003, despite his favorable policies and discourse regarding Mercosur and his demonstration of partial ideological convergence with Lula, the measures effectively taken were scarce.

Generally, though, there were no broader efforts of coordination and convergence. That way, the initial push towards common development appears to have been diluted, although it might have substituted the search for possible economic advantages brought about by the tightening of economic relations and by the joint international agency in specific situations. The weakening of President Rousseff, particularly from the campaign in 2014, did not formally change this trend, but it

[1] https://www.airway.com.br/embraer-encerra-producao-do-legacy-na-china/

undermined the capacity to direct international initiative towards a strengthening of the regional integration process. Some efforts were made by the Presidents Néstor and Cristina Kirchner, and Lula focused on favoring investments in state enterprises or with financing from the Inter-American Development Bank (AIDB) and the National Bank for Economic and Social Development (BNDES) which sought to enhance production chains, and which were partially continued during the Rousseff period after her inauguration in 2011. An important concrete step was the materialization of the agreement for the creation of a System in Payments for Local Currencies (SML), which became effective from October 2008. Nevertheless, the international financial crisis, by devaluating the Peso and the Real equally, raised immediate doubt about the implementation of this system. As we have seen, for a series of different reasons, protectionist trends became evident in relation to third countries, but there were also reservations with regards to the intra-bloc liberalization. Resistances within the financial area in Brazil, in the Ministry of Finances, mainly from the second mandate from 2015, and in the Central Bank, eventually prohibited all kinds of coordination focused on economic policy cooperation. The corporate business interests with national and protectionist concerns in mind were important in this regard. This brings us back to the analyses developed in previous chapters with regards to the Brazilian elites, concerning many aspects similar to those of other members states within the bloc.

According to Hirst (2006), the priority attributed by Brazil to South America still in the Lula period could be a way to substitute previous modes of integration based on a strategic alliance with Argentina. The economic and structural reasons which obstruct this alliance tend to prevail over political, cultural, and ideological affinities. Yet, the increased attention to energy integration and to the development of sensitive technologies—themes discussed on Lula's trip to Argentina in February 2008—points to forces within the state which continue to focus on a perspective of deep integration. These forces exist, including some within the business sectors, but they were gradually weakened by a strategy which at the time was difficult to understand.

From 2003, Brazil came to explicitly recognize the existence of structural asymmetries within Mercosur. The attempts to provide counterpoints to the other participants did not gain the necessary traction. Differently from Burges' (2005) interpretation, this lack has its origins mainly within the very national difficulties; it can hereby not be explained by the egoistic vision regarding the benefits of integration. This *vision* might have existed within business sectors, but it was not the line which prevailed in the formulation of state policies since 1985. The fact that it was only in 2006, (fifteen years after the Treaty of Asunción), that the Structural Convergence Fund was implemented, is due to the weakness characterizing all the members states, including Brazil. We also analyze this aspect in Item 2 of this chapter. As we discussed in Chap. 5, US$100 million were allocated to the Fund, and posteriorly this value was increased. These resources were meant to attenuate the unfavorable consequences for the smaller members of the bloc,—Paraguay and Uruguay.

During the Lula government, preoccupations existed with regards to the limits established for the Mercosur format, but this did not seem to be sufficient to surpass the structural weaknesses. "Mercosur faces the challenge of reinventing itself and attending to the expectations of all of its members. We have to devise mechanisms to definitively equate the asymmetries, including through the allocation of new resources. We need to face the questions related to the institutional strengthening and implementation within each country, concerning the decisions and agreements which we reach within the bloc. This new phase of Mercosur which we initiate will demand that its institutions correspond to our ambitions [. . .] but Mercosur, necessarily, means more institutionality" (Lula da Silva, 2006). We saw that, within Brazilian society, this perspective is not only non-consensual but also faces direct resistance, which explains the very real limits to state initiative. The mechanisms for opinion-formation supported by interests of political, ideological, and business groups eventually portray regional integration and cooperation, not only as an interest of specific political forces which seek to associate integration with corruption, hereby contributing to the substantial inversion of the trend of corrosion of regional solidarity. This has also affected other regional institutions.

As Lima (2006) notes, it is important to consider that the ascent to power of left-wing governments in South America did not necessarily lead to automatic alignments, as these governments tend to be more sensitive to demands made by their respective constituencies, independently of the effect which their actions might have for the processes of regional integration. An emblematic example in this regard was the Bolivian nationalization of the hydrocarbon resources promoted by Evo Morales in May 2006, which affected Petrobras' interests within that country. This episode provides an exemplary case, as it permits an evaluation of the possibilities and limits of cooperation which has certain similar worldviews and values as its basic presumption; a critique of social inequalities, a distancing from global centers of power, and generic socialist ideas. In the case of Bolivia, just as it had occurred in the 1940s and 1950s with tin, in the 2000s gas was seen symbolically as a value to be preserved to guarantee the emancipation of the poor and historically marginalized populations. The same is the case in Paraguay where, according to Canese (2008, p. 25), the state's policies aimed towards the" recuperation of hydroelectrical national sovereignty".

As has been highlighted, the Brazilian perception that affinities open certain pathways and promote the comprehension between trade partners should not impede recognition of the fact that regional and foreign policy mainly relates to that which can be considered as national interests. If interests are inherent to the state (Deutsch, 1978) and to the classes with a high degree of structural significance within the regional integration process, it is still theory which shows in which conditions these can coincide with integration initiatives. Political will is not sufficient. The capacity to produce spillover effects or spurring of mutual interests within the regional integration process becomes necessary; in the opposite case, the search for non-cooperative solutions will prevail. Lima (2006) argues that risks exist of an erosion of the domestic coalition responsible for one of the main contemporary Brazilian foreign-policy legacies: the approximation with Argentina. This phenomenon materialized in a gradual fashion throughout the 2010s (Tokatlian, 2020; Botto, 2015). "In this regard, a strong complementarity was generated between the progressive governments in Argentina and Brazil, in terms of national development models, which, different to its predecessors recuperated the ideas from ECLAC about closed integration. Nonetheless, a single grand dilemma remains evident: how can the egoistic inclinations of the nation-states be overcome through productive coordination? The advances in this direction were mainly symbolic, as the creation of mechanisms of temporary safeguards, the renovation of the lists of exceptions, and the implicit acceptance of the unilateral violations of the external common tariff' (Botto, 2019, pp. 65–66). According to the author, the developmental convergence was not sufficient to overcome the stagnation generated by the egoistic propensities, which was stimulated by corporate and autarchic interests. This gradually fed corporative and inwards-looking interests which, in turn, over the coming years stimulated the return towards traditional and well-known ties with central countries, not least the United States. This did no doubt occur due to worries about not abandoning the interest in less traditional relations with China and with Mercosur and other South American countries.

The expectations initially generated by the emergence of innovative political forces adhering to agendas aimed at promoting regional integration hinted at the chance of a new phase of attempts to advance Mercosur and South America. As Oliveira and Onuki (2006) argue, it is necessary to qualify the idea of the direct ties between left-wing political positioning and support for regional integration. In other words, in thesis, there was something which favored the association of objectives to which Nardin (1987) refers if we consider certain ideological postures. The inherent difficulties related to the integration process within the region, when added to the different conceptions about which pathways of development should be pursued, caused problems which were difficult to solve.

6.5 Final Considerations

The evolution of international political economy from the beginning of the 1990s and until the middle of the 2000s had strong impacts concerning the strengthening of universalism as a fundamental conceptual matrix for regional insertion of Brazilian foreign policy. Beyond projecting a special position for the country in the discussions of the main themes within the international agenda, the Brazilian global activism sought to strengthen multipolarity and international organizations as privileged instances for the ordering of international stability. That way, during this phase the country intensified its relations with new poles of power, which tended to become increasingly relevant within the configuration of the international system. We therefore highlighted the importance of these changes and particularly the new significant role of Asia, mainly China. Brazil strengthened its relations with all its partners.

The situation of uncertainty and irregularities within the international system suggested a strategy of flexible international insertion, open to shifting circumstances. This notion was present within Brazilian formulations in relation to

Mercosur, mainly in defense of the intergovernmentalism as an institutional principle for integration. This perspective, maintained constantly from 1991 until today, including during the Temer and Bolsonaro governments, has been reappreciated as it adapts to different interpretations, also with regards to regional integration.

During the prolonged period of confidence concerning relations with Argentina, Mercosur, and South America from 1985 to 2016, a significant aspect of Brazilian foreign policy in a world which has undergone significant transformations was the aspirations towards a guarantee of a minimal cohesion in Mercosur in order to use the integration process as a platform for the country's international insertion. The provision of sporadic benefits to the country's partners—seen by them as insufficient, and generally considered a consequence of the rise in the pressures received—was an important strategy which defined the management of this cohesion. But the Brazilian position appeared to have reached its limits; the needs for integration are much larger than Brazil's capacity to provide the compensations demanded by its partners, as Mariano (2007) already foresaw towards the end of the first Lula mandate. In fact, the capacity to become a paymaster was absent (Mattli, 1999).

As we argue, for Brazil and for Mercosur, the difficulties in pursuing regional integration were not related to political will but rooted within the deep changes within the international system. These changes refer to the economic structure, trade, and investment flows, technology, and political, military, and cultural power. Within Brazilian society and the Brazilian state, the interests and conceptions of autonomy, universalism, and the aspiration towards the end of unilateralism and the strengthening of multilateralism—objectives which in some phases overlap and converge with the project of regional integration, particularly in relation to Argentina and Mercosur—in the 2000s, appear to confront growing difficulties in converging. From 2009 and during the Obama years, the region contradictorily became the object of geopolitical tensions. On the one hand, the democrat administration resumed relations with Cuba, which were re-established in April 2014; before the Seventh Summit of the Americas, which took place in Panama in April 2015; on the other, it strengthened its signals that its interest in the region would persist, acting in opposition to governments not considered sufficiently friendly.

Even with the emergence of governments considered to be centre-left, with characteristics emphasizing autonomy and developmentalism, with similar political and social support bases and generic political affinities, there were no major pushes towards the processes of regional integration, particularly in Mercosur; on the contrary, in fact a cycle of disengagement in relation to the region appears to have been evident. Disputes,—often highly accentuated—ensued (gas from Bolivia, Itaipu, Botnia, Odebrecht Ecuador, Brazilian and Argentinean protectionist measures violating Mercosur agreements) which affected the very core of the integration process between full members and associate Mercosur countries, gradually weakening it. While interests and positions contrary to the integration process developed within societies, these appeared not in the form of political proposals which sought to expand or readapt the process, but as resistance. The national crises did not lead to adjustments in the integration process, but rather resulted in its weakening and the reduction of efforts of complementation.

It is worth underscoring that the weakness of the pro-integration epistemic groups permitted the strengthening of others, which, albeit not directly opposed to it, in the context of an international system in transformation began appreciating ideas, projects, and interests which did not converge with or strengthen the process of regional integration. In the Brazilian case, this happened from 1998. The accurate perception, that as the bloc deepens, there would be a corresponding loss in Brazilian sovereignty and autonomy in relation to the world, did never completely disappear, and it eventually became an important component within the state's and society's line of action. Inversely, the perception that the integration process would strengthen the country's global position did not prevail. Consequently, an option which could have limited Brazil's international movement and also would have contradicted the principle of universalism, was rejected. We saw that the Brazilian principles—autonomy and universalism—just like the role which elites attributed to the integration process converged towards the maintenance of a process within the Southern Cone, which was limited to an essentially intergovernmental customs union, that was compatible with the broadening of the bloc and with Brazilian ambitions. The way in which the elite and the state managed the issue of Mercosur, from 1991, explains the growing significance of the theme of South America for Brazil. The geographical broadening of the integration objectives is related to the same perception which the country holds of itself in relation to the world. When the insertion of a large share of South American countries supported the strengthening of political, ideological, economic and military initiative of the United States, the events during previous decades resulted in strong signals of weakening.

References

Albuquerque, J. A. G. (2007). O governo Lula em face dos desafios sistêmicos de uma ordem internacional em transição – 2003–2006. *Política Externa, Ed. Paz e Terra, 16*(1), 33–44.

Almeida, P. R. d. (1993). *O Mercosur: no contexto regional e internacional*. Edições Aduaneiras.

Amorim, C. (2015). *Teerã, Ramalá e Doha: memórias da política externa ativa e altiva*. Benvirá.

Araújo Castro, J. A. d. (1982). *Araújo Castro*. Editora UnB.

Araujo, E. (2017). Trump e o Ocidente. *Cadernos de Política Exterior, 3*(6), 323–358.

Araujo, H. V. (2004). *Os países da Comunidade Andina* (Vol. 2). FUNAG.

Barbosa, R. A. (1996). O lugar do Brasil no mundo. *Política Externa, Ed. Paz e Terra, 5*(2), 69.

Barros, P. S., & Gonçalves, J. d. S. B. (2019). Fragmentação da governança regional: o Grupo de Lima e a política externa brasileira (2017–2019). *Mundo e Desenvolvimento, 2*(3), 6–39.

BBC. (2020). *Argenchina: por que a desbancou o Brasil como maior parceiro comercial da Argentina*. https://www.bbc.com/portuguese/brasil-53862542

Bolton, J. (2020). *The room where it happened: a White House memoir*. Simon & Schuster.

Botto, M. (2015). *La integración regional en América Latina: quo vadis? El Mercosur desde una perspectiva sectorial y comparada*. Editorial Universitaria de Buenos Aires (EDUEBA).

Botto, M. (2019). Desarrollo e integraciónenLatinoamérica. Los desafíos de ayer y de hoy, mirados desde la experiencia del MERCOSUR (1991-2018). *Revista Estado y Políticas Públicas, 7*(12), 55–71.

Brasil-Argentina, ACE-14. (1990). Disponível em: http://www.mdic.gov.br/comercio-exterior/negociacoes-internacionais/132-acordos-dos-quais-o-brasil-e-parte/1818-acordos-brasil-argentina-ace-14 Acesso em 22 de junho de 2020.
Burges, S. W. (2005, October). Bounded by the reality of trade: practical limits to a South American region. *Cambridge Review of International Affairs, Routledge, 18*(3), 437–454.
Camargo, S. (2000). A integração do Cone Sul (1960–1990). In J. A. G. Albuquerque (org.). *Sessenta anos de política externa brasileira (*1930-1990*:* O desafio geoestratégico). Annablume, NUPRI/USP.
Canese, Ricardo. 2008. "A recuperação da soberania hidrelétrica do Paraguai". In: Codas, Gustavo (org.). *O direito do Paraguai à soberania.* : Editora Expressão Popular.
Central Bank of Brazil. (2020). https://www.bcb.gov.br/estatisticas/estatisticassetorexterno
Cervo, A. L. (2006). A ação internacional do Brasil em um mundo em transformação: conceitos, objetivos e resultados (1990–2005). In H. Altemani & A. C. Lessa (Eds.), *Relações internacionais do Brasil: temas e agendas*. Editora Saraiva.
CIA. (2019). Central Intelligence Agency. https://www.cia.gov/the-world-factbook/field/area/country-comparison
Clarín, 7/9/2008. *Lula, en exclusiva con Clarín: 'no existe ningunahipótesis de que Brasil se juegue solo'.*
Comtrade. (2022). United Nations Comtrade Database. https://comtrade.un.org/data
Confederação Nacional de Indústria (CNI). (2020). *Impactos jurídicos da saída do Mercosur* (p. 77).
da Fonseca, R. G., & Marconini, M. (2006). Desempenho e política comercial: inserção internacional e o comércio exterior brasileiro. *Revista Brasileira de Comércio Exterior, Rio de Janeiro*, n° 87.
Deutsch, K. (1978). *Análise das relações internacionais*. Editora UnB.
Valor Econômico, 16/11/2004. *Empresários discutem o Mercosur.*
ECLAC. (2003). *Estudio Económico de América Latina y el Caribe 2002–2003*. https://www.cepal.org/pt-br/node/26300
Escude, C. (2004). *La globalización y el sistema-mundial neomoderno frente a las armas de destrucciónmasiva y laseguridad humana: haciaun materialismo histórico de derechos.* Universidaddel CEMA Serie de Documentos de Trabajo N° 274 www.cema.edu.ar/publicaciones Área de Ciencia Política – Octubre, pp. 17 18.
Fonseca Júnior, G. (1998). *A legitimidade e outras questões internacionais*. Paz e Terra.
Gazeta Mercantil, 19/10/2006. *Brasil não perdeu prestígio. Ele nunca foi tão alto.*
Godio, J. (2006). *El tiempo de Kirchner: eldevenir de una revolución desde arriba*. Ediciones Letra Grifa.
Gonçalves, J. B., & Lyrio, M. C. (2003). Aliança estratégica entre Brasil e Argentina: antecedentes, estado atual e perspectivas. CEBRI Dossiê, vol. 2, ano, 2.
Guimarães, S. P. (2006). *Desafios brasileiros na era dos gigantes*. Contraponto.
Haas, E. B. (1964). *Beyond the Nation State*. Stanford University Press.
Hirst, M. (2006, setembro). Los desafíos de la política sudamericana de Brasil. *Nueva Sociedad, 205*, 131-140.
IMF. (2019). International Monetary Fund. World Economic Outlook, October 2019. https://www.imf.org/en/Publications/WEO/weo-database/2019/October
León-Manríquez, J. L. (2006, maio/junho). *China-América Latina: una relación económica diferenciada*. Nueva Sociedad, n° 203.
Lima, M. R. S. D. (2006). *Decisões e indecisões: Um balanço da política externa no primeiro governo do presidente Lula*. Carta Capital, 27/12/2006. Disponível em: http://observatorio.iuperj.br
Lula da Silva, L. I. (2006) *Discurso do presidente da República, Luiz Inácio Lula da Silva, por ocasião do encerramento da XXX Cúpula dos Chefes de Estado do Mercosur*. Córdoba, julho. Disponível em: http://www.Mercosur.gov.br/discurso. Accessed 12/2/2021.

Mariano, M. P. (2007). *A política externa brasileira, o Itamaraty e o Mercosur*. Tese deDoutorado. Programa de Pós-Graduação em Sociologia, Faculdade de Ciências e Letras – UNESP-Araraquara – SP.
Mariano, M. (2015). *A política externa brasileira e a integração regional: uma análise a partir do Mercosur*. EditoraUnesp.
Mattli, W. (1999). *The logic of regional integration: Europe and beyond*. Cambridge University Press.
Mello, F. de C. (2000). *Regionalismo e inserção internacional: continuidade e transformação da política externa brasileira nos anos 90*. Tese de Doutorado. Departamento de Ciência Política da Faculdade de Filosofia, Letras e Ciências Humanas da Universidade de São Paulo.
MDIC. (2020). Ministério da Indústria, Comércio Exterior e Serviços. https://www.gov.br/produtividade-e-comercio-exterior/pt-br/assuntos/comercio-exterior/estatisticas/base-de-dados-bruta
Ministério das Relações Exteriores. (1991). Brasil, Argentina, Uruguai e Paraguai criam Mercado Comum do Sul (Mercosur). Resenha de Política Exterior do Brasil, Brasília, n° 68, 1991 (Nota à imprensa de 26 de março de 1991).
Moreira, M. M. (1989). *O Brasil no contexto internacional do final do século XX*. Lua Nova, São Paulo: Cedec, n° 18.
Nardin, T. (1987). *Lei, moralidade e as relações entre os Estados*. Forense-Universitária.
Narlikar, A. (2003). *International trade and developing countries: coalitions in the GATT and WTO*. Routledge.
Oliveira, A. J., & Onuki, J. (2006). Eleições, política externa e integração regional. *Revista de Sociologia e Política, 27*, 145–155.
Onuki, J. (1996). *O governo e o empresariado argentino: a percepção política do Mercosur*. Dissertação de Mestrado. Departamento de Ciência Política da Faculdade de Filosofia, Letras e Ciências Humanas da Universidade de São Paulo.
Pinheiro, L. (2004). *Política externa brasileira, 1889–2002*. Jorge Zahar.
Prates, D. M. (2006, abril). A inserção externa da economia brasileira no governo Lula. *Política Econômica em Foco*, São Paulo, n. 7.
Samurio, S. E., Barros, P. S., & Severo, L. W. (2019). O protagonismo do Brasil na integração da Sul-americana: uma análise das relações comerciais 2000–2018. OIKOS (Rio de Janeiro), (Vol. 18, pp. 38–54).
Sanahuja, J. (2019). La crisis de integración y el regionalismo en América Latina: giro liberal-conservador y contestación normativa. In M. Mesa (Ed.), *Ascenso del nacionalismo y el autoritarismo enel sistema internacional* (pp. 107–127). FundaciónCultura de Paz.
Saraiva, M. G. (2018). As relações com a União Europeia (2008–2015). In D. Neto et al. (Eds.), *Política externa brasileira em debate: dimensões e estratégias de inserção internacional no pós-crise de 2008*. IPEA e FUNAG.
Tokatlian, J. G. (2020). *América Latina es punto de disputa entre EE.UU y China*. La Nacion, 25/julio/2020. https://www.lanacion.com.ar/opinion/biografiajuan-gabriel-tokatlian-america-latina-es-punto-de-disputa-entre-eeuu-y-china-nid2403147
UN. (2019). United Nations. https://hdr.undp.org/en/content/human-development-indices-indicators-2018-statistical-update?utm_source=EN&utm_medium=GSR&utm_content=US_UNDP_PaidSearch_Brand_English&utm_campaign=CENTRAL&c_src=CENTRAL&c_src2=GSR&gclid=CjwKCAjwxZqSBhAHEiwASr9n9KCDnv8qw213F1DYzinw1WZ7k1POnsFhbJtFPfvGP2QiILvAb5jF3BoCe4EQAvD_BwE
Vadell, J. (2008). *América do Sul recebe o dragão asiático. Paper*. International Studies Association (ISA).
Valasco, E., & Cruz, S. C. (2007). *Trajetórias: capitalismo neoliberal e reformas econômicas nos países da periferia*. Editora da UNESP.
Walt, S. (2020). All great power politics is local. *Foreign Policy*. https://foreignpolicy.com/2020/08/24/all-great-power-politics-is-local/
Waltz, K. N. (2000). Structural realism after the cold war. *International Security, 25*(1), 5–41.
Wise, C. (2009). The North American free trade agreement. *New Political Economy, 14*(1), 133–148.

Chapter 7
Between Alliances and Disputes: Brazilian Attitudes Towards OAS, CELAC, Unasur, and Mercosur

7.1 Introduction

During the first decade of the 2000s, the Brazilian economic growth,—which coincided with the two Lula mandates,—created a momentum for Brazil within regional and global affairs. In this period, changes took place with regards to the visions for Brazilian international insertion, and consequently, in the perceptions concerning its agency within the American continent. The Brazilian ascent occurred within the broader picture of a growing influence of the BRICS countries. Together with China, India, Russia, and South Africa, in the 2000s Brazil was viewed as a growing economy, and projections placed it within the five largest global economies by the mid-twenty-first Century. Although there might not have been any direct correlation, the economic growth created a thrust for the Brazilian political initiatives, both on a regional and a global scale. The economic deacceleration which has marked Brazil since 2011 appeared not to have changed this picture throughout the first Rousseff mandate. On the other hand, the 2000s presented concrete signals of a partial decline of the United States' economic influence within the region, which was met with intense trade and financial flows from Asia, mainly from China: just as we have seen in Chap. 6. The indefinite suspension of the negotiations of the Free Trade Area of the Americas (FTAA), in Mar del Plata, in 2005, left an environment with new possibilities regarding the regional relations, to which some refer as post-hegemonic (Sanahuja, 2012). Hereafter, the financial crisis of 2007/2008 affected the United States' economy, including its trade and investment relations.

Consequently, aspirations were made towards the intensification of the cooperation ties between the Latin American countries, which comprise political, security, environmental, and development-related issues (Velasco e Cruz, 2007; Bittar & Hershberg, 2012; Sabatini, 2012). This was also reflected in the structure and activities of regional organizations. Within this context, it is worth highlighting the creation of organizations with new purposes regarding inter-American relations,

T. Vigevani, H. Ramanzini Junior, *The Challenges for Building Regional Integration in the Global South*, United Nations University Series on Regionalism 18,
https://doi.org/10.1007/978-3-030-93348-7_7

particularly concerning specific issue areas, such as the Union of South American Nations (Unasur), and the Community of Latin American and Caribbean States (CELAC).

In the second half of the 2010s, the Brazilian domestic environment became marked by profound changes. Brazil underwent a fierce electoral dispute in 2014. Rousseff was re-elected for her second term and should have remained president for an additional four years (2015 to 2018). The elections were decided in the second round, in October 2014. Dilma Rousseff, leading a coalition headed by the Workers Party received 54.501.118 votes, compared to the 51.041.155 votes received by Aécio Neves and his electoral coalition headed by the Brazilian Social Democratic Party.[1] The small difference of 51.64% to 48.36% of the votes highlights the extremely disputed Brazilian political scenario at the time. For our purpose, which is to discuss the Brazilian politics of regional and inter-American integration, and more generally, foreign relations, this information is highly relevant. It can help to understand the changes which from that moment became evident. Some of these transformations made themselves felt in the short term, while others were more strongly felt in the medium term, thus contributing to explain the domestic rationality behind the country's foreign policy with regards to the Brazilian international orientation. The inverse was often also the case. Today, evidence suggests that certain internal dynamics are related to external factors. We still do not have a reconstitution or a systemic analysis of the facts, but the destabilization of the developmentalist-distributionist consensus has taken place within different countries in the region. The so-called *Lava Jato* probe played a very significant role in Brazil (Avritzer, 2019).

At the point at which she initiated her second term, in January 2015, Rousseff encountered a very different situation from the one she had faced in January 2011, when her first term began. Rousseff's second term was thus initiated without the strength that she had enjoyed at the beginning of her first presidential period. It is not our aim to discuss Brazilian domestic politics here, but these circumstances should be understood, because they have conditioned the country's foreign policy, as we shall see. They hereby strongly influenced the state's capacity to mobilize its symbolic and material resources. At the election for the Presidency of the Brazilian Chamber of Deputies, in February 2015, the Workers Party (PT) candidate was decisively defeated by a candidate from the Brazilian Democratic Movement Party (PMDB). The PMDB was part of the governmental support base but maintained a strong dispute with Rousseff. This erosion only gained pace from that moment and onwards, accentuating a growing movement of distancing of the political and economic elites from the Workers Party. As it had occurred during the two mandates of President Lula (2003–2010), the political and parliamentary opposition concentrated its attacks on the government on basis of corruption accusations. From early 2014, the focus was the Public Federal Prosecutor's investigation concerning corruption in Petrobras. In March 2015, this issue gained further traction as the Supreme

[1]Source: Folha de S. Paulo, 27/10/2014.

Federal Court initiated an investigation of 50 individuals, nearly all parliamentarians, the majority of which was connected to the parties within the government's ruling coalition. At the same time, different forces from the opposition mobilized the public opinion, in large measure supported by media campaigns, and counting with broad middle-class support (Rossi et al., 2019; Singer, 2020), as well as economic interests, particularly those with an accentuated privatization perspective.

During the election of October 2014, the president gained most votes in the poor population segments, not least amongst those with incomes until 2 minimum wages. The same had occurred during the elections in 2010, although at a smaller scale. Amongst richer population segments, Rousseff's support was in decline and was particularly low amongst those that earned more than 10 minimum salaries. The same trend became evident with regards to schooling, where Rousseff enjoyed a high degree of support from those with only a basic education level and little support from those with higher education. Finally, it is noteworthy that the president won in only two regions: the North and the Northeast. Within the most developed regions, and in the most economically important,—the South-East,—Rousseff lost, particularly in São Paulo, although she did win in two important states in this region, Rio de Janeiro and Minas Gerais. In the South and the Centre-West, the president gained fewer votes than the PSDB candidate, Aécio Neves[2] (Amaral & Ribeiro, 2015).

The question which we seek to answer in this book relates to how the evolution of the Brazilian and international political situation eventually impacted the foreign policy regarding regional integration, the Inter-American relations, as well as foreign policy more generally. For this purpose, we apply some concepts with roots in foreign policy theory: from 2019, level four in Hermann's (1990) typology of changes was reached. Herman (1990) presents four graduated levels of foreign policy chance: (1) Adjustement changes, when changes in foreign policy occur in the level of effort to achieve purposes that remain unchanged, (2) Program Changes, refers to changes in the methods or means by which the goal is addressed, (3) Problem/Goal Changes relates to cases when the initial problem or goal that the policy addresses is replaced and the purposes themselves are replaced, and (4) International Orientation Change, involves a shift and redirection in the actor's orientation towards the world. During the Temer government (2016–2018), significant changes were undertaken, although they did not completely invert the country's system of foreign relations. With the beginning of the Bolsonaro administration, level four was reached, the highest categorized by the author. For Hermann (1990, pp. 5–6), this fourth graduate level of change represents "international orientation change: the most extreme foreign policy change [which] involves the redirection of the actor's entire orientation toward world affairs. In contrast to lesser forms that concern the actor's approach of a single issue or specific set of other actors, orientation changes involve a basic shift in the actor's international role and activities. Not one policy but many are more or less simultaneously changed". With regards to Brazilian foreign policy, as we saw in Chap. 6 when we highlighted some of the reasons for the

[2] Source: O Estado de S. Paulo, 27/10/2014.

changes of the traditional and constitutional orientation of Brazil from the extreme right-wing Bolsonaro government in 2019, we partly claim that these should be attributed to the declared alignment with the positions of the United States under the Trump administration.

As we have seen, some explanations take their point of departure in economic interpretations. The Brazilian production structure, even with internal consumption rising, continues to be strongly dependent on raw materials exports. This has become very pronounced within the highly complicated current economic conjuncture. In the last year of the Lula government, the economic growth was 7.53%. From 2012, growth rates gradually diminished. In 2012, these reached 1.92%. In the following years, growth hovered at 3.00% in 2013, and 0.50% in 2014. In 2015, Brazil entered a recession and witnessed a negative growth of −3.55%, while in 2016, the year in which the impeachment of Rousseff occurred, a drop in GDP of −3.21% materialized. In the following years, during the Temer administration, growth reached 1.06% in 2017 and 1.12% in 2018. In 2019, with the inauguration of the Bolsonaro administration, the economy grew at 1.14% (IBGE, 2020).

Certainly, structural economic problems exist, which suggests long-term economic challenges, rather than conjunctural issues. The economic interpretation points to opposing diagnostics. Within the liberal perspective, these are formulated as a low propensity to save and excessive redistribution. Within the developmentalist perspective, the critical characteristics underscored by liberals are viewed as necessary for the promotion of a higher degree of income distribution, less inequality, and growth within the internal market. Few interpretations, such as Fernandes (1975), connect crises to structural sociological reasons: a bourgeois with a low capacity for visionary long-term planning, and a society which still is incapable of breaking completely with the traditions connected to favoritism, slavery, and insertion within the system of colonial domination.

The relation between domestic and foreign policy (Putnam, 1988; Rogowski, 1989; Rodrik, 2018) is a recurring issue within the analysis of international relations; a theme which we have treated in Chap. 6. According to Moravcsik (1997), domestic politics do not only define states' foreign agency: the interconnection of different foreign policies, determined by domestic policies, mainly with respect to the most important states, is what eventually structures the international system. That means that although it occurs in a non-linear fashion, this is constituted as a result of different national conditions. The theoretical problem which arises is, as Waltz (1979) would say, a question of structure, and when we study small and medium countries, their relative position within this structure. The perception of a part of the North-American establishment during the Obama government was that Brazil's posture would somehow stimulate centrifugal positions in relation to established geopolitics, thus, wielding the potential to break with traditional manners of interaction. The North American concerns are not homogeneous, but rather determined by different interests and worldviews. The Democrats have sought to promote certain kinds of rights, including human rights and environmental preservation, but have always mainly been concerned with the central question of North American hegemony. For Piccone (2011, p. 173) "Brazil assumed the leading position in terms of filling the vacuum left by a lack of consensus within OAS, launching its own initiatives to create the Union of South American Nations (Unasur), a new forum which excludes the United States". At the same time, it signals the absence of mechanisms to effectively engage with the defense of human rights, as these goals remain diffuse within the new organization. As we did in Chap. 6, we reiterate that throughout the Obama administration, geopolitical concerns increased the pressures for the reinsertion of Latin American states within its sphere of influence.

Discussing the bases of international relations, Carr (2001), considered as a precursor to the contemporary realist school, highlights their political character, underscoring how that aspect would be more important than the legal and moral elements, "all legal systems presuppose an explicit or implicit initial political decision, reached by vote, bargaining, or force, like that of the authority charged with making and unmaking the laws. This necessary political backdrop can be found behind all law. The ultimate authority of law derives from politics" (Carr, 2001, p. 233). In a similar way, it is also impossible to understand the foreign policy without considering the domestic situation in Brazil during the second half of the 2010s. The Rousseff government's foreign and regional policy also presents important elements of continuity with aspects of the country's historical international engagement and particularly with that developed during the Lula government, but the internal constraints clearly point to the country's virtual paralysis. During the second mandate, in less than one year and a half of government, Brazil had three successive Ministers of Foreign Affairs, Antonio Patriota, Luiz Alberto Figueiredo, and finally, Mauro Vieira. The second mandate is characterized by conjunctural elements, not least the limitations imposed by the relatively recent internal political environment, with its growing capacity to mobilize different public bodies in defiance of the government in power. The foreign, regional, and Inter-American policies were subjected to fierce attacks.

In this Chapter, we hereby seek to understand the Brazilian engagement on a hemispherical level through a more general and long-term perspective, in order to assess which paths it has been following, from the collapse of the developmentalist-distributivist system, which also are discussed in previous chapters. We evaluate to which extend the increase and the weakening of the effective or symbolic Brazilian capacity affects continental relations, and the way that government and society formulate their regional policies, both through the previous perspective or by distancing themselves from the region by seeking the external linking through a resumption of the alliance with the United States. In other words, we seek to identify factors that motivate the adoption of strategies with regards to bilateral, sub-regional, regional, continental, as well as multilateral strategies.

With this purpose in mind, the analysis and reevaluation of basic concepts of Brazilian policy help to understand the significance of the concentric circles within the processes of regional integration and cooperation. The notion of concentric circles is based on the articulation of the Brazilian positions in Mercosur, Unasur, CELAC and OAS. The concentric circles would be defined in relation to Brazil's level of commitment to each cooperation bloc. The more central the bloc, the stronger the commitment. With this, Brazil could seek to maximize the possible favorable relations of each arrangement and advance objectives considered strategic in each arena, also considering the different foreign policy strategies and development models of the other countries in the region. Thus, the creation of new spaces, such as Unasur and CELAC, relates to goals not achieved in existing spaces or with the emergence of new challenges. At the same time, this strategy raises implementation challenges concerning how each circle affects others in situations of overlapping agendas regarding topics such as democracy clauses. It is necessary to observe that the building of new cooperative mechanisms such as Unasur and CELAC does not necessarily result in greater commitment to regional institutions. The established agreements are considered as a platform for international action and as a means to strengthen cooperation and state sovereignty, making it harder to deepen Mercosur.

In the following, we resume the analysis of aspects of the policies of regional integration and concertation in Latin America, discussing Mercosur, Unasur, and the CELAC. Finally, we discuss the continental engagement, particularly in relation to the OAS and the United States. We argue that the serious problems that explode during the second term of the Rousseff government, and the difficulties of domestic political negotiation, added to the economic crisis, limited the Brazilian regional profile and that the pressures for alignment with central countries, particularly the United States, were intended from 2016, during the Temer government,. This orientation continued from 2019 with Bolsonaro but didnt achieved the pretended results.

7.2 The Concept of Autonomy and Brazilian Foreign Policy: The Role of Integration

In Chap. 4, we discussed the issue of autonomy within Brazilian foreign policy. In this section, we resume part of the discussion initiated in that chapter, but we also approach the concept from a broader International Relations and Latin American perspective. The literature on Brazilian foreign policy, mainly from the 1990s, sought to reinterpret the significance of autonomy, which was considered as an important explanatory variable. In general, we take our point of departure in Hélio Jaguaribe (1958), form his early works at the IESB. In a conceptual interpretation of the work of Juan Carlos Puig, Simonoff (2015) underscores the tight relation between, on the one hand, the concept of autonomy, and on the other, that of political integration or concertation. With this in mind, he discussed something which could be viewed as a form of instrumentalization of the concept of integration and its relation with autonomy. The author reaches a conclusion which we seek to debate by discussing the perspectives relevant to Brazil in the second half of the 2010s, which on the conceptual level remain perfectly valid by the beginning of the 2020s. They even present certain perspectives which span beyond the years immediately after 2016, outlining some probable scenarios of the following decades. For

Simonoff (2015, p. 136) "the idea of subordinating integration to autonomy is not out of the question, since it would converge with the need to define tools that would permit peripheral societies to achieve their goals". As we have seen, in the case of South America, the talks about subordinating integration to autonomy had profound consequences. In the name of autonomy, the integration process was weakened. Hereupon, after 2016, the country's autonomy was depreciated due to the explicit aspiration towards international insertion subordinated to the hegemony of a larger power. In the Brazilian case, this would not only occur in relation to a larger power but also to a particular political project of conservative forces which aim towards the restoration of North-American power with explicit policies of confrontation and polarization.

In the course of the 2010s, the strength which the forces of opposition to the Workers' Party governments reached within Brazil,—which should be viewed within the context of growing conservatism and illiberal authoritarianism (Levitsky & Ziblatt, 2018)—initially propelled the Brazilian Social Democratic Party (PSDB). Hereafter, with some similarities to Europe of the 1920s and 1930s, in the vacuum created by the self-proclaimed a-political movements, other declaredly right-wing movements were strengthened, which, although they varied, did display certain fascist characteristics. This necessitates a reevaluation of the regional integration and foreign policies, as they had been conceived up until then. It is therefore important to understand that the resistance towards regional integration was part of a radically alternative project of international insertion. Highlighting the advantages of regional integration would not affect the process of Brazilian disengagement when this occurred within a general context marked by the political defeat of the developmentalist-distributivist factions, as well as the liberal forces who had been the initial formulators of the integration project. The governments of Alfonsin, Sarney, Menem, Collor de Mello, Itamar Franco, Cardoso, Pedotti, and Lacalle can be characterized in these terms.

One of the paths to the reevaluation of the foundations of Brazilian foreign policy, from autonomy to regional integration, would eventually be the resumption and resignification of these very ideas after 2016. Just like it has happened in other countries, as part of this reevaluation, the critique of the prevalent positions during the PT governments would not be directed at the very concept of autonomy, but rather at its interpretations, thus, seeking a reappreciation of its roots which can be found throughout the twentieth Century, as we have discussed in Chap. 3. These roots have remained alive and in vigor until today. Applying Russell and Tokatlian's (2010) formulations, it is likely that the concepts of globalization and interdependence, as well as the ideas of insertion within global value chains, comparative advantages, etc. will be sought reinserted within the autonomy-integration equation, hereby elevating their significance. These ideas have been,—and are still,—strongly present within the Brazilian foreign policy, including during the Lula and Rousseff governments, but their significance, their interpretation, and their utilization have varied strongly across time. One of the arguments presented by José Serra and Nunes Ferreira (2016–2018) was that Mercosur and Unasur, and the forms of South-American integration, could constrain the Brazilian attempts to manage its foreign relations with point of departure in its own capacities. This reading contrasts with that of the ISEB and the Independent Foreign Policy, which, as we have discussed in Chap. 3, accentuated the Brazilian need to develop its industrialization and create a national economy, but without adopting a conflictive position in relation to its region (be this either the *La Plata River Basin*, South America, or Latin America).

In the Brazilian and South-American academic production within International Relations, autonomy is a notion which refers to a foreign policy that is free from the constraints imposed by powerful countries. It is an objective to be pursued within the foreign engagement and also an explanatory concept regarding international options. In Brazil, the issue of autonomy is important to intellectuals, because it also is potentially vital to the state. This idea and value is something which should be constantly reaffirmed and hereby differs from the situation in which some developed countries find themselves, due to the elevated degree of autonomy which their economic, political, or military weight provides for them. Although it is not the objective of this book, it is important to remember that even some "Americanist" governments are considered by certain actors as interested in the preservation of some degree of autonomy and present serious divergences, not least economic, in relation to the United States (Malan et al., 1977; Casarões, 2019). By way of example, we here refer to the governments of Dutra (1946–1950), Castello Branco (1964–1967) e Collor de Mello (1990–1992). Some authors attribute their "pro-americanism"—which is strongly present within their foreign policies—to certain forms considered necessary for the preservation of autonomy or national development, etc. The radicalization of the pro-americanism from 2019, with the resulting unconditional adherence, is attributed to that which Amorim (2020) refers to as an abnormal government.

Rather than being rooted in the juridical notion of sovereignty, in Brazil, autonomy is a distinctively political concept; an instrument to safeguard the country against the more detrimental effects of the international system. From the more powerful countries' perspective, external autonomy is not a primordial preoccupation. Mello (2000) considers the notion of autonomy as the basis for the articulation between the concepts of independence, diversification, and universalism within Brazilian foreign policy. Independence would hereby constitute a previous condition for autonomy, while diversification and universalism would refer to the means that should be promoted to reach this. In the Brazilian case, the term autonomy relates to the idea of broadening the scope for state actions, considering the conditions of the domestic and international system in any given period. It is, therefore, a relative notion, which depends on the domestic and/or international context in which the foreign policy is implemented.

Beyond this, by definition, the notion of autonomy is always a question of degree, as this aspect is particularly important within the discussions about regional integration, which, by definition implies a certain degree of relativization of autonomy. Within the Brazilian foreign policy perspective, there was a propensity to accept a higher degree of cooperation in the 2000s. For example, within the field of regional security, this becomes evident with regards to the sectorial limits of autonomy to further relatively modest objectives of South American cooperation. In the opposite case, the weakening of regional integration would suggest a rise of conflict. It is not surprising that the institutions of regional integration, cooperation, and articulation by weakening or outright deteriorating,—as it was the case with Mercosur and Unasur—open space for crises which cannot be solved through regional intermediation, and hereby also strengthen the possibility of attracting global conflict to the region. The situation with Venezuela from 2017 provides a very clear example of this (Teixeira Junior, 2020).

Since 2015, due to the changes which would be strongly accentuated within the Brazilian elite's positions, and which also wielded a strong impact on public opinion, the intensification of critique of Mercosur becomes accentuated, as this organization, as a customs union, is presented as an obstacle to the signature of agreements with other countries, particularly the most important market economies, not least the United States. This tendency was further strengthened by the difficulties which many countries in South America faced at this point. This was not only the case for Venezuela but also Argentina, which was symbolized by the election of Maurício Macri in 2015. In the words of Rubens Barbosa[3] (2014) "Brazil should reconsider its strategy for trade negotiations, freeing itself from ideological preconceptions, and aiming at the opening of new markets, not only amongst developing countries, but also within developed countries. Our priorities during the past 12 years, focusing exclusively on multilateral negotiations within the WTO, and on Mercosur and South America, do no longer serve Brazilian interests" (Barbosa, 2014). Indications of similar inclinations became evident with regards to other countries, contributing to the pressure towards change within certain sectors of Brazilian society, particularly the business community, but also within government and important strata of the public administration. According to the journal, *El País,*[4] referring to the special advisor for trade negotiations, Carlos Peréz del Castillo,[5] named by the Chancellor Rodolfo Nin Novoa right after the inauguration of President Tabarez Vázquez on March 1, 2015, "His appointment implies that the Foreign Ministry will try to have Uruguay, either with Mercosur or alone, seek new trade agreements." In fact, the same Peréz del Castillo affirms that "Mercosur as a central model for insertion of Uruguay is totally obsolete. We are going to stay in Mercosur, we are not going to leave, but much honesty is needed, because today it has no credibility ".

The notion of autonomy is characterized by the state's capacity to implement decisions based on its own objectives, without external interference of restriction, and by the ability to control the internal consequences of processes or events produced beyond its borders. In Latin America, from the 1970s, the idea of

---

[3] <http://opiniao.estadao.com.br/noticias/geral,uma-nova-politica-comercial-imp-,1,591,030> O Estado de S.Paulo, 11/11/2014; p. 2.

[4] <http://www.elpais.com.uy/informacion/cancilleria-quiere-libertad-buscar-acuerdos.html> El Pais, 4/3/2015; p. 3.

[5] <http://www.elpais.com.uy/informacion/mercosur-agotado-modelo-insercion.html> El Pais, 4/3/2015; p. 3.

autonomy has been conceived as a way to "liberate" the countries within the region from their external dependence. In fact, the application of this concept dates far back in time. For some countries, we can even trace it to the nineteenth Century. In Brazil, phases such as the nationalist Vargism, particularly in the period from 1951 to 1954 (Alves, 2007), the Independent Foreign Policy (the Quadros and Goulart governments) (see Chap. 3), and the Responsible Pragmatism (the Geisel government) (Lima, 2018) reflect the deep-reaching degree of the concept's embeddedness. Jaguaribe (1979, pp. 91–93) describes the international system as a hierarchical order. Although the countries with the capacity to plainly exercise their autonomy do not possess a complete guarantee of the total inviolability of their national territories, they can provide considerable obstacles for the agency of their enemies, adversaries, or simply competitors, and hereby enjoy sufficient room of maneuver to conduct their foreign policies. The most vulnerable and/or strategically weak nations, on the other hand, although formally independent and sovereign, have historically been constrained by great powers.

Autonomy is a function of the structurating conditions which Jaguaribe (1979, pp. 96–97) describes as "national viability" and "international permissibility". The first term refers to the existence of adequate human and social resources to be able to guarantee international insertion and a certain degree of socio-cultural cohesion within national borders. The second concept relates to the capacity to neutralize external threats and depends on the economic and military resources, as well as alliances with other countries. Jaguaribe (1979) also identifies two fundamental factors for the existence of autonomy within the periphery: technological and business autonomy, and favorable relations with the Centre. The formulations cited above by Barbosa and del Castillo present the significance of relations with central countries in a new perspective: not only as an important goal of states but as an alternative to the strengthening of intra-regional and South-South relations. Seeking to explain the evolution and the different uses and instrumentalizations of the concept of national interest, in the Brazilian case, the notion of autonomy relates to the idea of a broadening of the margins for agency or choice of the state, considering the conditions provided by the domestic and international system in any given period. It is, therefore, a relative notion. It implies a certain degree of relativization of autonomy. In the case of the Brazilian elites, the idea of autonomy was always, and still is, used instrumentally, according to the conditions at any given time (Pinheiro & Lima, 2018).

Ever since the end of the Cardoso government, the CNI has perceived regional integration as a limit to the business interests of certain production chains, and in 2020 it stated its favorable position in relation to Mercosur, underscoring the costs of a rupture with the customs union. During the presentation of a study conducted by this entity about the relevance of the bloc, Robson Braga de Andrade, the president of the Confederation of Industry, highlighted that "the CNI hopes that this publication will contribute to the debate about the deepening of the discussions regarding the adjustment of Mercosur, so that Brazil and its other members can reap the positive results of regional integration within this important common market" (CNI, 2020, p. 11). That is, according to the Confederation "considering only the

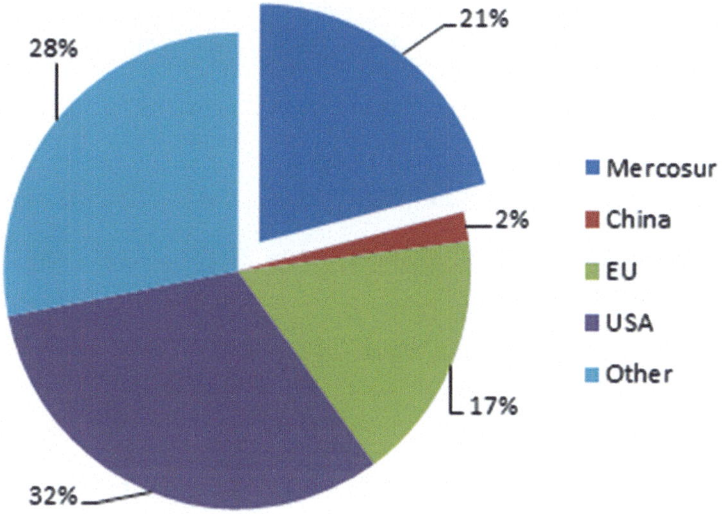

Fig. 7.1 Destination of Brazilian exports of manufactured products (2015–2019 average). Source: CNI (2020)

last scenario (exports of manufactured products) the relevance of Mercosur is evident, as it is more important, even than exports to the European Union" (CNI, 2020, p. 23). In the case of Brazil leaving the bloc, the study affirms that "a significant share of Brazilian exports of manufactured products (which today enjoy free access to the markets within of the Mercosur countries, with exception of the automotive industry and cane-ethanol sectors) will be impacted" (CNI, 2020, p. 23).

Only the United States import more manufactured products than the Mercosur in absolute terms. In a country such as Brazil, where the share of industry has been decreasing constantly since 1980, the argument concerned with the importance of the regional bloc gains weight. Even in periods marked by a contempt for the countries within the region (Casarões, 2020) and aspirations towards the intensification of relations with rich countries, such as those of the government which took office in 2019, the structural reasons for the interest in the regional bloc should he highlighted within this book which aims towards long-term assessments. Figure 7.1, which presents the average of Brazilian exports of manufactured products between 2015 and 2019, clearly indicates this. In other words, Mercosur is a market which represents 21% of the category of products with a higher value-added, and only the United States accounts for the purchases of more manufactures, reaching 32%. As we can read in Fig. 7.1, China reaches 2%, and the European Union 17%. This is one of the main reasons for the difficulties of forming a more coherent and stable Brazilian position.

Table 7.1 shows the growing primarization of the Brazilian economy, with the rise in the significance of raw materials within its export basket,—a trend which, as we have discussed, has been accelerating constantly since 1980. According to MDIC, in the 22 years from 1997 to 2019, raw materials have been growing from

Table 7.1 Brazilian exports by technological intensity—share

Products/Year	1997	2001	2005	2009	2013	2017	2019
Basics	18.6%	18.1%	20.6%	31.0%	38.0%	37.6%	42.0%
Low-tech manufacturing	34.6%	33.4%	29.5%	30.1%	25.7%	26.5%	23.9%
Medium-low-tech manufacturing	17.3%	15.4%	17.8%	14.7%	15.4%	12.8%	15.3%
Medium-high-techmanufacturing	25.2%	21.7%	25.1%	18.6%	17.2%	18.5%	15.0%
High-techmanufacturing	4.4%	11.4%	7.0%	5.5%	3.7%	4.6%	3.8%

Source: MDIC. Author'selaboration

Table 7.2 Brazilian imports by technological intensity—share

Products/Year	1997	2001	2005	2009	2013	2017	2019
Basics	12.8%	11.7%	17.4%	13.9%	14.2%	9.6%	9.1%
Low-tech manufacturing	11.6%	7.6%	6.9%	8.8%	8.6%	10.7%	9.3%
Medium-low-tech manufacturing	13.8%	15.3%	14.4%	14.7%	18.5%	19.4%	22.7%
Medium-high-techmanufacturing	43.1%	42.6%	39.4%	42.5%	42.1%	41.6%	42.0%
High-techmanufacturing	18.7%	22.9%	21.9%	20.1%	16.6%	18.8%	16.9%

Source: MDIC. Author'selaboration

18.6% to 42%. In the same period, the significance of low-tech, medium-low-tech, and medium-high-tech manufacturing has been declining. In the same way, the high-tech manufacturing products, although still varying from year to year, decreased from 4.4% to 3.8%. Here, it is important to underscore how these have remained at a very low level.

Table 7.2 presents imports according to technological intensity. The variations do somehow help to complement the picture presented above. In the same period considered from 1997 to 2019, the share of imports of basic products diminished from 12.8% to 9.1%. With regards to low-tech manufacturing and medium-high-tech manufacturing, the share has maintained a certain stability. The same is the case with regards to high-tech manufacturing, which has varied from 18.7% to 16.9%. A higher degree of variation can be found with regards to medium-low-tech manufacturing, the share of which has been varying from 13.8% to 22.7%. This consolidates the analysis with regards to the strong weakening of the industrial park, which even became evident in relation to products which had been the cornerstone of the process of import substitution in the twentieth Century; the industry of non-durable and durable consumer goods. As additional evidence of this tendency, it can be noted that in 2019, the Brazilian participation in the global industrial production fell to the lowest level of the historical series which was initiated in 1990. According to the CNI communication, "the loss of the participation of Brazilian industry within the global industrial production can be observed since the mid-1990s". Also according to the CNI "the data illustrate that the Brazilian economic crisis from 2014 to 2016 intensified this trend", which continued in the following years, making the Brazilian industrial production recede in relation to other countries, including other developing states, such as Mexico and Turkey, within the international classification (https://www1.folha.uol.com.br/mercado/2020/09/brasil-atinge-menor-participacao-na-producao-industrial-mundial-desde-1990-diz-cni.shtml).

The role of the interests of political elites which manage the states is fundamental in order to understand the presence or absence of the room to develop the centripetal forces which could produce the spillover phenomenon. The continuity of the process, in theory, presupposes the growth of the importance of integrated epistemic groups. Discussing the difficulties of the regional integration process, Schmitter (2000), Malamud and Schmitter (2006), and Lekrofridi and Schmitter (2015) show how these do not necessarily disappear throughout time. In the case of the European Union, Schmitter (2000) demonstrates how the apparent difficulties for the process to advance in the direction of a stable political confederate union would be evidenced by indefinite postponement of the formation of European parties, which took place nearly half a century after the Rome Treaty. This situation persists until today and has been aggravated by Brexit. In the same way, Malamud and Schmitter (2006) and Mariano (2015) discuss some of the particularities of Mercosur, and the difficulties related to a conventional theoretical interpretation of explaining its constant oscillations, which already has become evident in the developmentalist-distributivist period.

In his reflections about autonomy, in contrast to realist authors such as Morgenthau (2003) and Waltz (1979), Puig (1980, 1984) argues that the international system is not characterized by anarchy, but by an international hierarchy. According to Puig (1980, pp. 149–155) the obtainment of autonomy hinges on four stages: (1) the formal status of a sovereign state; (2) the obtainment of sufficient material benefits to launch a project of national development; (3) the acceptance of the politics of the great powers within their area of strategic interest in exchange for the exercise of autonomy within areas of equal importance for the Latin American countries, as for example, in the choice of their development models; and (4) the rupture of dependency with the Centre and actions of non-obedience. For Puig (1980), and for Jaguaribe (1979), autonomy requires sufficient degrees of "national viability", a considerable quantity of domestic resources, and an explicit commitment of elites to the national project. The two authors also share the idea that autonomy requires the mobilization of power resources within the periphery. Regional alliances to interact with the Centre, political and economic integration, and the improvement of negotiation strategies constitute the instruments for reaching this goal. In this perspective, regional integration can be a strategic objective. On the other hand, adequate doses of political realism necessitate the pragmatic dosage of efforts to reach these objectives.

Analyzing the existence of the four stages formulated by Puig (1980) remains an interesting exercise, particularly for Brazil. In the Brazilian case, we have certainly witnessed the first stage, the sovereign state. This stage exists to varying degrees in all of the countries within the region in the twenty-first Century. It is more difficult to define the state of the other three stages. The Brazilian reality of the 2010s, which became clearly evident in 2015 with the growth of the institutional crisis at the beginning of the Rousseff mandate, is that the capacity to realize an autonomous national project is under *judice*. The political elites spurred its fragmentation, advancing towards a declared institutional crisis. The combatting of corruption, which apparently constitutes itself strongly in an innovative international regime, imbricated with power relations implies secondary effects which are expressed as the instrumentalization in relation to internal political disputes, as it also has been the case in other countries, even in the developed world. The surge, or resurgence, of interests which do not consider the preservation of strategic decisions related to the state as an important objective, has consequently impacted the process of regional integration. The revelation of the international articulations in the production of proofs (The Intercept, 2020) particularly the use of the concept of lawfare, contributed to the election result of 2018, thereby demonstrating the weakness of national power.

In the Brazilian case, companies such as Petrobras, the EBX Group, and large construction enterprises from the heavy construction sector which were part of the Brazilian interest in the region regarding both Mercosul and Unasur (Neves, 2019), were structurally weakened or even destroyed. Without strong business structures, the consequences for the foreign policy regarding the region and the world were large. The result was the undermining of the material bases for an integration policy symbolically sustained by the concept of national interest, especially of the perspective which integrates national interests within the region. The relations with the United States gained importance within this context. The contemporary Brazilian crisis strengthened the sectors who accentuate the importance of the relations with the United States, as well as the European Union. Beginning in 2019, despite the country's position as Brazil's and Mercosur's major trading partner and a significant investor, the relations with China would be understood within the perspective of a trade war, formulated by the Trump administration. The relations with China were questioned by important parts of the government in Brasília.

In order to understand the different conceptions of autonomy debated in Brazil, it becomes important to return to its previous formulations. Adapting the concept of autonomy in the mid-1990s, Fonseca (1998) argues that the Brazilian diplomacy in parts of the Cold War period has been characterized by autonomy through distance. Yet, in the 1990s, this diplomacy would be forced to incorporate new values due to (1) the Brazilian democratization, (2) the end of the Cold War, (3) the acceleration of the process of globalization, and (4) the emergence of "new issues" within the international agenda (the environment, human rights, global trade reform, etc.). In sum, the very idea of autonomy would gain new connotations. According to the author, the first expression of autonomy by distance would be to maintain a certain distance,—albeit not always opposed to—the actions and values of the capitalist and developed West. In addition to this, it would imply a critical position in relation to the superpowers. On the other hand, in the contemporary world, autonomy cannot any longer be associated with "distance" from controversial issues in order to guard the country against undesirable alignments. On the contrary, according to Fonseca

Jr. (1998), autonomy can be traduced as "participation" due to a desire to influence the agenda through participation in decision-making processes.

In the same line of reasoning, Russell and Tokatlian (2003) argue that the acceleration of globalization during the last decades has substantially changed the space for action of Latin American countries. This new global context demands that autonomy would be defined in a different manner, implying the need for a transition from antagonistic autonomy (which is similar to autonomy through distance) towards relational autonomy (which is similar to autonomy through participation).

Relational autonomy can be traduced as a growing interaction, negotiation, and participation in the elaboration of international rules and norms. Autonomy is hereby no longer defined "*by a country's power to isolate itself and control external process and events, but instead by its power to participate in and effectively influence world affairs, particularly in all types of international organizations and regimes*" (Russell e Tokatlian, 2003, p. 16). For Russell and Tokatlian (2003, p. 19), relational autonomy should be reached through commitments and negotiations with large participation from the public opinion, strengthening the democratic aspect of this type of development of foreign policy. The partial abandonment of elements of sovereignty (a characteristic of relational autonomy) would take place to develop institutions and norms for the promotion of the common good. Within this perspective, we perceive the idea of propositive insertion within the logic of prevalent international regimes. In fact, when the signals of weakening of the idea of autonomy through diversification—which refers to a mode of international insertion by which the participation within existing international regimes is accepted, but still supplementing this with alliances focused on balancing traditional hegemonic powers (for example, the BRICS articulation),—regional integration and South American cooperation thus becomes less relevant. At that moment, in which the approximation with the United States returned to the debate, the discussion with regards to the insertion within regional groups with strong North-American leadership momentarily gained momentum, not least concerning the Transatlantic Trade and Investment Partnership (TTIP).

Within a study in which different possibilities for Brazil are evaluated through trade projections, particularly those related to the potential conclusion of the TTIP and Transpacific Partnership (TPP), Thorstensen and Ferraz (2014) underscore that the consequences within the trade-related realm would be particularly detrimental to Brazil, in case the country would not find ways of adhering to the TTIP. When Trump gained power in the United States in 2017 and withdrew the applications for approval of the TPP from Congress, and suspended the TTIP, the efforts made by Argentina and Brazil towards individual adhesion to liberal regimes were strengthened with the debate about joining the OECD (Thorstensen & Gullo, 2018). The same was the case with the Mercosur countries, though in a more disarticulated manner. The political ideas and strategies based on the aspiration towards autonomy, as underlined by Briceño Ruiz (2012, p. 54), appear to reach a moment of inflection. For him, at the beginning of the 2010s, "The recent reflections on national density and relational autonomy confirm that economic development and political autonomy continue to be central ideas within integrationist reflections about Latin America".

With its abandonment of the projects of autonomy and integration, Brazil's weight amongst the Latin American countries contributed decisively to the transformation of the equilibria and weakening of the South American bodies concerned with integration, cooperation, and coordination.

Each of the concepts debated when discussions revolve around autonomy, through either distance, participation, or diversification, were rooted in the Brazilian diplomatic tradition. Yet, the action strategies that derive from them are not necessarily successful in terms of ensuring benefits, for example, regarding commercial exchanges, the attraction of direct investments, the influence on international bodies, in the consolidation of efforts of regional integration, or to enhance the political prestige and influence on the issues of peace and war. Because of the way that the issue of autonomy has been inserted within the objectives of the external agency of the Latin American states, particularly in the Brazilian case, the regional integration experience encompasses important particularities. These even comprise of theoretical consequences to be considered.

The integration of the Southern Cone and South America, regarding Mercosur and Unasur, do somehow clash with the theories developed by neo-functionalists (Matlary, 1994; Haas, 2004) or by liberal-intergovernmental scholars (Moravcsik, 1994; Moravcsik, 2005). Simplifying, for the first, regional integration depends on the phenomenon of spillover, aiming at the attenuation of national power in favor of supranationality. For the second group, the combined interaction of national interests should support regional integration. For the liberal intergovernmentalists, national autonomy subsists, but the persistence and advancement of the regional integration process result from the combination of national interests. With regards to the Brazilian state and its policy-formulating instances, as we saw in Chap. 2, we can affirm that the different regional blocs should contribute to the strengthening of the autonomy of member states as an objective and consequence of the integration process. So it was in 2016. We hereby highlight that the regional blocs, and particularly Mercosur, were consistently incorporated within Brazilian foreign policy, with strong roots within the state and society, as we continuously have witnessed since the Tripartite Treaty of Itaipú of 1979 (Gardini, 2010). In a certain way, we reencounter Puig's (1984) formulation that the idea of regional integration should be compatible with that of autonomy, which has been reassessed by diverse authors such as Colacrai (2009), Bernal-Meza (2005) and Simonoff (2015).

For the neofunctionalists and liberal-intergovernmental scholars, regional integration arises from domestic actors' and groups' demands and from the interests of the state. It has as its presupposition a reasonable degree of economic interdependence between its members (Choi & Caporaso, 2002). With regards to the need for interpretation of regional integration from the foreign policy perspective (in this case concerning Brazil, but the line of reasoning has a much broader validity), we can conclude that the idea of autonomy does not entirely overlap with that of integration. Unless the idea of autonomy is conceived through a federative perspective,—the object of analysis of Schmitter (2000). The apparent movement of decline of regional integration in South America as witnessed within different processes towards the end of the 2010s is not only visible from 2016 in

Mercosur, but also from before that, in the Andean Community, as well as in the difficulties of deepening the Pacific Alliance. This interpretation contributes to the understanding of the Brexit process and of part of the problems which present themselves to the European Union (Hooghe e Marks, 2019).

In order to understand the Brazilian political development post-2016, it is worth remembering that the concept of autonomy hereafter has undergone a significant reinterpretation. During the Temer administration (May 2016–2018), there was a tentative return to autonomy through participation, albeit very modified. It implied a weaker prevalence of multilateralism and a stronger degree of adhesion to liberal international regimes. In the post-2019 period, the idea of autonomous positions has been outright rejected. In other words, in this case, as Pinheiro and Lima (2018) had previously formulated, confronted with a new articulation of internal interests and external incentives, would there be any possible return to a position of dependent international insertion? This could also be formulated as the recognition of the impossibility of autonomy: "In the autonomist view, by contrast, the country should not behave as a "small country" but rather "harden" its soft power, according to the expression used by the then chancellor Celso Amorim (2016, pp. 45–59), although this does not imply becoming a nuclear power. Due to this belief—that the country should take certain risks on the international scene, given a favorable international and national context—policies with an autonomist bias were moments of rupture and discontinuity in Brazilian foreign policy, every time Brazil adopted a critical position with respect to the status quo" (Pinheiro & Lima, 2018, p. 18). The authors analyze autonomy, and also evaluate the concept in relation to Jaguaribe and Puig, as an exception. It hereby does not necessarily follow that the post-2019 external engagement is related to traditional dependence, but rather to an abnormal exacerbation of this.

The Brazilian Minister of Foreign Affairs from 2019 to 2021, Araujo (2017, p. 354) has written that "In the Itamaraty, throughout decades we have learned, at all costs, to avoid the submission of Brazil to a bloc, in order to preserve the capacity to develop an autonomous foreign policy. We want to maintain relations with all blocs, but without exclusively being part of any of these. We, therefore, observe with great distrust, the idea of being part of a Western world, which necessarily excludes other civilizations, and which would leave us confined to a specific bloc. But this absolute non-alignment should not impede Brazil from aligning it with itself, and the very essence of its nationality, if we reach the conclusion that this essence is Western". For Araujo (2017) the Western essence is that of President Trump of the United States.

From the foreign policy perspective, there were important changes throughout the Workers Party years. These changes were introduced by the "presidential diplomacy" of Lula da Silva, which generally also was adopted by Rousseff. Even when the policy-formulating core of the diplomatic engagement, including Celso Amorim, Samuel Pinheiro Guimarães, and Marco Aurelio Garcia, and a number of diplomats, formulated and accompanied these changes, particularly the critiques of the hegemonic policies, in general, the administrative structure—which includes many other areas beyond foreign relations, ministries, and institutions—did not actively follow these changes. We thus conclude that, according to our interpretation within this book, if the post-2016 governments would orient their external engagement differently from that which marked the developmentalist-distributivist period, thus, somehow neglecting the autonomy perspective, they will certainly encounter a non-hostile structure.

The demands and interests, mainly those of an economic nature, aimed at regional integration, thirty years from the Treaty of Asuncion of March 1991, did not display any important qualitative growth, a question which we analyze in Chap. 6. Since the Brazilian and Argentinean exchange rate crises of 1999 and 2001, there has not been any strong demand for regional integration within Brazil, and neither has there been any vigorous growth of interdependence. We thereby do not deny that there were historical advances regarding certain issues: for example, the disappearance of the chance of war in the *La Plata Basin*, an issue of recurring preoccupation to the four Mercosur countries and a higher level of intra-regional investments, albeit declining since 2014. The present period, from the mid-2010s to 2020 points towards a situation of low-intensity cooperation and integration. The Brazilian institutional turmoil, which spelled a situation of crisis within certain large companies, such as construction enterprises and others, Petrobras, certain banks, the BNDES investments, and high-technology areas (aeronautics, security, etc.) resulted in a low demand for regional integration. Towards the end of the so-called post-hegemonic period in Brazil, the positions which link autonomy with regional integration were not strengthened in terms of their bases of political and material support. After this, the forces which defended a higher degree of insertion based on ties to "global" markets gained ever more importance. Which does not mean that they have reached their objective.

7.3 Integration and Political Concertation in Latin America: Mercosur, Unasur, and the CELAC

The Brazilian position in relation to the regional bodies since the end of the military regime in 1985 and 2016 can be interpreted as a strategy of concentric circles. We here underscore that, even in the first circle, the most restricted and most accentuated,—Mercosur,—the country did not abdicate from its autonomy. In fact, within this customs union, the Brazilian governments always refrained from submitting the country to common decisions, with only a few exceptions, due to the alleged risks of instability within member states. This structural positioning, which endured for 30 years (1985–2016), provided a justification for debating the very basic elements of Mercosur. This idea gained traction in parallel to the institutional crisis. In Brazil, from the exchange rate crisis from 1999 to 2001, which became increasingly accentuated during the Rousseff government, actors with a strong social, economic, and political weight openly defended the need to downgrade the current level of integration and free trade agreement, albeit with some caveats. As Bacha (2014, p. 11) writes:

> Given the broad internal market, which could open up for exports to other countries in the world, Brazil will enjoy conditions for engaging in beneficial negotiations concerning the compensatory opening of the markets of its trade partners. There is ample scope for opportunities, involving multilateral, regional, and bilateral agreements. It is certain that the country needs the freedom of movement, and, therefore, to make more flexible the rules for negotiations with third countries which have been observed in Mercosur.

In February 2015, the same author affirmed the need to resume the negotiations for the Free Trade Area of the America (FTAA), which had been interrupted in November 2005 in Mar del Plata.[6] The uncertainties that became evident from the point of the Brazilian and Argentinean crises in 1999 and 2001, respectively, which slowed the negotiations down, put the economic aspects of the regional integration process on hold. In Chap. 5, as we discussed the concept of "*salto in avanti*", we saw that these difficulties, within the Lula and Rousseff governments, which both adhered to the integration process but without strong backing from the political and business community, were partially substituted by social and political issues. Recurrent—albeit circumscribed—disputes, highlighted the need for new initiatives to strengthen the integration process if the objective shared by important forces with the capacity for action within Brazilian society had been aimed at the continuity and deepening of Mercosur. From 2011 and onwards, the governments did not push for further advances. In large measure, these governments depended on domestic political processes, which were the object of strong internal tensions within the four countries in the bloc. Just like it had been evident regarding other regional integration experiences, the absence of agency and initiative eventually obstructed the process. One example regards the controversy related to Venezuela's entry into Mercosur; it was accepted during the summit in Cordoba in July 2006. Considering the controversies within the Brazilian and Paraguayan parliaments, Venezuela was eventually accepted as a full member during the summit in Brasília, in July, 2012, which was realized without the presence of Paraguay. Even so, Venezuela's ratification of innumerous protocols which already were included in the body of the legal proceedings of the bloc was postponed for later negotiations.

In normal circumstances, the decision-making dynamic tends to gain more autonomy in relation to nation states. This depends on the interests at play, but also on state capacities. The low Brazilian engagement in the institutional strengthening of the bloc can be understood in this light, as the state—in this case, understood not as the government, but as the broader administration—does not desire to lose control of the process. The Brazilian positions are based on the logic of intergovernmentality and are more adapted to the expansion of the bloc than to its deepening. Intergovernamentality has thereby permitted Brazil to maintain a strong capacity to intervene in relation to the politics of regional integration, as it reserves a high level of autonomy for each state. This is hereby compatible with the element of

[6] Entrevista ao jornal Valor Econômico, 5/2/2015.

autonomy within Brazilian foreign policy in relation to its partners. It is highly important that this autonomy during the developmentalist-distributivist period permitted the densification of relations with other non-central large countries and groupings, such as the BRICS. From the perspective of the critics of regional and South American integration, it also spurred a process of reintegration in relation to central countries. The relation to the United States, but also the European Union, and the acceleration of the negotiations for entry into the OECD should be understood from this point of view.

The concepts of autonomy and diversification of partnerships defended by part of the elites and present in the institutional memories of the Ministry of Foreign Affairs (Mariano, 2007), led to continuous questionings about Mercosur. The perception that the deepening of the integration process within the bloc led to a loss of Brazilian sovereignty and autonomy continues to influence part of the state agencies. Courses of action which could have the consequence of limiting Brazil's international room of maneuver by constraining the diversification of its partnerships were thereby firmly rejected.

A more institutionalized Mercosur would not serve the interests of a considerable part of the elites, social, and economic regional groups, and political sectors which appear to already have their needs contemplated by the basic structure defined in 1991. As we saw, since the end of the 1990s, certain developments have defended its downgrading. In any case, even if the objectives are rescaled, as we have seen continuously with regards parts of the business community, not least the manufacturing sector, the interest in increasing trade and cross-border investment persisted. Within certain business communities, this interest is still highly central. In previous periods, during the PSDB and PT governments, large Brazilian companies sought regional markets. That was the case with Petrobras, Itaú, Bunge, Gerdau, AmBev, and others. It was also the case with construction companies such as Camargo Correa, Odebrecht, Andrade Gutierrez, OAS, Queiroz Galvão, etc. The crisis which exploded from 2014 to 2015 due to the investigations and juridical processes related to corruption in Petrobras eventually impacted the Brazilian position concerning regional integration very significantly. This would also gain regional repercussions. The weakening or even potential disappearance of some of these companies would diminish the already tested engagement amongst businessmen in relation to regional integration. All the theories about regional integration recognize the importance of this sector, be this either public or private, for the advance of the integration process.

Mercosur was important in specific situations, as during the negotiations with the European Union, in relation to which an agreement was formally signed in Brussels in June 2019. It was also important in the relations with the United States in the period until 2016, serving as a mechanism of resistance confronted with asymmetrical pressures. Traditionally within Brazilian diplomacy, there has been strong preoccupation related to avoiding commitments which later could become a liability. This has been evident within economic negotiations, but it is also true with regards to other fields. At the same time, it should be noted that although the international environment would suggest a strengthening of the integration process in order for

Brazil to obtain better conditions for negotiating with other countries, this has not always been the case. For example, typically, contradictory situations have also become evident: we saw in Chap. 6 that the European Union strongly appreciated the bloc to bloc relation. In the case of intra-bloc difficulties in Mercosur, the pressures towards national solutions will certainly be intensified, as we have seen. This continuously became evident until 2016. During the Temer period, the movement towards national solutions at the cost of the states within the bloc gained momentum. The decision to not permit Venezuela to assume the *pro tempore* presidency in July 2016 led to pressures on Uruguay, to transfer the position.[7] With the Bolsonaro administration, the tradition of the first destination for a newly inaugurated Brazilian president being Buenos Aires was broken. In March 2019, Bolsonaro traveled to Santiago, which was the first trip to a country within South America. His objective was to participate in a meeting with other regional chiefs of state to discuss the creation of Prosur. The presidents of Argentina, Colombia, Paraguay, and Peru were also present.[8]

Successive Brazilian governments have accepted the idea that integration means ceding a certain degree of sovereignty, but the concessions actually made have always tended to be restricted: this explains the defense of the Customs Union with limited policies regarding the confrontation of asymmetries (Arbix, 2015). The low degree of complementarity was not confronted through coherent policies aimed at regional development, or common projects and strong initiatives to create production chains. Whenever they did become evident, internal governmental initiatives were limited (Froio, 2015). To the degree that these asymmetries remain evident, the general trend is that the customs union will not be completed, and eventually will be weakened due to a logic according to which conflicts are overvalued, as the means for their overcoming have a direct relation with the changes of the states' positions. Though far from being the only responsible party regarding these difficulties, the Brazilian position also encountered resistance to further integration amongst the other members of the bloc. The positions of Argentina, Paraguay, Uruguay, and Venezuela in relation to Mercosur also accentuated these limits. We highlight Brazil, as the role of paymaster, according to Mattli (1999) would befall this country,—although it has never openly assumed it.

Differently from Mercosur, Unasur arose in a context of regional diversity. These diversities even also concerned the politics of insertion within the international economy. Diversities were accepted and considered normal, and therefore Unasur did not have economic integration as its objective, thus discarding all kinds of proposals regarding a common market. The goal was to overcome differences, without neglecting them, and to maintain a space for interaction. Unasur represented a second concentric circle for the Brazilian policy, which due to its

[7] https://internacional.estadao.com.br/noticias/geral,serra-e-fhc-viajam-ao-uruguai-para-evitar-que-venezuela-lidere-o-mercosul,10000061190

[8] https://g1.globo.com/politica/noticia/2019/03/23/bolsonaro-chega-de-volta-ao-brasil-apos-viagem-ao-chile.ghtml

intergovernmental and flexible characteristics, without any unavoidable institutional commitments, was consolidated over a few years. Its *raison d'etre* thereby gradually became evident, from Brasília's perspective.

From Lula da Silva (2006) perspective, in a speech at the opening ceremony of the II Meeting for Chiefs of State and Governments of the South-American Community of Nations, the predecessor of Unasur: "a project as broad as that of our community has to comprise institutions that permit the realization of our projects. If we want a strong community, it is imperative to imbue it with the necessary instruments". The goal was the existence of a South-American, and thereby not a Latin-American and even less so, a hemispheric instrument. Hence, in this space, in the formulation of the Brazilian state, of its politicians, and its leading officials, consensus could be achieved with regards to certain issues. A consensus which becomes possible as order is sought and permits the maintenance of the independence of individual states. More importantly, this consensus can also be obtained as a result of the composition of regional power. The preservation of autonomy, cooperation, and selective integration thereby merge, and a common space in which these relations correspond to another geography emerges, which attenuates, but does not eliminate, the weight of extra-regional factors. This would be possible in South America, but not in Latin America, and even less so, within the continental sphere. Applying the concepts discussed in this book could provide a way for propelling regional autonomy; not by confronting objectively more powerful states, but rather by creating a space for regional affirmation with regards to issues in relation to which certain capacities would be formed, without neglecting the power relations on the global level.

Within this South American sphere, some countries have obtained a higher degree of decision-making capacity. For the heads of state, for the elites who supported the government, and for the diplomacy, Brazil obtained a higher degree of decision-making capacity. As we have highlighted, the Brazilian formulation of a South American space has gained continuity, and has been in consolidation since 1993, and even before that. It thus lasted throughout different governments of Itamar Franco, Cardoso, Lula, and Rousseff. We clearly understand that it corresponds in time to the Mexican policy of insertion within the North American space, as Mexico has broken with its secular tradition of anti-Americanism. In a situation of growing difficulties regarding Mercosur and even in a situation of changes in relation to the United States, which we analyze below, Unasur could work with regards to different interests. It could preserve a reasonable autonomy for internal regional negotiations. At the same time, from the Brazilian foreign policy perspective, concerning the governments cited, the bloc could help preserve a space which in all circumstances until then had been viewed as central to the regional stability and even with regards to the international system.

Within the Brazilian foreign policy perspective, according to Guimarães (2006, p. 275) it is imperative to work "consistently and persistently in favor of the emergence of a multipolar global system in which South America would constitute one of the poles and not be relegated as a mere sub-region for another economic and political pole". The continuity of domestic conflict in South American countries, including within the three largest countries in Mercosur (Argentina, Brazil, and Venezuela) shows the existing difficulties even during the post-hegemonic period, of reaching the level of a pole. In the relations between the countries, which constitute three groups in which the countries of Unasur divided themselves during the first half of the 2010s - Mercosur, the Pacific Alliance, and the Bolivarian Alliance for the Peoples of our America (ALBA)—consistent problems exist. Some are of a historical origin, like those between Chile and Peru, while others are connected to very specific problems of the moment, which we today, *ex-post facto,* can consider as related to international tensions. During the Obama administration, the extra-regional influence, not least from China, gradually became viewed as potentially dangerous for the North American geopolitical interests.

Even in situations of important changes, like those that took place from 1990 to 2015, for Brazil, the South American space has been divided in a consistent manner, as Santos (2014, p. 184) accentuates in a historical perspective from the Itamar Franco government.

> The concept of Latin America was consolidated from the construction of a common imaginary by intellectuals from the region—with Brazil often receiving or being attributed with a peculiar role within this identity-based architecture,—but also as the representation of the "other" for the North American society, as an asymmetric counter-concept of its self-attributed virtues. Yet, the adhesion of Mexico to NAFTA in 1992 contributed to eroding the concept of Latin America, by decisively approximating one of its most important poles, Mexico, to the "other" within this continent: the United States.

In comparison to the Brazilian policies towards Mercosur, in the case of Unasur, during the developmentalist-distributivist years, autonomy appears to mainly be related to certain specific cooperation objectives. This occurs at least within three different dimensions: financing for regional integration, even considering the Brazilian restrictions in relation to the *Banco do Sul*, infrastructure integration (incorporation of IIRSA and the establishment of COSIPLAN); and defense (the South American Defense Council). This regards more or less articulated attempts to connect national autonomy with the objectives of South American cooperation and integration. The efforts of cooperation and integration related to these three dimensions are based on the objective to strengthen states' autonomy, either from the perspective of increasing states' room of maneuver within the international system or with regards to effectively exercising sovereignty over the national territory (Borda, 2012). It is important to highlight that the process of creation of the South American Defense Council is linked not only to the objective of strengthening cooperation regarding issues of defense and security but also relates to the intent of establishing a counterpoint of influence in relation to the United States in South America, and more precisely, the Andean region.

In other words: Mercosur is designed as a customs union aiming towards a common market (of the South); therefore, by definition, there is a horizon of abdication of elements of autonomy and sovereignty, hence, we define this as the first concentric circle. As we have discussed, part of Mercosur's problems refers to this issue. Not only with regards to Brazil, but repeatedly also concerning Argentina, Paraguay, Uruguay, and also Venezuela in the period in which it participated within the bloc. Just like their respective societies, concerning both elites as well as the population more generally, regional states consider that the focus of their development depends on national capacity, understood not in terms of an absolute, but rather, as a relational capacity. The dominant political groups in each state, albeit they do change throughout time, appreciate their local power. The elites, in line with their ideological positioning and their insertion within the global web of power, appreciate their local sovereignty, even as they recognize their weakness and dependency on the global level. In the case of Unasur, exactly because this construct privileges the idea of national autonomy and sovereignty over the territory of each state, it managed to make very different and ideologically distinct interests converge for some years.

Concluding this part of the analysis of Brazil's position in relation to Unasur until 2016, we resume Russell and Toklatian's (2003, p. 19) idea of relational autonomy. This is partially useful in order to think about how the principle of autonomy relates to the country's positions within Unasur. This is how we chose to treat it, in contrast to the concept's original significance as it was developed by its authors, a high degree of participation from public opinion, interest groups, and domestic actors in the definition of Brazil's positions did not become evident. Brazilian policies towards South America, although they did not neglect domestic preferences, were until 2016 much more determined by state institutions, and by the presidency and the ministry of foreign relations, as has been discussed by the authors who study the concept of presidential diplomacy. In the case of Unasur, the participation of the Ministry of Defense was also important. The necessary domestic support for the implementation of agreements, in general, has been sought *ex post facto,* which is one of the particularities of regional integration in South America which complicates the use of theories of a neofunctionalist or liberal-intergovernamental nature in order to understand this.

The idea of relational autonomy should be understood and used in combination with Pinheiro's (2004) analysis of the double pattern of Brazilian foreign policy, defined as pragmatic institutionalism. That means that there are different spheres of analysis. On the one hand, autonomy is sought through distance or through diversification. On the other, autonomy is sought through cooperation, establishing a relation between the two which aims to guarantee benefits, and remove risks. During the Lula and Rousseff governments, the idea of the importance of institutional construction gained traction, not least within the presidential perspective, without dismissing double patterns. As the Brazilian crisis strengthened the positions of those who defended negotiation of free trade agreements with central countries and large blocks (TTIP and TPP), or the rapid adaption to the OECD standards, the search for institutionality within South-American organizations would lose priority. This would happen without Brazil needing to abandon its preoccupations about modes of cooperation, and even regional integration. The country has been significantly benefitted by the export of higher value-added goods to the region and this position does nor disappear amongst business organizations, even after 2019, as a CNI study (2020, p. 13) indicates: "the trade with the bloc has a high economic significance for Brazil. Mercosur is the destination of 45% of Brazilian goods exports to Latin America and 21% of total exports of manufactured products to the world. Beyond that, it is also an important destination for investments made by Brazilian multinational companies".

In the analysis of integration policy and Brazil's hemispheric relations, the Community of Latin American and Caribbean States (CELAC), established in 2010, arises as the third concentric circle. Some member states have viewed these organizations as a possible alternative forum to the OAS. The previous president of Ecuador, Rafael Correa, made the greatest advances in this direction. For him, the CELAC should substitute the OAS.[9] The Brazilian position stands out as the most moderate and articulated. The Brazilian government during the Workers Party period recognized the importance of the organization but did not believe that it should be turned into an alternative to the OAS, and neither should it serve as a base for confrontation against it.

For Brazil, the OAS arises as an organization which joins all Latin American and Caribbean countries, and, in the words of Garcia, "without excluded countries" (2013, p. 61). This is, in fact, a process of creation of forums without participation by the United States or Canada, but a more pragmatic conception of the international realm implies an avoidance of confrontation or even policies which directly aim at the weakening of the OAS or other instruments of a continental nature. We thus clearly perceive the underlying idea of this third concentric circle. The Brazilian government perceives that a higher degree of identity exists regarding the CELAC than in the case of the OAS. This interpretation of the Brazilian position is shared by a wide spectrum of authors, including some close to the opposition at the time. With point of departure in a position differing from the government at the time, Sorj and Fausto (2013), partly agree with the conclusions reached regarding these motivations:

> The central objective of the Brazilian engagement within its regional environment is political stability. In general, Brazil has been successful in mediating conflicts between the anti-American agenda led by Chávez—supported by the rest of the ALBA countries—and other countries in the region. Moderating impulses, Brazil has become central in the development of institutions that seek to limit the importance of the OAS, even regarding the United States, without proposing its disappearance. In turn, the existence of regional organizations without the effective presence of the giant in the north propels the Brazilian influence. (Sorj & Fausto, 2013, p. 65).

In the Brazilian government's understanding, the CELAC would provide continuity to the initiatives previously developed by the *Contadora* and Rio Groups (created in 1983 and 1986). It is possible to affirm that the CELAC is viewed as a representative of a continental group of states which share certain affinities, and which is capable of organizing certain initiatives, including parts of the relations with the rest of the international community, as well as the United States. China considers the CELAC as its institutional interlocutor within Latin America.

---

[9]Infolatam. Equador: Rafael Correa apresenta a Insulza suas propostas para reformar a OEA. 30 de novembro de 2012. Available from: <http://www.infolatam.com.br/2012/11/30/equador-rafael-correa-apresenta-a-insulza-suas-propostas-para-reformar-a-OAS/>. Acessed on: 28 mai. 2013.

Within this perspective, some interpretations suggested that Brazil would seek the formation of an alternative pole with extra-regional competitive potential (Burges, 2008; Gardini & Lambert, 2010; Malamud, 2005). What would be the basis for an analysis of Brazilian regional foreign policy which highlights the country's intended role in relation to its surroundings, underlining the disinterest in offering something in exchange which would otherwise be expected from a paymaster? The Brazilian foreign policy, particularly the regional and hemispheric policy, clearly shows that there was not any ambitions stretching beyond the country's real possibilities. Despite the strong differences in relation to aspects of foreign, regional, and hemispheric policy, including in relation to Mercosur and Unasur, within civil society and between political forces with roots in the 1988 Constitution, we find a reasonable consensus about certain fundamental issues, particularly in relation to the needs not to overestimate national capacities. Issues which are inscribed in the Article 4 of the constitutional text that regard the principles defining Brazilian international relations: "I—national independence; II—the prevalence of human rights; III the peoples' self-determination; IV—non-intervention; V—equality between states; VI—the defense of peace; VII—the pacific solution to conflicts; VII—repudiation of terrorism and racism; IX—cooperation between the peoples' for the progress of humanity; X—concession of political asylum".[10] The only paragraph of article 4° states that "The Brazilian Federal Republic will seek the economic, political, social, and cultural integration between the peoples' of Latin America, aiming at the formation of a community of Latin American nations".

In this book, we do not focus on formal aspects; we conduct an analysis of Brazilian foreign policy in relation to the process of regional integration. We cite the Article 4 because it reflects the perception of a large part of society, beyond political, social, and economic elites. The evolution of an increasingly polarized national political context from the 2014 elections, as we have seen, led to rising tensions in the following years. It is therefore important to remember that there was a minimum foreign policy consensus, including with regards to the issue of regional and hemispheric insertion. This does not equal ignoring the large divergences, as well as the very different worldviews of the PT and the PSDB, two parties with roots in the 1988 Constitution. The radicalization occurring since then, which led to the Bolsonaro government in 2019, has in fact introduced extra-constitutional variables in Brazil. These variables do in some aspects coincide with interests of Brazilian elites, but cannot to confounded with these.

If this interpretation was true during the Cardoso and Lula terms, those of Rousseff accentuated the impossibility of the country assuming a foundational role within the region, beyond what Brazil could assume on basis of its dimensions, particularly economic, as we have seen in Table 6.1 of Chap. 6. This in part derives from the recognition of the constraints, partly due to the deterioration of the political and economic crisis which weights decisively in terms of limiting Brazilian influence. With different oscillations, above all in the developmentalist-distributivist period,

[10] https://www.senado.leg.br/atividade/const/con1988/CON1988_05.10.1988/art_4_.asp

this structural crisis of the Brazilian economy would endure until the 1980s, thus spanning some 40 years (Bresser Pereira, 2019), comprising of deindustrialization, and a continued fall in the savings capacity and competitiveness. The belief in the possibility of Brazilian intermediation, or even in the power of conviction,—the soft power—in certain cases is overestimated even by interest groups and segments within the North American government which use this to accentuate pressures within the region.

The Brazilian government contributed strongly to the proposal for the constitution of the Summit for Latin American and the Caribbean for Regional Integration and Development (CALC) which would merge with the Rio Group to become the CELAC. This contribution was not isolated, and neither can it be said to have played a completely decisive role: it contributed to different existing efforts without which, the CELAC would not have been constituted. The Mexican President, Felipe Calderón, also played an important role due to the country's interest in avoiding reliance on one single external link: NAFTA and the United States. CELAC is important to Brazil, but it demonstrated a lower degree of density than Mercosur and Unasur.

7.4 The Hemispheric Level: The OAS and the Relations with the United States

As we saw in Chap. 2, relations with the United States have always been important for Brazil. In this regard, there are no exceptions; these relations are,—and have always been,—very important for all the hemispheric countries. This has been the case during the 20th and 21st Centuries, in all continents. Once again, they became an important focus of political contestation in Brazil throughout the second Rousseff government. The indications in this regard appeared both in Brazil and in the United States. The pressures for change were not mainly directed towards the country's international engagement or bilateral relations,—although they might have spurred avenues leading in this direction,—but rather from the understanding that the leading groups and Brazilian elites would have concerning this environment and these relations. In other words, they are directly related to the country's internal conditions, and secondly, with the attitudes of North American sectors with interests in Brazil, within either the business community or government. The North American positions are important, but the most relevant focus relates to how they influenced domestic power relations from the point at which internal disputes were sharpened in Brazil.

As we have demonstrated in previous chapters, the idea of autonomy has been a guideline which always was present within Brazilian politics. The United States' agency within hemispheric politics, and by itself, has always presented a challenge to the exercise of autonomy within this sphere. At the beginning of the twenty-first Century, new circumstances became evident, particularly with regards to the possibility for a gradual change within the international equilibrium. What is important to highlight in this respect, due to the consequences which it could imply for the relations within the Americas, is the relative decline of the United States, although it continues to be, by far, the main global power. It is important to remain aware of the significance of the Chinese economic, political, and even strategic presence (Vadell, 2011). In any case, if the long-term consequences of this process were not already evident in the years of the second Rousseff administration, they gradually did gain a higher degree of visibility. One of these consequences was the dichotomy between an acceptance of the Chinese presence within the region in the economic field, as a large importer of commodities from many Latin American countries and a large investor, not least in infrastructure, and an increase in tensions which persist within the technological and geopolitical realm. The North-American pressures, albeit not direct, had the effect of destabilizing various governments, with consequences regarding the integration process.

The analysis of the Brazilian position within the continent should keep this array of factors in mind, which explains the ambiguity throughout time. On the one hand, within the Lula governments and during the first Rousseff mandate, the aspirations towards the strengthening of sub-regional organizations, in order to enhance autonomy in relation to the United States, and on the other hand, maintain a low profile within the OAS, which was used as a forum for discussing specific issues. Historically, the OAS has been a locus for the development of relations with the United States, but it was far from the only one, and even the main institutional vehicle for this purpose. The relations between Brazil and the United States materialize mainly within bilateral forums. We can hereby understand the relative significance of the OAS for Brazil. If until 2016, this can be understood through the notion of a fourth concentric circle, its role has not entirely changed for Brazilian governments since then.

Within the OAS a decrease in the North American influence can be observed, which for some authors is considered as disinterest. This is not a conjunctural phenomenon and has been evident since the 1990s and throughout all of the Insulza period (2005–2015), and into the Almagro tenure (2015–2025). According to Herz (2011), in the so-called post-hegemonic period, the organization cannot still be viewed as a North American foreign policy instrument as it was in the past. For the author, the situation in the United States within the OAS is much different, because of the emergence of the left within many countries, due to the diversification of their foreign policies, and because of the lack of compatibility between North American interests and the region's objectives regarding issues such as migration, terrorism, and the combatting of drug trafficking, beyond the lack of a clearly emanated strategy on behalf of Washington (Herz, 2011). The evolution of the North American influence within the organization also presents ambiguities. On the one hand, this appears to diminish, particularly due to the absence of policies for the region, but, one the other, it continues to wield a great significance. As Bell and Armstrong (2015) highlight, the budget still comes from Washington, amounting to approximately 42% of the total value (Meyer, 2013). This proportion will not change within the short and medium-term, considering that the relative quotas of each country are based on criteria related to the weight of their own economies. It is even more important to consider that in the second half of the 2010s, until 2020, the conditions which had led to the weakening of the OAS ceased to exist with regards to the majority of regional governments, which in the case of Brazil is illustrated by the government in power from 2019. This does not mean that the OAS necessarily will resume its regional centrality. In the Trump period, in fact, the foreign policy orientation based on unilateralism sought specific agreements. This implied the broadening of trade agreements and bilateral cooperation and initiatives directly aimed at the United States, as Bolton (2020) describes in Chap. 8 ("Chaos as a way of life") with regards to the administration's worries about Venezuela. Even with respect to the policies of aggressive unilateralism, the countries within the region are not relevant,—Brazil amongst them.

Discussing the possible strategies for Latin America in relation to the United States, Russell and Tokatlian (2007, p. 22) defend that the countries within the region could make use of "a binding multilateralism [which] implies the utilization of international instruments to oppose proposals or actions by the United States which violate international legality, and to induce them, along with other countries, to adhere to agreements and international regimes which depend on their participation in order to be efficient, and to coordinate with other countries in order to broaden capacities of collective action in relation to Washington" (Russell & Tokatlian, 2007, p. 22). This analysis contributes to the explanation of the general perspective of Brazilian policy during the governments from 1986 to 2016. But it does not help to explain the position in relation to the OAS, due to the specificity of relations within this organization. In the case of hemispheric organization, considering the power asymmetries, the historical, and the recent experience throughout the past 30 years have suggested that multilateral politics do not imply the desired effects by the country's governments. The Brazilian government's preoccupation with the North American bases in Colombia, the lack of convergence during the crisis in Honduras, and the way the United States insisted in discussing drug trafficking and Colombia guerillas are all issues which point to clear difficulties in using the OAS, even without abdicating from the recognition of its usefulness in relation to certain issues of common interest. It thus becomes evident that the OAS is less convergent with the community of values which nurture the relations with Mercosur, Unasur, and CELAC. It is noticeable that the Brazilian governments who seek to tighten economic and geopolitical relations with the United States favor bilateral relations in detriment of multilateral ties. The OAS would not return as the center of attention, and Brazil has contributed to the consolidation of the North American geopolitical interest within other multilateral institutions with a hemispheric format, such as the Inter-American Development Bank (IADB) (Folha de São Paulo, 03/08/2020—*Declaração sobre a candidature norte-americana à presidência* do BID).

The chance that this situation within the OAS should change considerably towards the end of the 2010s, still within the Obama and Rousseff terms, was eventually discarded. Both on the Brazilian as well as the North American side, the trend was to favor bilateral relations in detriment of multilateralism, as we have seen in the Brazilian case. The tendencies towards a defense of multilateralism and autonomy from 2015, eventually became weakened. In the case of the United States, ambiguities became evident. In many instances, the government's position, particularly the Obama administration, converged in the direction of improving relations, even with governments not positively minded towards the United States. Different groups within governments, the business community, and liberal think tanks were central in this respect. An individual who played an important role in this regard was the Vice-President, Joe Biden. In the case of the illegal tapings of the Brazilian president made by the National Security Agency (NSA), in relation to which the Brazilian government formally requested an apology in 2013, some initiatives were made to accommodate the situation, of which the former Minister of Foreign Relations, Mauro Vieira was a central part. At the same time, conservative sectors, not least within the Republican Party acted aggressively, especially against certain aspects of the Brazilian foreign policy: as an example, they were strong critics of the BRICS bloc. The serious difficulties in which the Obama government found itself, confronting a hostile Congress in the final phase of its second mandate, in 2015 and 2016, indicates that in much the same way that there were no consistent lines of action in relation to Brazil, the same was the case concerning foreign policy. In the case of the Republican Party, directly destabilizing positions regarding hemispheric politics were adopted.

The bilateral presidential meeting in Panama in April 2015, and the negotiation to resume preparations of the Brazilian state visit to Washington should be viewed within this context. The differences compared to previous periods during Rousseff's second term did not go unnoticed in Washington. Analyzing the Brazilian problems[11] in an editorial, the New York Times highlights that:

> So far, those hopes appear to have been misplaced. Ms. Rousseff has been an underwhelming leader on domestic matters and, perhaps most disappointing, on the world stage. While the other three large emerging economies, China, Russia and India, are pursuing muscular foreign policies, under Ms. Rousseff's watch, Brazil's voice in the international arena barely registers above a whisper.

The journal concludes that a way to improve stability in Brazil could be to act in order to complement contested North American interests in Latin America. The policy formulators of the democratic Obama government sought to attract the Rousseff government to their sphere, without confronting it. The editorial hereby concludes:

> Nonetheless, Brazil can play a pivotal role in two Latin American countries that are of growing importance to the United States. In Venezuela, Brazil may be the most influential external actor capable of bridging the dangerous divide between the government of President Nicolás Maduro and the opposition, which Mr. Maduro has confronted by jailing its leaders. Mr. da Silva, a charismatic politician who reveled in diplomatic deal-making, often used his significant leverage on Mr. Maduro's fiery predecessor, Hugo Chávez.

[11] <http://www.nytimes.com/2015/03/22/opinion/sunday/brazils-dim-voice-on-the-world-stage.html?_r=0>

> In Cuba, Brazil could play a constructive role in the economic and political evolution of the island as the Castro era comes to an end. Brazil has already invested in a huge new seaport that could help resurrect Cuba's anemic economy. New York Times (21/3/2015).

In a similar vein, in Washington, the objective was to highlight how the countries' economic interests would point towards an improvement of relations, which should lead to a new level of convergence and cooperation. Meacham (2015), from the *Center for Strategic and International Studies* points to a possible avenue:

> In simple terms, Brazil and the United States have abundant reason to cooperate. Brasilia's economic needs coupled with Washington's desire to codify the relationship justify that cooperation.... Washington's preference for FTAs is not immediately compatible with Brasilia's tendency toward rules-based multilateral trade.... Add to this the complications of Brazil's membership in Mercosur, which explicitly limits members' ability to seek free trade agreements outside of the bloc as we've seen with the Mercosur-EU free trade agreement process, and it becomes clear that any meaningful free-trade effort can only result from careful diplomatic maneuvering. Conclusions: The two biggest economies in the Western Hemisphere can't continue to operate in economic parallel. The potential gains from broader bilateral trade cooperation are enormous, and both Washington and Brasilia appear increasingly open to having the discussion. In the face of domestic turmoil and dissatisfaction, Dilma could seize bilateral trade as a new goal—and one that could deliver tangible results that could play well at home given growing public support. Even embroiled in political crisis, working with Washington could be a much-needed way out.

The Brazilian economic and political development in the 2000s was important, but it does not directly point to the attenuation of the strong asymmetries in relation to the United States. There was no objective on behalf of Brazilian governments to compete or create antagonistic blocs. They rather sought to negotiate and assumed oppositional positions with regards to certain national interests, which included the combatting of poverty, the lowering of persistent inequalities, the defense of adequate policies for environmental protection, preserving the development policies, etc. We have seen that there was a policy of constructing an autonomous pole within the international system, but not in direct opposition to the United States. Some North American voiced recognized this.

> It is time to work more closely with Brazil in the search for common interests regarding the strengthening of global governance, the promotion of regional stability, environmental protection, and public health, the liberalization and expansion of international trade within agriculture and services, and regarding energy security (Lowenthal, 2008, pp. 37–38).

Throughout the Workers Party governments, there were no significant tensions between Brazil and the United States. At least since 1990, this relationship has not undergone any structural changes. Yet, this does not mean that disagreements did not exist, particularly with regards to issues related to the recurrent North American unilateralism, without impeding policies of understanding and cooperation (Patriota, 2008). Within the economic and trade fields, there were certain disputes, such as the Brazilian contestation of the North American cotton subsidies within the World Trade organization (WTO), which was definitively ruled favorable to Brazil by the Dispute Settlement Body, in June 2008,—in general, disputes regarding "normal" controversies between countries. The controversies of economic and commercial nature have always enjoyed bipartisan support in Brazil.

At the same time, a certain margin for disagreement also became evident, which in the 2010s grew within some fields. An area in which this lack of understanding has been felt with increasing intensity is exactly with regards to hemispheric relations, which is important to consider in the analysis of the Brazilian position in relation to the United States, as it also reflects on issues concerned with the OAS. This has produced spillovers on Brazil's politics of regional engagement and highlights the importance of the present discussion with regards to the four concentric levels. Here, it becomes important to remember the conference of Chiefs of State in 2005 in Mar del Plata, "there is no doubt that the period from 2009 has shown the fundamental distance which separates Brazil from the United States with regards to the regional order of the Americas" (Neves et al., 2011, p. 149). For the Brazilian governments, the consequence has been the weakening of the very instances which should provide an institutional home for these relations; the OAS. The existence within Latin America,—particularly amongst some countries in South America,—of positions which coincide in the aspiration towards a higher degree of autonomy in relation to the United States, would eventually strengthen the Brazilian perception which had existed ever since the military governments, regarding the partial weakening of the OAS. This perception, which was reinforced during the Lula and Rousseff governments, led to increased tensions in the relations with the United States until 2016. A thorough discussion of these relations demands a more precise understanding of the structures of formulation of the North American foreign policy. The governmental agencies do not always act in a coordinated fashion. For some, the tensions were understood as an obstacle to be surpassed. Others acted from the beginning of the developmentalist-distributivist governments in order to weaken Brazilian governments since then. The case of the NSA, which is subordinated to the *Department of Defense* and the *Justice Department* serves as examples. Other more prominent cases concern private institutions, from corporations to think tanks.

Considering this Chapter's goal of demonstrating the Brazilian position in relation to regional and hemispheric organizations, it becomes important to understand their evolution over time. The crisis of the OAS is not a new fact of the 2010s. In part, it has been confounded with the strengthening of North American unilateralism, or with the increased autonomy of some of its member states. It has been weakened in different historical moments. From the crisis of Honduras in July 2009, it has been facing difficulties of maintaining itself as an institutional point of reference. In the period of the Workers Party, Brazil adopted a posture aimed at managing hemispheric relations which were incompatible with the North American positions. Although it is not the decisive factor, this lack of convergence merged with the impasse which can be simultaneously observed as a cause for the weakening of the OAS. With regards to the Brazilian positions in this phase can be mentioned the crisis in relation to the Interamerican Commission for Human Rights (IACHR) as a consequence of the precautionary measure which recommended the immediate suspension of the licensing of the Belo Monte hydroelectric dam in April 2011, and the position at the Sixth Summit of the Americas in April 2012, when all Latin

American countries left the United States, and partially Canada, isolated in their defense of the position that Cuba should not participate in the following summits, and in not supporting the Argentinean claim with regard to its sovereignty over the Ilhas Malvinas/Falklands Islands. Analyzed *post facto,* this posture contributed significantly to the resumption of relations between the United States and Cuba. From December 2014, a new phase was initiated, including the reciprocal diplomatic recognition. Not even the election of Trump and the new escalation of tensions between the United States and Cuba did, until the end of 2020, lead to a total rupture with Cuba, neither on behalf of the United States or the other states on the continent, including Brazil.

The partial resolution of the issue regarding Cuba did not lead to a reinvigoration of the OAS. This justifies the designation of the organization as the fourth concentric circle within the Brazilian foreign policy on the continent until 2016. The Brazilian position cannot be classified as one of opposition to the OAS and its different working areas but should be considered as a low-profile posture. In a similar way, it is also consensus that the United States did not find a vehicle for systematizing continental relations. The constitution of Unasur in 2008 opened the path for the existence of a temporary capacity for conflict resolution in relation to regional and domestic disputes in South America. Its weakening and posterior disappearance impeded the existence of instruments which could guarantee stability and resistance by making the region an object of geopolitical disputes with the potential to create international instability. Unasur had contributed to the resolution of specific conflicts, in 2008, with the institutional crisis in Bolivia, and the diplomatic crisis between Colombia and Ecuador, and in 2010 in the crisis between Venezuela and Colombia, as well as in other institutional crises in Ecuador in 2010, in Paraguay in 2012, and between 2012 and 2017 in Venezuela. In these cases, the OAS did not at any point have the capacity to intervene in a mediating role with sufficient credibility. According to Teixeira Junior (2020), this situation opened the way for a higher degree of instability, making the region the object of geopolitical tensions which, amongst other, comprise of the United States, China, and Russia.

Since Jair Bolsonaro took office in 2019, there has been a strong ideological alignment with President Donald Trump. Since 2019, this alignment with the US has been a priority for Brazil's foreign policy. The alignment with the US has historical roots in parts of Brazilian elites, notwithstanding the fact that the bandwogoning policies have always produced limited results. Bolsonaro made significant efforts to build a personal relation with President Trump, which nonetheless has resulted in very limited benefits for Brazil. Joe Biden's victory against Trump in the 2020 US elections,—which Bolsonaro was one of the last leaders to recognize,—leaves the Brazilian president without a key international reference for an agenda against the so-called globalism. In addition, Bidens approach towards trade, human rights, deforestation in the Amazon and stimulus towards global action against climate change may cause frictions with Bolsonaro's perspective. With the United States under Biden, the room of maneuver for Bolsonaro's international agenda has been reduced, leaving Brazil under Bolsonaro more isolated in world affairs.

Part of the Brazilian elites, particularly those that merged against the PT governments, replaced a regional integration perspective for an insertion in the world focused on the liberal system. An example is the search for participation in the OECD in a different perspective from the BRICS and the regional integration mechanisms. Furthermore, the military elite that has participated in the Temer and Bolsonaro governments seeks insertion in the US-led security system. As happened in other historical moments, the results tend to be of low relevance, which seriously weakens Brazil's international bargaining capacity and also reduces its regional influence.

7.5 Conclusion

In this chapter, we have used the concept of concentric circles, which facilitates an understanding of the Brazilian position in relation to regional bodies. Geopolitical and structuralist scholars attribute much importance to the idea of the international system and a state's positioning within this. States' foreign relations have hereby been treated hierarchically. We believe that the hierarchical conception which we present within this chapter explains the Brazilian perception of the early 2000s until 2016, particularly, of the presidency and the Ministry of Foreign Affairs: Mercosur represented the first circle, Unasur the second, CELAC the third, and the OAS the fourth. This was based on a choice aiming at rationality. There was an objective of focusing on the interests of social actors, particularly those determined by corporative and economic aims, though without neglecting those of the population in general, linking them to certain national and historical objectives of the country. The rationale of the integration policies was determined by the binominal of autonomy and development. The hierarchization of the forms of integration, collaboration, and cooperation,—all internally related—should have the objective of maximizing capacities.

Understanding the international and hemispheric position of Brazil implies considering the concept of autonomy, which has been viewed as an essential principle for safeguarding the country against the most detrimental effects of the international system. It provides the foundation for the articulation between the concepts of interdependence, diversification, and universalism. In the Brazilian case, the term autonomy relates to the idea of the broadening of the state's margins of maneuver, considering the perspective of the conditions of the domestic and international system at any given period. This idea appears as an explanatory factor with regards to the international positions,—even in different governments. Seeking to understand the reasons which could have led to the extreme changes, the fourth level of Hermann's (1990) scale, international orientation change, initiated in 2016, but more decisively deepened in 2019, will be an important point of departure in order to proceed to new phases of the research, not least to understand if there are structural reasons or whether it regards a short-term moment of Brazilian foreign policy. Giving continuity to the central ideas within this book, it is possible that the aspirations towards autonomy would cease to be a fundamental aim within Brazilian foreign policy. As we have observed, the internal difficulties of political negotiation, even the climate marked by a lack of negotiations, as well as the economic crisis create barriers for the Brazilian role within the region. Within all of the spheres analyzed, the regional policy developed from the end of the military governments in 1986 until 2016, during thirty years, was challenged by pressures for a more intense approximation with central countries. Will its failure, with the victory of those opposed to it, lead to a definitive rupture with the social bases on which the previous foreign policy was based? Or are we confronted with an unstable equilibrium? The weakness of a national development project is closely linked to a polarized world-view, of war, to which those who manage the state appear to accommodate themselves.

Discussing the Brazilian position in relation to the regional organizations, a historical issue appears to reemerge: the relation with the United States. During the Cardoso and Lula governments, particular conditions, such as favorable international trade, the strengthening of the generically anti-hegemonic countries in South America, the capacity for international projection, the participation within the BRICS, and the growing relevance of China all allowed for the maintenance of friendly relations with the United States, always within the level of diplomatic normality. This occurred in a context of strong positioning against unilateralism within different arenas, be this either trade, geopolitics, or multilateral organizations including the UN, etc. The Brazilian political and economic crisis which would result in the impeachment in 2016 strengthened new positions. The sharpening of the crisis occurred at a moment in which important and profound transformations also took place in the United States. In Brazil, with regards to foreign relations, there was a growth of demands made by business interests and political factions, which impacted the central administration, and called out for the adhesion to international regimes formed by the central states. These positions were expressed through the defense of the adhesion to international regimes which, until then, had been under the United States' leadership, as it became evident with regards to the OECD.

References

Alves, V. C. (2007). *Da Itália à Coréia: decisões sobre ir ou não à guerra*. Belo Horizonte Editora da UFMG.

Amaral, O. E., & Ribeiro, P. F. (2015). Por que Dilma de novo? Uma análise exploratória do Estudo Eleitoral Brasileiro de 2014. *Revista de Sociologia e Política, 23*(56), 107–123.

Amorim, C. (2020). *Reflexões sobre a geopolítica depois da pandemia*. Carta Capital, 15 de junho de 2020.

Araujo, E. (2017). *Trump e o Ocidente*. Cadernos de Política Exterior, no. 6, ano III.

Arbix, G. (2015, December 17). *Entrevista dada a Tullo Vigevani*. Aragusuku e Jose Luiz Pimenta.

Avritzer, L. (2019). *O pêndulo da democracia no Brasil*. Todavia.

Barbosa, R. (2014). *Uma nova política comercial*. O Estado de S. Paulo, 11 de novembro de 2014. https://opiniao.estadao.com.br/noticias/geral,uma-nova-politica-comercial-imp-,1591030

Bell, A., & Armstrong, F. (2015). *OAS: New leadership, old challenges. Aulablog*. Center for Latin American and Latino Studies (CLALS), American University.

Bernal-Meza, R. (2005). *América Latina enel mundo*. Grupo Editor Latinoamericano.

Bittar, S., & Hershberg, E. (2012). *North-South relations in the western hemisphere. Mid-Atlantic council of latin American studies*. American University (Paper).

Bolton, J. (2020). *The room where it happened*. Simon & Schuster.

Borda, S. (2012). Desafios y oportunidades de la Unión de Naciones Suramericanas – UNASUR. Documentos CRIES. No. 18. Bresser Pereira, L. C. (2019). 40 anos de desindustrialização. *Jornal dos Economistas*, junho de 2019. Disponivel em: http://www.bresserpereira.org.br/articles/2019/278-40-anos-desindustrializacao-J.Economista-FOR.pdf.

Briceño Ruiz, J. (2012). Autonomia y desarrolloenelpensamiento integracionista latinoamericano. In J. Briceño Ruiz, A. Rivarola, & Á. Gragea (Eds.), *Integración Latinoamericano y Caribeña*. Política y economia. Fondo de Cultura Económica de España.

Burges, W. S. (2008). Consensual hegemony: Theorizing Brazilian foreign policy after the cold war. *International Relations, 22*(1), 65–84.

Carr, E. H. (2001). *Vinteanos de crise: 1919–1939*. Editora Universidade de Brasília.

Casarões, G. (2019). Eleições, política externa e os desafios do novo governo brasileiro. *Pensamiento Propio, 24*, 231–274.

Casarões, G. (2020). The first year of the Bolsonaro's foreign policy. In A. Mori (org). Latin America and the global order: dangers and opportunities in a multipolar world. Ledizioni Ledi Publishing.

Choi, Y. J., & Caporaso, J. A. (2002). Comparative regional integration. In W. Carlsnaes, T. Risse, & B. Simmons (Eds.), *Handbook of international relations*. Sage Publications.

Colacrai, M. (2009). Los aportes de laTeoría de laAutonomía, genuína contribuciónsudamericana. La autonomía es hoy una categoria en desuso o se enfrenta al desafio de una renovaciónenun contexto interdependiente y más complejo? In G. Lechini, V. Klagsbrunn, & W. Gonçalves (Eds.), *Argentina e Brasil, vencendo os preconceitos. As várias arestas de uma concepção estratégica* (pp. 33–49). Revan.

Confederação Nacional da Indústria. (2020). *Impactos jurídicos da saída do Mercosur,* Brasília.

Fernandes, F. (1975). *A revolução burguesa no Brasil: ensaio de interpretação sociológica*. Zahar.

Folha de São Paulo, 03/08/2020. *Declaração sobre a candidatura norte-americana à presidência do BID*. Disponível em: https://www1.folha.uol.com.br/opiniao/2020/08/declaracao-sobre-a-candidatura-norte-americana-a-presidencia-do-bid.shtml

Fonseca, G., Jr. (1998). *A Legitimidade e Outras Questões Internacionais*. Paz e Terra.

Froio, L. (2015). *Paradiplomacia e o impacto da alternância de governos na atuação internacional dos estados brasileiros*. Tese de Doutorado, DCP, UFPE.

Garcia, M. A. (2013). Dez anos de política externa. In E. Sader (Ed.), *Dez anos de governos pós-neoliberais no Brasil: Lula e Dilma*. FLACSO Brasil.

Gardini, G. L. (2010). *The origins of Mercosur*. Palgrave Macmillan.

Gardini, G. L., & Lambert, P. (Eds.). (2010). *Latin American foreign policies: Between ideology and pragmatism*. Palgrave/Macmillan.

Guimarães, S. P. (2006). *Desafios brasileiros na era dos gigantes*. Contraponto.

Haas, E. (2004). *The uniting of Europe: Political, social, and economic forces*. University of Notre Dame Press.

Herman, C. F. (1990). Changing course: When governments choose to redirect foreign policy. *International Studies Quarterly, 34*(1), 3–21.

Herz, M. (2011). *The Organization of American States (OAS): Global governance away from the media*. Routledge.

Hooghe, L., & Marks, G. (2019). Grand theories of European integration in the twenty-first century. *Journal of European Public Policy, 26*, 1113–1133.

IBGE. (2020). https://agenciabrasil.ebc.com.br/radioagencia-nacional/economia/audio/2021-11/ibge-revisa-pib-de-2019-de-14-para-12

Jaguaribe, H. (1958). *O nacionalismo na atualidade brasileira*. ISEB.

Jaguaribe, H. (1979). Autonomia Periférica e Hegemonia Cêntrica. *Estudios Internacionales, 46*(abril-junho), 91–130.

Lekrofridi, Z., & Schmitter, P. (2015). Transcending or descending? European integration in times of crisis. *European Political Science Review, 7*(1), 3–22.

Levitsky, S., & Ziblatt, D. (2018). *How democracies die.* Crown Publishing.

Lima, S. E. M. (2018). *O pragmatismo responsável na visão da diplomacia e da academia.* Brasília.

Lowenthal, A. (2008, Março/Maio). Recomendações da política americana para a América Latina. Política Externa, 16(4): 33–40.

Lula da Silva, L. I. (2006). *Discurso do presidente da República, Luiz Inácio Lula da Silva, por ocasião do encerramento da XXX Cúpula dos Chefes de Estado do Mercosur.* Córdoba, julho. Disponível em: http://www.Mercosur.gov.br/discurso. Acessed 12 Dec 2021.

Malamud, A., & Schmitter, P. (2006). *The experience of european integration and the potential for integration in Mercosur.* Paper Joint Sessions of the Workshops of the ECPR, Nicosia, Cyprus, 25–30 April.

Malamud, A. (2005). Mercosur Turns 15: Between rising rhetoric and declining achievement. *Cambridge Review of International Affairs, 18*(3), 421–436.

Malan, P. S., Bonelli, R., Abreu, M. d. P., & Pereira, J. E. d. C. (1977). *Política Econômica Externa e Industrialização no Brasil, 1939–1952.* IPEA/INPES.

Mariano, K. L. P. (2015). *Regionalismo na América do Sul: Um novo esquema de análise e a experiência do Mercosur* (1st ed.). Editora Unesp.

Mariano, M. P. (2007). *A Política Externa Brasileira, o Itamaraty e o Mercosur.* Tese de Doutorado. Programa de Pós-Graduação em Sociologia. Faculdade de Ciências e Letras – UNESP -Araraquara – SP.

Matlary, J. H. (1994). Integration theory and international relations: What does the elephant look like and how should it be studied? *Paper, Second ECSA World Conference.*

Mattli, W. (1999). *The logic of regional integration: Europe and beyond.* Cambridge University Press.

Meacham, C. (2015, março 23). *Protests, corruption, and recession: Is Brazil ready for trade cooperation with the United States?* Center for Strategic and International Studies (CSIS). http://csis.org/.

Mello, F. de C. (2000). *Regionalismo e Inserção Internacional: Continuidade e Transformação da Política Externa Brasileira nos Anos 90.* Tese de Doutorado. Programa de Pós-Graduação em Ciência Política. FFLCH/USP.

Meyer, P. J. (2013). *Organization of American states: Background and issues for congress.* Congressional Research Service.

Moravcsik, A. (1994). Preferences and power in the European community: A liberal intergovernmental approach. In S. Bulmer & D. Scott (Eds.), *Economic and political integration in Europe: International dynamics and global context.* Blackwell Publishers Oxford.

Moravcsik, A. (1997, September). Taking preferences seriously: a liberal theory of international relations. *International Organization, 51*(4), 513–553.

Moravcsik, A. (2005). The European constitutional compromise and the neofuncionalist legacy. *Journal of European Public Policy, 12*(2), 349–386.

Morgenthau, H. (2003). *A política entre as nações: a luta pelo poder e pela paz.* Editora UnB.

Neves, B. C. (2019). *Integração da infra-estrutura sul-americana.* Dissertação de Mestrado PPGRI-San Tiado Dantas.

Neves, C., Augusto, J., & Spektor, M. (2011). Obama e o Brasil. In A. Lowenthal, L. Whitehead, & T. Piccone (Eds.), *Obama e as Américas.* Editora FGV.

Patriota, A. A. (2008, Junho/Agosto). O Brasil e a Política Externa dos EUA. *Política Externa, 17*(1): 97–109.

Piccone, T. (2011). A agenda da democracia nas Américas: o caso para a ação multilateral. In A. F. Lowenthal, L. Whitehead, & T. J. Piccone (Eds.), *Obama e as Américas.* Editora FGV.

Pinheiro, L. (2004). *Política Externa Brasileira, 1889–2002.* Jorge Zahar.

Pinheiro, L., & Lima, M. R. S. (2018). Between autonomy and dependency: The place of agency in Brazilian foreign policy. *Brazilian Political Science Review, 12*(3), 1–22.
Puig, J. C. (1984). Introducción. In J. C. Puig (org.) *América Latina: Políticas Exteriores Comparadas*. Grupo Editor Latinoamericano. . Tomo I.
Puig, J. C. (1980). *Doctrinas internacionales y Autonomía Latinoamericana*. Instituto de Altos Estudios de América Latina. UniversidadSimón Bolívar.
Putnam, R. (1988). Diplomacy and domestic politics: The logic of two level games. *International Organization, 42*(3), 427–460.
Rodrik, D. (2018). Populism and the economics of globalization. *Journal of International Business Policy, 1*(1–2), 12–33.
Rogowski, R. (1989). *Commerce and coalitions: How trade affects domestic political alignments*. Princeton University Press.
Rossi, P., Mello, G., & Bastos, P. (2019). *The growth model of the PT governments: A Furtadian view of the limits of recent Brazilian development*. Latin American Perspectives.
Russel, R., & Tokatlian, J. G. (2010). *Autonomía y neutralidad en la globalización. Uma readaptación contemporânea*. Capital Intelectual.
Russell, R., & Tokatlian, J. G. (2003). From antagonistic autonomy to relational autonomy. *Latin American Politics and Society, 45*(1), 1–24.
Russell, R., & Tokatlian, J. G. (2007). A América Latina e suas opções estratégicas frente aos Estados Unidos. *Política Externa, 16*(3), 7–27. Dezembro-2007/Fevereiro-2008.
Sabatini, C. (2012, March/April). *Rethinking Latin America*. Foreign Affairs.
Sanahuja, J. A. (2012). Regionalismo post-liberal y multilateralismo em Sudamérica: El caso de UNASUR. In *Anuario de laintegración regional de América Latina y elGran Caribe 2012*. Coordinadora Regional de Investigaciones Económicas y Sociales.
Santos, L. C. V. G. (2014). *A América do Sul no discurso diplomático brasileiro*. FUNAG.
Schmitter, P. C. (2000). *How to democratize the European Union and why bother?* Rowman & Littlefield Publisher.
Simonoff, A. (2015). Integración y autonomia em el pensamento de Juan Carlos Puig. In J. Briceño Ruiz & A. Simonoff (Eds.), *Integración y cooperación regional en América Latina: una relectura a partir de la teoria de laautonomía*. Biblos.
Singer, A. (2020). The failure of Dilma's Rousseff developmentalist experiment: A class analysis. *Latin American Perspectives, 47*(1), 152–168.
Sorj, B., & Fausto, S. (2013). Brasil: Actor geopolítico regional y global. In B. Sorj & S. Fausto (Eds.), *Brasil y América Latina: ¿Quéliderazgo es posible?* (pp. 23–68). Fundação iFCH/Centro Edelstein.
Teixeira Junior, A. W. M. (2020). Geopolítica e Postura Estratégica dos Estados Unidos na Crise da Venezuela. *Análise Estratégica, 15*, 7–24.
The Intercept. (2020). *As mensagens secretas da lava-jato*. https://theintercept.com/series/mensagens-lava-jato/
Thorstensen, V., & Ferraz, L. (2014). *The impacts of TTIP and TPP on Brazil. Paper*. Fundação Getúlio Vargas.
Thorstensen, V., & Gullo, M. (2018). O Brasil na OCDE: membro pleno ou mero observador? In *Workingpaper series 478*. Faculdade Getúlio Vargas. https://bibliotecadigital.fgv.br/dspace/bitstream/handle/10438/23926/TD%20479%20-%20CCGI_08.pdf?sequence=1&isAllowed=y
Vadell, J. (2011). A China na América do Sul e as implicações geopolíticas do consenso do pacífico. *Revista de Sociologia e Política, 19*(Suplementar), 57–79.
Velasco e Cruz, S. C. (2007). *Trajetórias: capitalismo neoliberal e reformas econômicas nos países da periferia*. Editora Unesp.
Waltz, K. N. (1979). *Theory of international politics*. McGraw-Hill.

Chapter 8
Final Remarks

Within the introduction of this book, we raised three questions related to Brazilian foreign policy regarding regional integration more broadly, and Mercosur in particular.

1. The first concerns the distinction between a worldview within which the process of regional integration occupies a central place, and another according to which the integration process is viewed as instrumental, albeit, important.

   As we saw in Chap. 2, our analysis shows that domestic actors in favor of the integration process in the 1980s gained the initiative and capacity to overcome long historical periods in which the issue of regional integration had only been partially prioritized. This group of actors, which encompassed diplomats, military officials, scientists and energy technicians, politicians, and business entrepreneurs interested in expanding markets, permitted the approximation between Argentina and Brazil, and a change in the patterns of relations between these two countries.

   The difficulties related to the process of construction of public policies converged with the regional integration process and the strengthening of economic interdependence at the end of the 1990s. This included the resistance which became evident throughout the 2000s. These difficulties, even in the developmentalist-distributivist period, permitted the strengthening of actors which demonstrated an increasing inclination towards ideas, projects, and interests contrary to the process of regional integration. We demonstrate that within the nucleus of the Brazilian state and its elites, positions oscillated over time between ideas which associated the process of regional integration and Mercosur with central and structural interests, and others which perceived them as instrumental. This alternation permitted that which we define as a strong attenuation of interests throughout time, contributing to the decline of policies focused on regional integration, which eventually also became evident towards the end of the 2010s.

T. Vigevani, H. Ramanzini Junior, *The Challenges for Building Regional Integration in the Global South*, United Nations University Series on Regionalism 18,
https://doi.org/10.1007/978-3-030-93348-7_8

2. The Second question led us to provide an explanation of how an integration model with a strong commercial focus gradually was substituted by another, as a consequence of which the weakening of the possibilities for a higher degree of economic integration led to the so-called post-hegemonic conceptions. These were mainly related to political, social, and cultural integration, which we discussed in more detail in Chap. 5.

   Paradoxically, the regional integration process, which in some cases provided a high degree of leverage and autonomy, as in the fourth Summit of the Americas in Mar del Plata in 2005, or in relation to the South American integration process, took place in a historical period in which the phenomenon of globalization remained hegemonic, albeit with growing difficulties, as became evident in the Doha Round negotiations, initiated in 2001 and still not concluded after nearly 20 years. The weakness of Latin American states and their low agency capacity accentuated the difficulties of regionalism. The internal economic forces favorable to the integration process within the Mercosur countries, and in Brazil, in particular, were eventually weakened. This helps to explain why the integration process remained an integrated part of the foreign policy agenda, albeit with a low degree of intensity of continuity. We treated this in detail in Chap. 6. The great political changes in the United States and in other central countries in 2017, as the consequences of Brexit for the European Union would highlight, were phenomena which weakened liberal international cooperation. Instead of confronting the Trump administration through new initiatives of deep South American cooperation, the context of growing political polarization contributed to deepening the crisis within most states in the region. More recently, under the Biden administration, the perspectives for liberal international cooperation may be resumed within US foreign policy, but there is no evidence that this may impact the current scenario of political fragmentation and reduced economic interdependence in South America.

   Retrospectively, we can ascertain that the international context, of either growth or crisis, did not favor South American regional integration. The developmentalist-distributivist period – conceptualized by some authors as post-hegemonic – with regards to the initiatives directed towards the regional sphere, did not permit the confrontation of destabilizing factors. General agreement and similar worldviews on behalf of the political leadership during that period with regards to Mercosur, and hereafter Unasur, were not sufficient. The destabilizing factors, or those that did not favor regional integration, were innumerous. Those exogenous to the region could be highlighted as the consequences of the policies of the United States or the economic relations with China based on the exports of commodities. Endogenous factors were the weakness of the states and their low capacity to develop economic interdependence. In Chap. 5, we showed that the structural difficulties were partly substituted by the idea of a social, political, participative, and cultural Mercosur. We refer to this transformation as a "*salto in avanti*".

   The attempts of cultural integration, and of sharing of experiences of social policies (regarding education, health care, social security, etc.), and the aspirations made towards a higher degree of political integration (through the Parliament) and compensatory initiatives (Focem), not least the affinities between the political leadership, are all relevant aspects, but by themselves, they are still insufficient to guarantee regional integration. A regional integration process becomes consolidated when economic interests or epistemic communities reach their central objectives. A factor which explains the continuity of Mercosur are these economic interests. From the Brazilian point of view, on the one hand, they explain the low intensity, and on the other, Mercosur's continuity, as became evident in a document from the National Confederation of Industry (CNI, 2020), discussed in Chap. 6. In this book, we do not discuss the interests of Argentina, Paraguay, and Uruguay, but the dimension of the regional market, particularly the Brazilian, stimulated a similar tendency in the direction of low-intensity integration. At the same time, the limited scale of these interests did not permit the establishment of an integration dynamic that would generate spillovers. Throughout this research, neither could we detect any initiatives amongst Brazilian regional policy-makers directed towards the use of Mercosur or the region minded upon the creation of economic leverage on behalf of the country in relation to the world more broadly, as otherwise suggested by Krapohl (2020).

As we have seen in this book, Mercosur and the Brazilian policies examined underscore that in the process of regional integration between developing countries, it becomes difficult to define compensatory policies which would facilitate the social adherence to a regional bloc. In the second half of the 2010s, the assent of conservative governments, closely adherent to pro-market positions, resulted in a higher degree of disarray of regional bodies. Particularistic national preferences were hereby strengthened. This vision thus became predominant, and coincided with the crisis and destabilization in Brazil, but also within other regional states, as well as the aim of strengthening ties with central countries, understood as the underlying motivation for national preference formation in a context of intensifying global geopolitical rivalry. As we have discussed in Chap. 2, in Brazil, the idea of Brazilian singularity in relation to neighboring states reemerged.

3. The third question presented in the introduction refers to the compatibility of a vision of regional integration based on the idea of deepening of the process, and another which emphasized its enlargement. What is the rationale behind the prioritization of Mercosur in parallel to the creation of other regional instances, such as Unasur and Celac, or others with a technical or sectorial character? In Chap. 7, we analyzed Brazilian positions and the relations between Mercosur, Unasur, Celac and OAS, illustrating the rationale for supporting this architecture and the consequences which the decreasing role of Brazil in the region had for for these blocs. As we have discussed in Chap. 4, high-ranking public officials and the political and economic elites partly nurtured the perception that the deepening of Mercosur, and in general of a process of regional integration with a supranational perspective, would lead to the loss of sovereignty and autonomy in Brazil's relations with the world. This idea always remained present, even when it did not prevail within the initiatives of the governmental core, presenting itself as a

political component within regional policies which enjoyed support from certain social actors, – particularly the business community and conservative political forces. Inversely, the perception that Mercosur would strengthen the country's global position did not advance. As we have seen, the guiding principles within Brazilian diplomatic tradition – autonomy and universalism – converged towards the continuation of Mercosur as a customs union of an essentially intergovernmental nature and adapted to the enlargement of the bloc, but incompatible with its deepening. A consequence of these choices was the vulnerability to external pressures, a fact which helps to understand the gradual downgrading of the bloc's importance within Brazilian foreign policy from 1999, and mainly, from 2016. The traditional arguments related to autonomy and universalism also motivate the Brazilian positions regarding the creation of Unasur and Celac. The dimensions of Latin America, South America, and the Southern Cone structured the conceptual notion of concentric circles which is present within Brazilian foreign policy and which between 1985 and 2016 certainly had Mercosur as their main dimension.

The rationale behind this evolution exists and has not been connected to specific political forces. In Chap. 4, as we examined the origins of the concept of South America, we demonstrated how it corresponded to a deeper-lying foreign policy imperative which reaches beyond the policies of any particular government. A significant manifestation of this evolution already became evident during the Itamar Franco administration in 1993, through the proposal of creation of the *Área de Livre-Comércio da América do Sul* (ALCSA), presented not in opposition to the Southern Cone, but on the contrary, as complementary to this. In the Cardoso government, this agenda gained continuity aiming at regional political articulation, including with regards to security and infrastructural regional integration. In 2008, during the Lula da Silva government, there was a formalization of Unasur, which explicitly did not include commercial and tariff elements. In the case of Celac, the initiative was not Brazilian, albeit it was actively supported by the country. The goal was to build upon common interests, mainly in relation to Mexico, aiming at maintaining its regional insertion and Latin American ties.

Concluding the answer to the third question, relating to the potential compatibility between a vision of regional integration based on the idea of deepening of this process and another aiming at its enlargement, studying the Mercosur trajectory, we underline that these are distinct dimensions and therefore also hardly compatible. Despite this, both require a certain degree of institutionalization framework to advance the process of regional integration, although to different degrees. Until 2016, within Brazilian foreign policy, the emphasis on broadening without the sufficient institutional strengthening was one of the elements which obstructed this process. From a regional integration perspective, it is important that a country or a group of countries are clearly aware of the dimensions of broadening and deepening of this process, and that they act decisively concerning its implementation. Even prioritizing the broadening of this process demands backing from efficient and properly designed regional institutions. Within the introduction and in Chap. 4 and

5, we argued that the institutional design and the difficulties of advancing in relation to a community of interests within the bloc also relate to the absence of a paymaster. In the case of Mercosur, Brazil did not have a specific policy to assume this role, partly due to its own structural weaknesses. According to the data presented in Chap. 6, from 1991 to 2018, the intra-bloc trade fell from 9% to 8%. This means that the trade-related objective would not be reached.

This general assessment of Mercosur and regional integration, which we have centered on Brazilian foreign policy, has illustrated the difficulties of resolving the varying controversies of economic and commercial character. There were even setbacks in the integration of production chains – with a partial exception of the car manufacturing industry. From a political and social perspective, the case of the Mercosur Parliament is an example of a body that was inserted within the regional integration agenda, but which eventually was paralyzed due to the lack of interest in its concretization and to the absence of political entrepreneurs. There was not sufficient capacity, let alone interest, in the consolidation of different agendas which presented themselves throughout time. In some cases, such as it was evident regarding the Social Participation Unit (UPS), this did function reasonably well in the period of Social Summits.

In the Brazilian case, on which we have concentrated the analysis, the non-implementation of decisions and the low capacity for overcoming controversies also has its reasons. The rational choice theory highlights that "non-decisions" are part of the game. We conclude this book at a moment at which the Asuncion Treaty (March 1991) is about to reach its 30th years anniversary. With the benefit of hindsight, we can state that the setbacks in the Brazilian positions with the Temer government, but mainly, during the Bolsonaro administration, had reasons which can be found in previous historical periods. Chapters 2 and 3 explain the difficulties which the advancement of the issue of regional integration has faced in Brazil.

Crises are inherent to the process of regional integration, as are the disagreements regarding the division of gains and costs deriving from the increased cooperation between countries. In the case of Mercosur, the crises within the bloc, mainly from 1999, led to a lower degree of institutional investment on behalf of member states, as well as the downgrading of expectations concerning the integration process. Parts of these difficulties resulted from obstacles to the spillover and slowness of the bicycle movement. Based on empirical data and theoretical arguments, we have highlighted the Brazilian difficulties of deepening regional integration. Parts of the elite segments have been favorable to this process, which they have supported under certain circumstances. When geopolitical factors made themselves more clearly evident, governments, albeit still committed to the region, could not proceed in the direction of initiatives which would demand domestic support and density. We do not present this impediment as historically determined, or an inevitability, but rather as the result of the convergence between elite traditions and geopolitical logic, highlighting central vulnerabilities.

Concluding this book in a context in which regionalism is confronted with a very different moment compared to that which was evident at the point when Mercosur was formed, it becomes worthwhile to consider certain conceptual and contextual questions, in relation to which some brief considerations are in order. Resuming one of the central ideas within this book, is there a chance that the aspiration towards autonomy would cease to be a central pillar within Brazilian foreign policy? This has only previously been the case in 1964. The result would be a decisive Brazilian retraction in its relation with South America.

Instability and regional fragmentation inevitably results in a situation in which regionalism becomes incapable of contributing to sustaining legitimate governments or mediating solutions in situations of strong radicalization, such as in Venezuela (Barros & Gonçalves, 2019). This situation increases the region's vulnerability, particularly with regards to external actors, meaning that some countries reassumed the role of geopolitical battlegrounds. Brazil is not immune to global geopolitical disputes. On the contrary, the country has switched from proactive positions of balancing towards a posture of bandwagoning and alignment, with its government placing the country within the sphere of North American interests, under that country's umbrella. This position of alignment becomes evident from the recent postures assumed by the Bolsonaro government in relation to Venezuela and from the way that the 5G technology will be absorbed in Brazil. Distancing itself from regionalism contributes to the weakening of international cooperation and increases the space for intervention by extra-regional actors.

As we conclude our research in the early 2020s, we observe that a historically recurrent theme concerning regional organizations emerges within the Brazilian position: the relation with the United States. The Brazilian political and economic crisis, which resulted in the impeachment of President Dilma Rousseff in 2016, strengthened a novel array of positions, most of which related to geopolitical insertion and liberal economic measures. The intensification of the Brazilian crisis occurred at a point at which important and profound changes took place in the United States. In Brazil, there was a growth in the demands presented by the business community, conservative political forces, and public bureaucratic entities which impacted the central administration, defending the adhesion to international regimes shaped by central countries. These positions resonated through the clamors for Brazil to join international regimes led by the United States, like those developed within the OECD sphere (Mello, 2020).

The changes underway in Brazil from 2016, in the direction of a higher degree of approximation with the United States and a downgrading of the relevance of Mercosur proves that the previous policies were incapable of strengthening the interdependence or institutional framework within the bloc, in order to guarantee its continuity in situations of political instability. The difficulties analyzed concerning the materialization of the integration process, from 1991 to 2016, in part explain why radical changes, such as those observed within the Bolsonaro administration, have only led to a limited response on behalf of public opinion, at least until 2020.

Does the decline of a project of structured regional insertion of Brazilian international engagement equal the definitive rupture of the social, economic, and moral bases on which this policy rested? Or, are we confronting an unstable transformation? Seeking to understand the reasons which might have led to external changes, the fourth level of Hermann's (1990) typology, "international orientation change", which took place in 2016, and which was more decisively accentuated in 2019, it will be necessary to advance towards a new phase of the research, not least in order to understand if there are structural reasons or whether this concerns a short-lived moment within Brazilian foreign policy. What appears to us as indisputable, is that the regional integration process and a cooperative position in relation to neighboring countries are imperative to the development and stability within the region, and within Brazil.

References

Barros, P. S., & Gonçalves, J. D. S. B. (2019). Fragmentação da governança regional: o Grupo de Lima e a política externa brasileira (2017–2019). *Mundo e Desenvolvimento, 3*, 6–39.

Confederação Nacional Da Indústria (CNI). (2020). *Impactos jurídicos da saída do Mercosul* (p. 77). CNI.

Hermann, C. F. (1990). Changing course: When governments choose to redirect foreign policy. *International Studies Quarterly, 34*(1), 3–21.

Krapohl, S. (2020). Games regional actors play: Dependency, regionalism, and integration theory for the global south. *Journal of International Relations and Development, 23*, 840–870.

Mello, F. d. C. (2020). The OECD enlargement in Latin America and the Brazilian candidacy. *Revista Brasileira de Política Internacional, 63*(2), 1–17.

The manufacturer's authorised representative in the EU is Springer Nature Customer Service Centre GmbH, Europaplatz 3, 69115 Heidelberg, Germany. If you have any concerns regarding our products, please contact ProductSafety@springernature.com

Printed and bound by CPI Group (UK) Ltd, Croydon, CR0 4YY
30/09/2026
02225498-0002